TRANSLATION
DETERMINED

TRANSLATION DETERMINED

Robert Kirk

CLARENDON PRESS · OXFORD
1986

Oxford University Press, Walton Street, Oxford OX2 6DP

Oxford New York Toronto
Delhi Bombay Calcutta Madras Karachi
Kuala Lumpur Singapore Hong Kong Tokyo
Nairobi Dar es Salaam Cape Town
Melbourne Auckland

and associated companies in
Beirut Berlin Ibadan Nicosia

Oxford is a trade mark of Oxford University Press

Published in the United States
by Oxford University Press, New York

British Library Cataloguing in Publication Data
Kirk, Robert
Translation determined.
1. Quine, W. V. 2. Translating and interpreting
I. Title
418'.02'0924 P306
ISBN 0-19-824921-7

Library of Congress Cataloging in Publication Data
Kirk, Robert.
Translation determined.
Bibliography: p.
Includes index.
1. Quine, W. V. (Willard Van Orman)—Contributions in the philosophy of translating.
2. Translating and interpreting—Philosophy.
3. Meaning (Philosophy)
I. Title.
P306.92.Q5K57 1986 121 86-5230
ISBN 0-19-824 921-7

Printed in Great Britain
at the University Printing House, Oxford
by David Stanford
Printer to the University

To Janet and Lucy

Preface

Quine's famous doctrine of the indeterminacy of translation can seem obviously true, obviously false, or just confused and confusing. One may well be excited by its implications not only for philosophy but for cognitive psychology, linguistics, and anthropology. But it is perplexing. It has proved extraordinarily hard to state clearly; and it is enmeshed in a system of related but distinguishable doctrines, of various degrees of plausibility, whose interconnections are hard to discern. And although today, a quarter of a century after it was first presented in *Word and Object*, the doctrine is widely influential—indeed some philosophers treat it like an established mathematical theorem—there still seem to be no solid arguments either for or against it. So there are excellent reasons for devoting a book to it, even if the book's conclusion is that the doctrine is false.

Someone who has been bitten by a shark and survived, they say, won't talk about it except to other victims: no one else would understand. Being bitten by the indeterminacy doctrine is different in this respect as well as others. You will talk about it to anyone who will listen, but quite often those who have already been bitten will say you don't understand. So in this book I have paid special attention to the question of just what the doctrine is, or can sensibly be taken to be (for with this subject matter it would be particularly rash to insist on a realist approach). No previous acquaintance with Quine's work is presupposed. The book is addressed primarily to philosophers and students of philosophy, but I hope it is also accessible to linguists and psychologists.

Over the twenty years since I was first bitten I have benefited from discussing the indeterminacy doctrine with many people, and to all of them, starting with Peter Downing and John Watling of University College London, I want to express my gratitude. Special thanks are due to the members of the Philosophy Department at the University of Nottingham for their stalwart participation in numerous staff seminars on these questions, above all to Robert Black and Michael Clark for both stimulating criticism

and encouragement. Finally it is a pleasure to record my deep indebtedness to Quine himself, whose profound and disconcertingly radical writings first drew me into philosophy.

Acknowledgements

I wish to thank Gerald Duckworth & Co. Ltd., and the Harvard University Press, for their permission to use the quotation from Michael Dummett's *Truth and Other Enigmas* which appears as the epigraph to Part II; and also the MIT Press for permission to use the sentence from W. V. Quine's *Word and Object* which is the epigraph to Part III.

Contents

Part I. What is the Indeterminacy Doctrine?

Part II. The Case for Quine's Doctrine

Part III. The Case Against Quine's Docrine

Part IV. Implications

Abbreviations

Those works of W. V. Quine that are listed below will be referred to on the pattern of '*WO*, p. 27'. References to his other works, and to the works of all other authors, will match 'Davidson, 1979, p. 14'. Details of all works cited are given in the Bibliography.

EN   'Epistemology Naturalized' (1969).
ESW   'On Empirically Equivalent Systems of the World' (1975)
FM   'Facts of the Matter' (1977).
MR   'Methodological Reflections on Current Linguistic The-
            ory' (1970).
MVD   'Mind and Verbal Dispositions' (1975).
NNK   'The Nature of Natural Knowledge' (1975).
OR   'Ontological Relativity' (1968).
RIT   'On the Reasons for Indeterminacy of Translation' (1970)
RR   *The Roots of Reference* (1974).
SO   'Speaking of Objects' (1958).
TDE   'Two Dogmas of Empiricism' (1951).
TPT   'Things and their Place in Theories' (1981).
WO   *Word and Object* (1960).

Introduction

Suppose a French physicist remarks:

(1) Le photon n'a pas de masse.

Then any linguist acquainted with physics would accept

(2) Photons have no mass

as a translation. The words are so smoothly keyed into an internationally shared physical theory that there can be no room for substantial disagreement. Not only is (2) a perfectly acceptable English translation of (1): none that was not equivalent to (2) could fit the evidence. So it seems.

Quine challenges these assumptions. If we were perverse and ingenious enough we could devise an alternative to the generally accepted scheme for sentence translation between French and English. This rival scheme's version of (1) would be quite different from (2)—so different we should not accept it as even loosely equivalent to (2). The same would apply to the rival scheme's translations of countless other sentences, yet, by means of cunning compensatory adjustments, it would fit all the possible evidence as well as our usual scheme. Similarly for all translation of whole sentences. That is his thesis of the indeterminacy of translation.

This unsettling claim is part of Quine's wider campaign against our tendency to think of meaning and synonymy as matters of objective fact.[1] Of course we can't avoid talking about the meanings of words and sentences, and it is natural to assume that questions like 'Does this sentence mean the same as that?' have uniquely correct answers. But for various reasons he thinks such assumptions are wrong—for example, he thinks the idea of sameness of meaning is not genuinely explanatory—and the indeterminacy thesis makes this contention vivid. If there can be two or more mutually incompatible schemes of sentence translation which nevertheless fit all the possible evidence, it is hard to see how

[1] Romanos gives an excellent sympathetic account of the background and significance of this campaign.

translation relations can be matters of fact. And if this is correct, relations of sameness of meaning are not matters of fact even when they are supposed to hold between sentences of the same language. (This is the intralinguistic or 'domestic' version of the thesis.)

By now, uninitiated readers are likely to be bemused. Is this Quine's doctrine, or a caricature? Or have I perhaps—has Quine— just dressed up some platitude? There are real difficulties in arriving at a satisfactory statement of the main indeterminacy doctrine, as we shall see; and one of my aims is to get clear just what it amounts to, and to disentangle it from superficially similar views, many of them platitudes. (Part I: chapters 1–3.) There would have been no difficulty if Quine had given us actual examples of the alleged indeterminacy. But he has not, so conceivably he might not approve even of what I have said about sentences (1) and (2). The lack of examples is put down to several causes, including the enormous practical difficulty of devising a whole alternative scheme; for it seems that nothing less than a reasonably complete scheme would be convincing. His idea is that sentences at a fairly high theoretical level are so remotely and deviously associated with the possible evidence that a strikingly non-standard translation scheme could incorporate enough compensatory adjustments to avoid conflict with any evidence. So any example would have to be worked out in detail from the theoretical upper storeys right down to the observational ground—just to make sure it was in contact with the evidence at the right places. Some alleged examples (not Quine's, of course) will be discussed in chapter 8.

Let me emphasize that I am not interested in Quinean exegesis for its own sake, but only in uncovering, or constructing, whatever interesting philosophical doctrine best fits his statements on indeterminacy. We ought not to rest content with a boring interpretation so long as an interesting one is available. (Disagreement over the interpretation of the thesis is not itself, joking apart, an argument in its favour, since that is compatible with the most extreme Platonism about meaning.) Two useful tests for weeding out interpretations of the indeterminacy doctrine which cannot sensibly be ascribed to Quine are: 'Is this a mere truism?' and 'Is this compatible with an objectivist view of synonymy?' For whatever he means (or may reasonably be taken to mean), he has not all this time been labouring a truism, and he does use the indeterminacy doctrine as a weapon against objectivism in semantics. Now the particular interpretation that I shall eventually settle on in chapter 3 may not be exactly what Quine himself would be happy to endorse, since if I am right he has not always observed certain important distinctions. Nevertheless I think he would be even less happy to accept the only apparent alternatives to this interpretation.

Having arrived at what I believe to be a reasonably clear account of the central indeterminacy doctrine, I shall try to disentangle and examine the arguments for it, such as they are. This will require us to consider how it is related to certain other main Quinean doctrines. I shall conclude that none of the arguments, and none of the other doctrines, gives it much support, if any. This is true even of arguments based on certain established formal results in metamathematics and set theory. (Part II: chapters 4-8.)

Though not a Quinean, I am sympathetic to several of Quine's main doctrines. But contrary to the general view[2] I regard the indeterminacy doctrine as an aberration—a rotten plank in the Quinean ship—and in Part III I shall try to show that it is false. Chapter 9 gives my reasons for thinking other objections to the indeterminacy doctrine have not been successful; chapter 10 supports Quine's own view that the general indeterminacy thesis stands or falls with the domestic version; and chapter 11 outlines an argument against the latter, avoiding (I hope) assumptions inconsistent with his other main doctrines.

Finally I shall consider the implications of the falsity of the indeterminacy doctrine, concluding that it leaves the other main tenets of Quine's philosophy of language undisturbed. (For example, rejecting the indeterminacy doctrine commits us neither to the analytic-synthetic distinction nor to a sharp distinction between semantic and other facts. See chapter 12.)

Appendix A lists, with references, the main variants of the indeterminacy doctrine that will be considered in this book, and some different theses which seem relevant. As a foretaste I baldly give the main ones here.

I. Our ordinary notion of sameness of meaning is such that rival teams of linguists, applying this notion to a given pair of languages but deliberately disregarding all constraints of simplicity and practicality, could produce rival manuals of

---

[2] Powerfully urged by Romanos.

sentence translation which fitted all the physically statable evidence (or facts), yet were mutually incompatible. (This is the main indeterminacy thesis.)

II. As I, with 'schemes of reference' substituted for 'manuals of sentence translation'. (The 'inscrutability of reference'.)

III. Relations of sameness of meaning for sentences—even for exact translations—are not generally matters of fact. (I call this the 'non-factuality thesis'.)

IV. Statements of sentence synonymy make sense only relative to a scheme of translation. (The 'relativistic thesis'.)

V. There is no set of constraints statable in Quine-acceptable terms which, applied to the totality of Quine-acceptable evidence, determines a uniquely correct scheme of sentence translation between a given pair of languages.

VI. Sentence synonymy cannot be defined or analysed in Quine-acceptable terms.

VII. Different criteria for sameness of meaning can yield conflicting results.

VIII. Translation manuals which agree in their assignments of truth values to sentences, even in all possible worlds, can conflict with one another.

IX. Schemes of reference for a given language which agree in their assignments of truth values to sentences, even in all possible worlds, can conflict with one another.

X. In translation between conceptually distant languages there is not generally any fact—as to which of two inequivalent rough versions of a given sentence is correct—to be right or wrong about.

XI. For some pairs of (*a*) sentences, or (*b*) terms, offered as translations of one another, the behaviour of speakers of the translated language gives no basis for saying either that the proposed translation is acceptable, or that it is not acceptable.

XII. There can be empirically equivalent but mutually incompatible theories of the world.

For reasons to be given in Part I it is only theses I–IV that can be regarded as constituting Quine's indeterminacy doctrine. The others, though no doubt acceptable to him, must be distinguished from that doctrine. While I shall argue that I, II, III and IV are false, I think the rest, with the possible exception of XII (depending on how it is understood), are probably true—indeed many of them are platitudes.

The task of disentangling the central indeterminacy doctrine from other views will be begun in chapter 1. However, uninitiated readers may be hesitating to embark on what must look suspiciously like a Snark hunt. So the chapter is also an attempt to convey some idea of the significance of the indeterminacy doctrine.

Part I

What is the Indeterminacy Doctrine?

> Everything doth not hit alike upon every man's
> imagination
>   LOCKE

I

Clearing the Ground

Quine's indeterminacy doctrine is so radical that people often mistake it for a disguised platitude. I shall therefore begin this chapter by clearing away some of the commonest trivializing mis-interpretations. Then I shall try to give an idea of its implications by showing why various apparently promising lines of attack and defence fail. This will lead to a brief account of Quine's wider views on philosophy and language. I shall comment on the relations between the indeterminacy doctrine and certain other major topics: Wittgenstein's ideas on interpretation and rule-following; realism and anti-realism; and other current approaches to the notion of meaning. Finally I shall say something about translation manuals.

1.1 Trivializing interpretations

(a) If we had only the inscriptions on the Rosetta stone to go by, there would be no limit to the number of incompatible schemes that could be devised for translating between the three languages represented on it (hieroglyphic, demotic Egyptian, Greek), each scheme fitting all the evidence of the inscriptions. And quite generally, for any given body of data about people's actual linguistic and other behaviour, we could devise any number of incompatible semantic theories for their languages, all compatible with those data—assuming, contrary to fact, that we knew what a semantic theory should look like. But since that is a platitude we must not suppose it is Quine's point. His claim, in contrast, is that two schemes of translation could be incompatible even when both fitted not just whatever evidence we happened to have, or even the totality of actual linguistic behaviour, but *the totality of possible evidence*. (The question of just what the evidence is must wait until chapter 3.)

(b) Even for translation between such relatively close languages and cultures as French and English there is scope not just for disagreement between rival translators, but for irresoluble dis-agreement—disagreement which resists any amount of instruction in the facts about the two languages. In translating poetry, for example, a point can be reached where what is at stake is not knowledge of the two languages but literary judgement and taste. But the possibility of irresoluble disagreement over matters of taste is not news. Again, the indeterminacy doctrine is not about that sort of disagreement. It involves fundamental disagreement about the sense of what is said, about literal meaning, or what Quine sometimes calls cognitive meaning. His thought is that rival schemes will offer, as their respective versions of a sentence of the one language, sentences of the other 'which stand to each other in no plausible sort of equivalence however loose' (*WO*, p. 27[1]).

(*c*) The indeterminacy doctrine is also sometimes mistaken for the platitude that in translation between relatively remote languages and cultures, widely different, even non-equivalent, sentences in one language may be equally acceptable as rough equivalents of a single sentence of another. Differences of culture or theory can ensure there is no 'fact of the matter' as to which translation is right: neither is uniquely correct. Similarly, of course, for the translation of terms.

This is thesis X in the list at Appendix A. Although it can come as a stunning revelation to schoolchildren, it is excessively familiar to linguists (see e.g. Lyons 1977, pp. 235-8, pp. 253-8). For more than one reason this familiar point cannot be what Quine is getting at, although in some passages he puts considerable emphasis on it (SO, pp. 5 f., 25, OR, p. 29).

One or two examples may be useful. In Book III of the *Republic* Socrates is commonly translated as proposing to banish the 'flute' from the ideal state (*Rep.* 399D). In fact this instrument is the aulos. 'Clarinet' and 'oboe' would be just as acceptable—though as inaccurate—as 'flute', because the aulos, unlike any of these, has twin pipes. And although these pipes are cylindrical—like the clarinet and flute but unlike the oboe—they have double reeds, like the oboe and unlike both clarinet and flute (which of course has no reed). So unless we simply borrow the original Greek word, English has no way of translating it that is both neat and accurate. And there is nothing to choose between the various mutually incompatible rough translations—no fact of the matter as to which is best.[2]

---

[1] For abbreviations see p. 000.

[2] In this particular case there is Quine-acceptable behavioural evidence which relates

This lack of neat, exact translations goes with the fact that, in traditional terms, there is no exact coincidence of concepts. Conceptual differences between languages are not of course confined to cases where there are physical differences between cultures—auloi there, clarinets here. It is a platitude that different languages divide the world up differently—the same world (as people uncorrupted by philosophy would say). For example 'Colour words are notoriously ill-matched between remote languages, because of differences in customary grouping of shades' (*WO*, p. 41). John Lyons, discussing the difficulties of translating 'The cat sat on the mat' into French, points out that none of the French words 'tapis', 'paillasse', 'carpette', etc. has the same denotation as any of the English words 'mat', 'rug', 'carpet', etc. (1977, 237 f.). But there is no need to react by concluding that French and English do not talk about the same things, the same reality. In general the question of what terms refer to is distinct from the question of how they are to be translated. It seems enough to say we use different words to refer to the same individual things (but see chapter 5). (After all, the French do not talk our carpets out of existence by using their own words for them.)

Developed theories bring further difficulties. In Aristotle's theory of reproduction he uses a concept *kyēma*, which he defines as 'the first mixture of the male and female elements' (*De Generatione Animalium*, $728^{B}34$). It appears that 'zygote' or 'embryo' would be equally good (or bad) as rough translations in terms of modern biology; but they are by no means equivalent.[3]

Now, the main reason why cases of the sorts we have noticed must not be supposed to exemplify Quine's indeterminacy thesis is that they leave unscathed ordinary assumptions about the *objectivity* of synonymy, and of intentional notions generally, contrary to what Quine thinks his indeterminacy thesis does (*WO*, pp. 206, 207, 220 f., FM, p. 193. Cf. 1.3 and 1.4). That there is no fact of the matter as to which of two conflicting rough translations is correct is a truism entirely compatible with the view that both translated and translating sentences have meanings fully deter-

rather directly to the one-word observation sentences 'Aulos', 'Flute', etc., and ensures that they are not exactly intertranslatable. (On observation sentences see 2.1 and 3.9.) But as we shall see, that is not the main objection; and in any case such direct evidence will not generally be available.

[3] The example is from Furley 1958, pp. 55 f. For interesting discussions of the translation of this and other technical terms in the same work, see Peck's translation (1953, xliv-lxvii).

mined by the totality of possible evidence. Indeed, this truism is compatible with extreme Platonic theories of meaning. Even on such theories, different languages may use different concepts, different ways of dividing up reality, but that would not prevent the concepts themselves from possessing adamantine objectivity. Since Quine is neither labouring a truism nor endorsing Platonism, the indeterminacy doctrine must be something other than that it is not a matter of fact which rough translation is correct. He holds that 'there is not even . . . an objective matter to be right or wrong about' (*WO*, p. 73). On his view it is not an objective matter of fact what the translated sentence means, nor which 'concepts' people employ. So if the indeterminacy thesis is not to be merely trivial, it is what we think of as *exact* translation that must be held to be subject to the indeterminacy. (For another reason why Quine must hold that exact translation is subject to the indeterminacy see 1.5. On exact translation see 3.10.)

(*d*) Quite likely the ancient Greeks themselves would have been at a loss whether to apply 'aulos' to modern flutes, clarinets or oboes. Greek language use may have left this indeterminate. If so, this is still not an instance of Quinean indeterminacy, but of what I shall call common or garden indeterminacy of sense. It is one kind of linguistic indeterminacy whose existence could not reasonably be denied. It holds, of course, for whole sentences as well as for shorter expressions. We have a case of it if the behaviour of the linguistic community simply gives no basis for saying either that the expression in question applies, or that it does not apply, in the particular circumstances envisaged.[4] This sort of indeterminacy is clearly not what Quine's thesis is about because it too implies no failure of objectivity in translation. An exact translation will match indeterminacy of sense with indeterminacy of sense: anything else would just be a variety of rough translation.

Allied to this common or garden indeterminacy of sense is common or garden indeterminacy of reference. The use of terms may fail to fix a determinate range of application. Aristotle's 'kyēma', regarded from the point of view of today's biology, is a good illustration. But this common phenomenon too must not be con-

---

[4] This is thesis XI in the list at Appendix A. Cf. Dummett (1973), p. 624, and, for discussion of Wittgenstein's views, Baker and Hacker (1983, pp. 209-27). There is a tendency to count this sort of indeterminacy as vagueness. I am inclined to use 'vagueness' for something rather different, but nothing in my discussion will turn on whether common or garden indeterminacy of sense is counted as vagueness.

fused with its exotic Quinean counterpart, the alleged inscrutability of reference, to be examined in chapter 5.

(*e*) The next sort of trivialization is more a matter of oversight
than of deliberate interpretation. It is to assume one has an example
of Quinean indeterminacy when all one has done is to apply to
interlinguistic translation a looser standard of equivalence than
one has applied intralinguistically. The 'aulos' example can be
used to illustrate this sort of case too, although the present point
is not the same as the one noticed at (*c*) above. If you translate
'aulos' by 'flute' and say it could also have been translated by
'clarinet', you may be tempted to think you have an example of
Quinean indeterminacy because 'flute' and 'clarinet' are not equivalent. But if you refuse to count 'flute' and 'clarinet' as equivalent
by what right do you insist that each is equivalent to 'aulos'? In
fact 'flute' seems no closer to 'aulos' than to 'clarinet'. You are
inconsistent if you nevertheless insist the two English words do
not mean the same, while claiming they both translate the Greek
word. Once seen the inconsistency is obvious, but it is easily
overlooked.

(*f*) Notoriously it is a mistake to assume that a translation acceptable for one purpose will be acceptable for all purposes.[5] But
by now it will be clear why discrepancies between translations
which result from different purposes on the translators' part will
not illustrate the indeterminacy thesis. The existence of such cases
is entirely consistent with extreme Platonist theories of meaning,
and has no philosophical interest. Besides, as Quine shows by his
own insistence on the greater scope for indeterminacy at the higher
levels of physical theory (*WO*, pp. 76 f., EN, p. 89, RIT, ESW,
p. 314), his sort of indeterminacy is supposed to exist even when
scientific sentences are being translated 'literally' for normal scientific purposes.

A variant of this error is to assume the indeterminacy thesis is
illustrated by the different results we get from applying different
criteria for the adequacy of a translation manual. (See thesis VII
in the list at Appendix A.) For example, if as translators we aimed
to maximize the foreigners' agreement with ourselves, we might

---

[5] For example: 'In Lahu, a language of Burma and Southwest China, one cannot translate
literally the hymn "Stand up, stand up, for Jesus" without being somewhat silly, for Lahus
simply do not "stand up" for their leaders. On the other hand, one can say "to stand firm",
and this is the expression used' (Nida, 1964, p. 219).

well get renderings of their sentences which conflicted with the results of trying to maximize ascribed rationality.[6]

The above are, I think, the main interpretations of the indeterminacy thesis which would make it merely trivial. I consider next some seemingly obvious ways of defending or attacking it.

1.2 Why bilinguals won't help

You might think it obvious that radical disagreements about translation would be impossible between people who knew both languages really thoroughly. Surely a bilingual, or if necessary a committee of bilinguals, could track down and eliminate all possible sources of disagreement that involved more than matters of mere nuance or style? Not according to Quine. He maintains that his thesis applies to schemes of translation guaranteed by bilinguals just as it does to those devised by less well equipped mortals (*WO*, p. 71, p. 74). As to the fact (if it is a fact) that bilingual people do not actually disagree to the extent envisaged, this is no doubt to be explained much as Quine explains the fact that there are no actual examples of rival schemes of translation between natural languages: the territory has already been divided up between the existing schemes. Devising a rival would require an entire duplicate enterprise of translation, for which there is no adequate motive (*WO*, p. 72). There is also the fact that bilinguals, like linguists, tend to invoke considerations of simplicity, plausibility, and practical convenience, which drastically restrict their choices in practice without being theoretically necessary (*WO*, pp. 74 f.).

1.3 Why looking for the use won't help

One apparently promising line of objection to the indeterminacy thesis is suggested by the maxim 'Don't look for the meaning, look for the use'. The difference between meaningful sentences and mere empty noises might be characterized by saying that the expressions of a language have uses governed by syntactic and semantic conventions or rules; and the existence and efficacy of these uses and conventions might be explained in terms of people's intentions, beliefs, and wants. Sameness of meaning for sentences

---

[6] Peter Hylton appears to adopt this interpretation of the indeterminacy thesis. 'The point of indeterminacy is . . . that the maxims which a linguist uses are not determined by physics. Different maxims, yielding different translations, would be equally compatible with physics; it is the use of just *these* maxims which is left indeterminate even after physical theory is fixed' (1982, p. 180). Cf. also Christopher Hookway (1978).

might then be explained in terms of, say, sameness of relevant convention, in which case two non-equivalent sentences of one language could never both be acceptable as exact translations of a single sentence of another.

But this line of thought is doomed. It is not just that there are serious doubts whether syntactic or semantic conventions or rules could in general be characterized independently of decisions on how to translate the expressions involved—a difficulty which remains even if intentions and beliefs, not conventions, are taken as basic. (Cf. e.g. Davidson 1974a and 1974b.) The trouble is that this sort of objection depends on the assumption that sentences involving intentional notions report matters of fact.

Quine concedes that if intentions, purposes, beliefs, conventions, and the like could be counted as among those matters of fact to which schemes of translation must conform, then translation would be determinate. He does not dispute, for example, that if it were a matter of fact that Alf applied a certain word to all and only the objects he believed to be horses, then we could say Alf's word meant the same as 'horse'; or that if it were a matter of fact that Beth was disposed to assent to a certain sentence if and only if she believed that particles can be created out of the void, then Beth's sentence probably could not be translated except by 'Particles can be created out of the void'. But Quine rejects the assumption that such things are matters of fact (*WO*, p. 221, RIT, p. 181).

1.4 The implied non-factuality of propositional attitudes

By now it will be clear that there is a great gulf between Quine's position and traditional scepticism about other minds, and also the related notion of a 'hermeneutic circle'.

According to traditional scepticism we can never know, in any particular case, whether our interpretation of another's thoughts or feelings is right or wrong; but still there is something to be right or wrong about. The other person has certain particular thoughts and feelings: it is just that we cannot tell what they are.

Dilthey's idea of a hermeneutic circle emphasized the alleged methodological difficulty that in order to be able to interpret people's behaviour you have to start from assumptions about the meanings of their words, or about what they believe or desire, which cannot be established without circularity.[7] Quine uses sim-

---

[7] See Hodges (1952, pp. 138-42) for an account of Dilthey's doctrine of the hermeneutic circle, stressing his holism.

ilar reasoning, but his claim is radically different. It is not that we
cannot tell whether we have hit upon the right interpretation.
Rather, it is that there is nothing to be right or wrong about (cf.
WO, pp. 73, 221; OR, pp. 30, 47; FM, p. 193). We still use our
interpretations, of course, ascribing beliefs, desires, etc., in the
light of more or less adequate behavioural evidence. But in Quine's
view even the totality of possible evidence—indeed, even the totality of facts—is in general compatible with countless mutually incompatible schemes of interpretation.

At this point you might be reminded of a well-known objection to
behaviourism, and wonder whether (ironically, in view of Quine's
behaviouristic bias) it might serve to *support* the indeterminacy
thesis. This is the so-called 'perfect actor' objection. A perfect
actor who believed a certain proposition to be false might (it is
claimed) be disposed to behave in any conceivable situation in
ways entirely consistent with holding that proposition to be true.
If this is right, the same overall pattern of behaviour, and indeed
of behavioural dispositions, might represent quite different systems
of propositional attitude. And if this in turn is right, little more is
required, it seems, to get to the indeterminacy thesis. All it takes is
the claim that nothing *beyond* behavioural dispositions could serve
to give propositional attitudes their individuality. (Quine declares
his allegiance to this claim in OR, p. 29.) Many will find the claim
plausible. However, for at least two reasons this argument ought
not to bring in any new recruits to the indeterminacy doctrine.

One reason is that the assumption that the *totality* of the actor's
behavioural dispositions would match those of the naive believer
is on reflection highly implausible, especially when we take account
of dispositions to form new dispositions. (And the thesis being
supported would clearly lose its interest if we were not allowed to
take into account dispositions to form dispositions, since such
higher level dispositions can hardly be said to be irrelevant.) For
example, the actor will presumably possess dispositions to acquire
new dispositions that conform to any new information the actor
may acquire about how people with the belief in question are
actually likely to behave; but naïve possessors of that belief will
typically be robustly indifferent to such information. The second
reason for rejecting the argument is that it seems to depend essentially on the very assumption it is designed to undermine: that
the contents of beliefs and other propositional attitudes are matters

of fact which guide behaviour. For it is only on this assumption that the actor can plausibly be said to behave in the ways envisaged. So while the objection may have seemed plausible at first, in the end it appears to beg the question. (See 1.7 for some further relevant discussion. For Quine's talk of dispositions in connection with language, see Appendix B.)

1.5 Domestic indeterminacy

By now another line of objection may have occurred to you. Suppose for argument's sake that, as Quine's position implies, it is not a question of fact whether I believe that particles can come into existence from empty space. Given this assumption, together with some other defensible assumptions about truth and reality, it cannot be true or false that I actually hold this belief. Consequently it cannot be known that I hold it. But surely, the objection goes, I might know very well that I had this belief. Admittedly there may be beliefs I hold without knowing it; but this is surely not among them. It is a typical example of what would normally be counted as a belief consciously held on rational grounds—perhaps because I have read an article by reputable physicists which gives good reasons for it. I know I hold this belief, the objection goes, hence it is true that I hold it, hence it is a matter of fact that I hold it, hence Quine is just wrong.

The Quinean reply to this line of objection is not, of course, to deny that in these circumstances we should all agree that I believed that particles can come into existence from empty space, and that I believed that I knew I held this belief. The reply is that no determinate content is thereby given to these claims because the indeterminacy holds not just for translation between different languages but intralinguistically.

According to the general thesis of the indeterminacy of translation, one permissible scheme of translation between English and some other language might render my sentence X by Y, and a rival scheme might render it by Z, when Y and Z were agreed not to be equivalent. So while the first scheme represented me as believing that $[Y]$, the second would represent me as believing that $[Z]$— something altogether different. (Here square brackets round a letter stand in place of an actual use of the sentence for whose name that letter stands.) In that case there would seem no reason to say

my belief had any objective content, at least if that content must
be given in the other language.

Still, we might hope to be able to give a determinate content to
my belief in my own language, English. Couldn't we simply say I
believed that [X]? This move is blocked by the intralinguistic
version of the indeterminacy thesis, according to which it would
be consistent with the totality of possible evidence about both my
language and myself to represent my X as meaning something quite
different. The claim is that the set of sentences of a single language
could be mapped onto itself in such a way that someone who
uttered a given sentence X could be interpreted, consistently with
all the possible evidence, as meaning what the interpreter would
mean by the sentence Y onto which X was mapped, even though
X and Y were agreed not to mean the same. (*WO*, pp. 27, 78; OR,
pp. 46 f.)

It appears to follow that interpreting our compatriots' utterances
of X 'homophonically', that is, mapping X onto itself, is just one
out of many equally permissible ways of interpreting them. Now
Quine is willing to admit talk of sameness of meaning relative to
some specified scheme of translation or interpretation, for this is
surely no more than to concede that it is a matter of fact which
sentences are correlated by a given translation manual (3.12). Relative to the homophonic scheme, then, he can concede that I may
be said to believe that X, and to know I believe that X. But on his
view the homophonic scheme is not uniquely permissible, so we
cannot say absolutely that I believe that X.

Admittedly there is something strangely disturbing about this
idea. It is bad enough to be told we cannot know what others
believe; but to be told we cannot know even what *we* believe—
how, in that case, can we make any rational appraisals of our own
beliefs, or indeed of anything? And what would it be like to be
given a non-standard scheme of translation for English and imagine
it applied to oneself? Surely, we tend to think, there must be
objectively different psychological states associated with X and Y
(cf. Bradley, 1969, p. 124). We tend to think that our sentences—
those particular types of mark or sound-patterns—help to guide
us in our decision-making, and hence in our behaviour. And because we assume each particular sentence makes its own distinctive
contribution to these processes, we find it hard to understand how
it could fail to be a matter of fact that a sentence has one meaning

rather than some quite different meaning. Moreover, because it is obvious that there is nothing sacrosanct about the sounds or marks we happen to use in our language, we find it hard to see how it could fail to be a matter of fact, in some cases, that two quite different sentences should nonetheless have exactly the same objective psychological role, and so, presumably, objectively the same meaning. But the intralinguistic or 'domestic' version of Quine's thesis seems to make such thoughts question-begging. I shall return to it later (3.13, 3.14, chapter 11). (Incidentally, the fact that Quine associates his general indeterminacy thesis with its domestic version is yet another reason why the thesis cannot be understood as thesis X: the platitude that rough translations can conflict. Within a single language there can be no question of anything but total congruity of concepts: the homophonic scheme is presumably as exact as it is theoretically possible to be.)

1.6 Why the utility of language is no objection

If, in Quine's view, sentences generally lack what might be called objective meanings, how is it that we can make them do useful work? How is it, for example, that we can successfully order potatoes rather than stewed prunes? Or how is it that by saying to a child 'The moon is round like a ball' we can get the child to behave and reason—as it seems to us—appropriately to the moon's being spherical, rather than to some other body's being, say, cylindrical? How is it that by the use of words we can get the builder to lay slabs rather than set up pillars? Indeed, if there is no determinate fact of the matter as to what Quine's own utterances mean, why does he bother to write sentences which some of us take to express profoundly interesting philosophical views? (If there is nothing to be right or wrong about, how can he complain that his views have sometimes been misrepresented?) If sentences do have determinate meanings, then presumably our success in using them is explicable in terms of our common knowledge of those meanings. But if sentences lack determinate meanings this success appears very mysterious.

Part of one possible Quinean reply has been anticipated: talk of translation and sameness of meaning generally is acceptably 'objective' provided it is relativized to a given scheme of translation. It is a matter of fact that, relative to the usual scheme for getting from French to English, 'Le photon n'a pas de masse' means the same as 'Photons have no mass'. And relative to the homophonic scheme we may say it is a fact that an English speaker's utterance of 'There are black holes in our galaxy' means there are black holes in our galaxy—and we may justifiably add that the speaker *believes* there are black holes in our galaxy.

However, a serious objector is unlikely to be satisfied with this concession. It seems to give away too much. If we can really count it as a matter of fact that the given sentence has that meaning relative to the homophonic scheme, what is to prevent us saying that for a sentence to have a determinate, objective meaning in our own language just *is* for it to have such and such a meaning relative to the homophonic scheme? After all, Quine himself has said that the homophonic method is 'fundamental to the very acquisition and use of one's mother tongue' (*WO*, p. 59; cf. OR, p. 46), thereby conceding its privileged status.

Quine has several possible replies. One might be to suggest that our practical success with language is to be explained by our all tending to use the homophonic method for interpreting our compatriots' utterances. Another might be to say that practical success does not depend on the method of interpretation, and can be accounted for in other ways. But neither of these replies would be very impressive. The first seems to make him vulnerable to the objection mentioned in the last paragraph, in which case the domestic version of the indeterminacy thesis is put at risk. Since domestic and general theses stand or fall together (chapter 10) the second reply might be preferable. But that would commit him to maintaining that the use of non-homophonic interpretations would not lead to any significant practical difficulties—an implausible claim. For it seems that our interpretations of others' remarks often guide our behaviour: different interpretations, different behaviour.

I think these difficulties ought to lead us to consider a different reply. The objection challenges Quine to account for the practical success of language if sentences generally lack objective meanings. He can reply, first, that other notions than that of meaning may well be adequate to explain that success; second, that not much indeterminacy infects the interpretation of sentences closely linked to practical activities. To grasp the significance of these points, and generally to improve our understanding of Quine's doctrine, we need to take account of his whole approach to philosophy.

1.7 Quine's naturalism

Following Dewey, Quine has described himself as a naturalist. We are natural objects among others, and all our activities, mental and physical, including our scientific theorizing, are part of the natural world and should be studied empirically, in the spirit of natural science. Philosophy is part of this scientific enterprise and cannot claim a privileged position or independent authority (OR, p. 26, 1968b, p. 303, TPT, p. 2). On all the evidence available, and in spite of the still unfathomed complexity of our brains, we are made up of the same sorts of elementary particles as shoes, ships, and sealing wax. Thus there is 'no change without a change in the positions or states of bodies' because nothing capable of change has any but physical components (FM, p. 187, NNK, pp. 68 f.).

For any particular event which is explicable at all, therefore, there is in Quine's view an explanation in terms of physics. Not that this is an unexamined dogma. The point is that the best evidence to date supports it (cf. TDE, pp. 44 f., *WO*, pp. 264 f., NNK). Admittedly, even if the workings of the human brain were fully understood, there would be no *practical* prospect of explaining human behaviour in terms of physics and physical structures. So no doubt the idioms of meaning and propositional attitude are 'practically indispensable'. However, when we use these idioms we should recognize, if we are philosophers, that they have no place in a language designed to 'limn the true and ultimate structure of reality' (*WO*, p. 221). This rejection of intentional notions is backed up by reference to the indeterminacy thesis, among other considerations: Quine does not dogmatically assert the scientific unsoundness of intentional idioms and attempt to justify the indeterminacy thesis on the basis of that free-floating dogma. Another set of reasons for rejecting intentional idioms is given in 'Two Dogmas of Empiricism'. Those who believe that the notions of synonymy, analyticity, etc., can be given reasonably clear sense must show how that can be done without falling foul of the difficulties set out in that article. (See chapter 12 for more on the relations between the indeterminacy thesis and Quine's philosophy of language.)

In the absence of detailed information about the structure and functioning of people's brains, we can make sensible guesses about their *dispositions* to behave in certain specifiable ways when their sense organs are subjected to certain specific types of stimulation.

Such talk of dispositions, though to some extent speculative, and not as acceptably scientific as Quine would prefer (*RR*, pp. 10, 13; MVD), is at any rate exposed to the possibility of empirical checking in the light of advances in the neurosciences. In this respect, disposition talk contrasts favourably, in Quine's eyes, with the intentional idioms of believing, intending, hoping, wanting, etc. There are no reasonably clear principles for the use of these idioms—they fit where they touch—indeed, they are subject to the indeterminacy if anything is. Certainly they cannot furnish satisfactory scientific explanations of behaviour (MVD *passim*). If we want scientific explanations of behaviour we must either wait for explanations in neuroscientific terms (a long wait!), or try to devise suitable notions based on behavioural dispositions. (Quine's ideas on language and dispositions are discussed further in Appendix *B*.)

We are now in a position to see why Quine is not going to be impressed by the objection that the success of language is mysterious unless sentences have objective meanings. He can reply that it is question-begging to assume that the only way to explain behaviour adequately is by invoking our ordinary notions of meaning and synonymy. In his view, other types of explanation are in principle available, whereas we impose our schemes of intentional explanation on patterns of behaviour to which rival schemes could also have been applied. So meanings lack scientific explanatory power, and the objection cannot be pressed without a critique of his whole philosophical approach (which is not of course what I am going to offer).

1.8 Why 'confronting the facts' won't work

Our success in using language to deal with the world may still seem enough to guarantee the impossibility of significant conflict between schemes of translation. Why can't we decide between rival schemes by simply confronting them with the facts? If in an Italian restaurant I request 'Burro' and am given butter, that confirms my belief that the waiter has understood me and that my Italian phrase-book is correct. If instead I am offered something else— a donkey perhaps—then it seems likely that the waiter hasn't understood me (maybe he is Spanish).

Quine is not vulnerable to this line of objection. He concedes, as anyone must, that the practical utility of language requires some sentences to be closely linked with non-verbal reality (2.1). Other sentences, however, are more remote from it—their connections with the world are mediated by multifarious links with other sentences—and in general the degree to which a sentence is subject to the indeterminacy depends on its remoteness from non-verbal reality (*WO*, pp. 76 f.; EN, p. 89; ESW, p. 314). Any permissible Italian-English translation manual must render 'Burro', taken as a one-word Italian sentence, by 'Butter', or by something not significantly different. But the more theoretical a sentence, the less tightly its translation is constrained by independently identifiable facts. Rival schemes which conflict only at higher levels of theoreticity cannot in general be 'confronted by the facts' because one cannot in general tell, independently of any scheme of translation, what the users of a given language count as the facts, or how they assess their relevance (see e.g. *WO*, p. 64, EN, p. 89, *RR*, pp. 35 ff., ESW, p. 314, and chapter 4 below).

1.9 The museum myth, and alternative approaches to the idea of objectivity in semantics

The indeterminacy thesis implies that relations of sameness of meaning are not matters of fact. *A fortiori* it is sharply opposed to the myth of the mind as a museum in which 'the exhibits are meanings and the words are labels' (OR, p. 27). But the inadequacies of this primitive myth are not a reason for endorsing the indeterminacy thesis, nor are those who reject the thesis thereby committing themselves to the myth.

There has been an understandable temptation to assume that if, contrary to what Quine believes, statements of sentence synonymy can be objectively true in the sense of not being subject to Quinean indeterminacy, they must somehow correspond to facts about hidden mental entities—ideas, meanings, or whatever. The submerged assumption is that objectivity in a given domain demands realism about the existence of things in that domain. Evidently Plato was driven by something like this thought. But reflection on two other sorts of case should destroy its appeal. One is notions like axis, equator, and centre of gravity. The fact that a certain body has a certain determinate axis of rotation in no way implies the existence of some entity (a chain of atoms?) which *is* its axis of rotation. Nevertheless, there is a clear sense in which it is an objective matter of fact that it has that axis of rotation. The other case is

that of colours. It is widely and reasonably maintained that, given
the colour concepts we have, the truth values of statements about
colours are determined by the totality of truths statable in terms
of physics (except in borderline cases, of course, but that is beside
the point: see 1.1(*c*)). But clearly those who take this view are not
thereby committed to hold that a thing's having a certain colour is
a matter of its standing in a relation to an entity which is its colour.
So, just as two bodies may have the same axis of rotation without
there being any entity which is that axis, and two surfaces may
have the same colour without their colour being an entity, there
seems no reason why those who reject the indeterminacy doctrine
should not also reject the primitive notion that meanings are some
kind of entities.

   Those who reject the indeterminacy doctrine might quite possibly go along with Quine himself in maintaining that the only
evidence relevant to justifying claims about sameness of sentence
meaning is evidence about people's behavioural dispositions. Their
disagreement with Quine might then lie in their insistence that the
totality of facts about behavioural dispositions, broadly construed,
rules out the possibility of significant conflicts between rival schemes of sentence translation—that this totality actually does determine sentence synonymy. This is not an obviously absurd position:
support for it can be looked for from various directions. For example, we might attempt to follow Gareth Evans's lead and carefully
trace the different effects on behavioural dispositions that would
be expected to flow from different types of interpretation of various
predicates, hoping thereby to reveal how the dispositions ruled
out the possibility of significant conflict (Evans, 1975). Or we
might hope to show more directly that constraints on translation
guarantee uniqueness. (The argument of chapters 10 and 11 is
another approach to showing that behavioural dispositions determine translation.)

   Here it is pertinent to note that to reject the indeterminacy
doctrine, and to maintain that the truth values of statements about
sentence synonymy are determined by the totality of truths about
behavioural dispositions (or physically statable facts, or whatever:
see 3.1), does not commit us to maintaining that statements about
sentence synonymy are *translatable* or even analysable in those
terms. That is, it does not commit us to rejecting thesis VI in my
list: rejection of the indeterminacy doctrine (theses I–IV) is quite

compatible with acceptance of VI. We need only maintain that those facts which could be stated in the preferred vocabulary are what make the other true statements true. (This appears to be Quine's own view about other sorts of statements when he says 'There is no change without a change in the positions or states of bodies', FM, p. 187.) In this sense the other truths are *strictly implied* by the physically statable truths: it is absolutely impossible that the physical truths should have been as they are while whatever truths are statable in other terms—chemical, biological, or whatever—were other than they are.[8]

Truths about colours and contours provide useful illustrations. There is every reason to think that sentences such as 'Some tables are brown' and 'Some trees are gnarled' cannot be translated into any set of truths expressed in terms of, say, particle physics, no matter how complicated the translations might be. Nor does it even seem plausible to suggest that we might be able to give necessary and sufficient conditions for the truth of such sentences in those terms, or in any other Quine-acceptable terms. Yet it is clearly possible to maintain that the truth or falsity of such statements is strictly implied by the totality of truths statable in Quine-acceptable terms: that it is absolutely impossible that the totality of Quine-acceptably statable truths should have been as it actually is, while the truth values of such statements were other than they actually are.

Finally, let us note that there is a myth about reference similar to the one about the 'meaning museum'. The museum myth is that meanings are language-independent mental items to which words can be assigned rather as labels are assigned to museum exhibits. The myth about reference is that we can pin words to things by means of special mental acts of referring, rather as labelled arrows

[8] Not that Quine would put it in these terms. But the trouble with his dictum 'no mental difference without a physical difference' (FM, p. 187) as it stands is that it could have been accepted as *contingently* true even by Descartes. That the other truths are such as to be strictly implied is itself a contingent matter, unless physicalism is true a priori. But it is not contingent that you cannot have just *these* physical facts without the other facts. It seems best to bring out this point by using 'strictly implies', in spite of its strongly un-Quinean flavour. The more fashionable 'supervenes' is often defined to give a relation which is not strong enough, thus: 'properties A supervene on base properties B if, necessarily, if something with B has A, then everything with B has A'. This relation leaves it mysterious why the A properties actually occur, since it allows that if there had contingently been nothing with both A and B in the actual world, there could have been something with B but not A. See Blackburn (1984a, pp. 182–7). In contrast the relation I am talking about requires it to be necessary that whatever has B has A. (Kirk, 1979 and 1982b.)

can be shot at trees. These acts of mental archery connect the word 'Paris' to Paris, 'orange' to oranges, 'rabbit' to rabbits, and so on. Naturally Quine holds that there are no such mental acts. But he goes further. He applies the indeterminacy doctrine to terms as well as to the translation of whole sentences. Just as the totality of possible evidence leaves room for conflicting translations of sentences, so, he maintains, it leaves room for conflicting assignments of referents to terms. However, it should now be clear that just as rejection of the thesis of the indeterminacy of sentence translation does not automatically commit us to the museum myth, so rejection of the corresponding thesis for reference does not commit us to the myth of mental archery. (See also chapter 5.)

1.10 The indeterminacy thesis and the Brentano–Chisholm thesis

We have just seen that opponents of the indeterminacy doctrine need not maintain that synonymy statements are translatable or analysable in Quine-acceptable terms. So they will not be happy with Quine's assertion that 'Brentano's thesis of the irreducibility of intentional idioms is of a piece with the thesis of indeterminacy of translation' (*WO*, p. 221)—at least if 'irreducibility' means the impossibility of translating or analysing intentional idioms in Quine-acceptable terms. (Cf. thesis VI in the list at Appendix A.)

Quine regards the Brentano–Chisholm thesis as showing, not 'the indispensability of intentional idioms and the importance of an autonomous science of intention', but 'the baselessness of intentional idioms and the emptiness of a science of intention' (*WO*, p. 221). Now the Brentano–Chisholm thesis is certainly not a platitude. It is both interesting and important, though by now pretty generally accepted. But still there seems no way to interpret that thesis and the indeterminacy thesis as mere variations on a single theme. Quine appears to have been somehow led to conflate two distinct issues: the objective versus the subjective, and extensionality versus intensionality. Part of the trouble springs from the slippery notions of reduction and explication. I am taking the Brentano–Chisholm thesis to be that intentional idioms cannot be reduced to extensional (non-intensional) idioms in the sense that they cannot be translated, defined or analysed (that is, given analytically necessary and sufficient conditions) in extensional terms. Thus interpreted, the thesis is very attractive. But it seems to be sharply distinct from the indeterminacy doctrine, which, as we have seen, implies that many statements in intensional terms do not generally state matters of fact at all. In contrast, the Brentano–Chisholm thesis is clearly compatible with an extreme objectivism about meaning.

There is an assumption which, if sound, would go a long way towards justifying the claim that the two theses are equivalent. It is that if one theory, *A*, describes and explains in its way everything described and explained by a second theory *B*, but not conversely, then the sentences of *A* must be translatable by, or at any rate have logical equivalents in, sentences of *B*. Suppose we temporarily concede this translatability assumption, then, and make two further assumptions. One is (*a*) physicalism: the view (noticed in the last section) that all truths about the things, properties and phenomena that really exist are strictly implied by the totality of facts statable in terms of physics, but not conversely. The other assumption is (*b*) that physics is extensional. Both (*a*) and (*b*) are acceptable to Quine (see FM) and I do not wish to dispute either of them.

Now if, as (*a*) has it, all truths about what really exists are strictly implied by the facts statable in purely physical terms (but not conversely) the translatability assumption requires all truths not framed in purely physical terms to correspond to logically equivalent sentences which *are* framed in purely physical terms. But if physics is extensional, as (*b*) has it, the Brentano–Chisholm thesis rules out the possibility of just such equivalents, from which in turn it follows that statements made by means of intensional idioms do not state matters of fact. And that gives us the non-factuality component of the indeterminacy doctrine (thesis III) as a special case.

The translatability assumption, or something very much like it, evidently lay behind positivistic reductionism. It is natural if you like the idea that statements of kinds which seem problematic (e.g. statements about the external world, or about psychological states) can be explicated as logical constructions out of statements of apparently less problematic kinds (e.g. statements about immediate experience or behaviour, or statements in the vocabulary of physics). Possibly Quine was influenced by something like the translatability assumption, although so far as I know he nowhere states or defends it. (How could he?) But the translatability assumption lacks appeal. Apart from the historical failure of all attempts to produce actual translations or logical equivalents of the kinds allegedly possible, there are well known considerations which go strongly against the particular suggestion that everyday mental language statements are translatable into behavioural or physical language. A further potent thought has been that the translatability assumption appears to fail dramatically in the particular case of digital computers, a case where several clearly distinct levels of descriptions and explanation apply to the same concrete entities. For it is an excessively familiar fact that exactly the same program and exactly the same inputs could in principle have accounted for the behaviour of any of an indefinitely wide range of physically very different machines. (See also Appendix B.) It therefore seems that in general no particle-level translations or even logical equivalents could be constructed for program-level descriptions and explanations. Yet whatever facts about the machine's behaviour are explicable in terms of its program and inputs will also have *some* explanation in terms of particle physics.

If this is right, the translatability assumption must be abandoned. But without it, I do not see how the Brentano–Chisholm thesis could be represented as equivalent to the indeterminacy thesis.

1.11 Quine and Wittgenstein

Many readers of *Word and Object*, struggling to fathom the indeterminacy doctrine, will have been puzzled by the footnote in which Quine comments:

Perhaps the doctrine of indeterminacy of translation will have little air of paradox for readers familiar with Wittgenstein's latter-day remarks on meaning. (*Word and Object*, p. 77.)

The context is a consideration of theoretical sentences like 'Neutrinos lack mass', which according to Quine lack linguistically neutral meaning, and of which, above all, it is true that 'understanding a sentence means understanding a language'. But why does he associate himself with the views of someone who, it seems, could not possibly have accepted his indeterminacy doctrine? Can Quine's doctrine really be just a continuation of Wittgenstein by other means?

It is true that Wittgenstein introduces us to a close relative of Quine's radical translator. ('Suppose you came as an explorer into an unknown country with a language quite strange to you . . . '— *Philosophical Investigations*, sect. 206. See the next chapter.) More to the point, Wittgenstein also introduces us to the idea that no facts about me alone could determine what rules I was following, or what I meant by a given expression: perhaps all such facts are compatible with countless mutually incompatible interpretations (op. cit. sects. 143-206: see below). So certainly Quine's indeterminacy doctrine is akin to some of the ideas Wittgenstein considers. However, Wittgenstein does not seem to want us to conclude that translation is indeterminate.

It will be helpful to exploit Kripke's remarkable interpretation of Wittgenstein on rules and private language. (That Kripke's interpretation is disputed—as usual with such interpretations—will not affect the points I want to make, since if Kripke is wrong Quine will look even more remote from Wittgenstein than would otherwise appear.)

Kripke represents Wittgenstein as having propounded, and offered a solution to, a remarkable sceptical paradox—'the most radical and original sceptical problem that philosophy has seen to date' (Kripke, 1982, p. 60). The paradox, briefly, is that there could not possibly be any facts about a given person's past history which justified present claims about what that person had meant, in the past, by a given expression. For no matter what the expression may be, and no matter what may have been said or done, the totality of facts about the person's past is compatible with a perverse interpretation which diverges from the standard one for at least some possible circumstances in which the person has not yet used the expression. According to Kripke, Wittgenstein's 'sceptical solution' is this. He accepts that there are no facts about me which justify my claim that in the past I meant by this expression what I now say I meant by it. Nevertheless I am not wrong when I claim to be justified in saying what I meant and mean by the expression, because the customs and practices of my linguistic community—given that we all share the same 'form of life'—provide both what constitutes my meaning this rather than that, and also what constitutes my being justified in thinking I meant this rather than that. (A brutal condensation; but I hope it is adequate for my purposes. I take it that sameness of 'form of life' in the relevant sense is sameness of innate predispositions and tendencies, which result in sameness of what it is found natural to do, and agreement in what is counted as 'going on in the same way'. See also 10.7.)

Now Kripke's Wittgensteinian sceptic's point looks very much like Quine's thesis of the inscrutability of reference (thesis II), although, as Kripke points out, there are notable contrasts. Moreover it is at least plausible to say that if there is inscrutability of reference, there is also indeterminacy of sentence translation (5.9). But before saying more on the relations between Quinean indeterminacy and the scepticism Kripke describes, I want to mention and comment on three main contrasts Kripke detects between Wittgenstein's and Quine's treatments of these matters.

(*a*) 'Quine bases his argument on behaviouristic premises' (op. cit., p. 55), while Wittgenstein's sceptical point is supposed to hold even if all possible introspective evidence is taken into account. (*b*) 'The way the sceptical argument is presented is not behaviouristic. It is presented from the "inside" '. And (*c*) 'the important problem for Wittgenstein is that my present mental state does not appear to determine what I *ought* to do in the future.' 'Since Quine formulates the issues dispositionally, this problem [viz. whether anything determines what my dispositions ought to be] cannot be stated within his framework' (op. cit., p. 57).

My comments are these. (*a*) Quine does indeed make some behaviouristic assumptions. However, it is far from clear that he needs to use them in arguing for the indeterminacy doctrine. Moreover, he cannot now be said to assume that only behaviour can be relevant (see 3.1). Kripke's second contrast (*b*) does seem to hold, at least in respect of presentation: Quine does not put his case 'from the inside'. (*c*) It certainly seems that the question whether anything determines what my dispositions *ought* to be cannot be stated in just those terms from within Quine's framework. However, the question whether anything determines whether a given scheme of interpretation is uniquely correct can be stated from within Quine's framework (see chapter 3), and there is at least a prima facie case for saying that if the answer to this second question is affirmative, so is the answer to the first.

But there is more to be said. Kripke's Wittgensteinian sceptic assumes that only facts about *me*—my past history, my intentions and behaviour—could be relevant to what I formerly meant by a given expression. Here I think we have a much more significant contrast between that sceptic and Quine than any of the other three. For Quine's thesis is that even the totality of facts about a whole linguistic community, and indeed the totality of facts about the whole world, would fall short of determining what anyone meant by a sentence, or that one particular translation manual was uniquely correct. This contrast can be stated as follows. Kripke's Wittgensteinian sceptic maintains that:

(A) There are no facts in a particular person's life history which determine what they mean by any given word, or justify the claim that they mean this rather than that.

And the same sceptic goes on to conclude that:

(B) There is nothing which determines what anyone means by anything, or justifies the claim that anyone means this rather than that.

Wittgenstein himself appears to accept (A). But surely he resists (B), assigning a vital role to the whole linguistic community, its form of life, and its customs and practices. Quine, however, not only accepts Kripke's sceptic's (A): he also insists on (B), since on his view the whole conception of meaning is a misconception. Here we have a very sharp contrast indeed between Wittgenstein and Quine.

As Kripke points out, Quine often puts the issues in terms of behavioural dispositions, and many people tend to think that reference to the individual's dispositions could be used to refute the sceptic. Kripke argues strongly against this suggestion (op. cit., pp. 22–37). To pursue this issue far would involve too many questions of Wittgensteinian exegesis, but some further comments are needed. First, the thesis Kripke ascribes to Wittgenstein, that rule-following and meaning are possible only for those who share the language of a community, does not by itself commit him to the view that the totality of dispositions would leave room for conflicting rival interpretations of that person as a language user. If Wittgenstein's idea is that the difference between thinking you are obeying a rule and obeying it is constituted (other things being equal) by your membership of a linguistic community, then he is so far free to concede that the dispositions of that community, and of each of its members, would leave no room for rival schemes of interpretation. So at any rate that thesis by itself provides no support for the indeterminacy doctrine. Now Kripke stresses that dispositions will neither *justify* my responses (e.g. to questions like 'What is 123 + 456?'), nor *tell* me what I ought to do in each new instance' (op. cit., p. 24). He also argues that Wittgenstein would have rejected a dispositional *analysis* of what it is to mean, e.g., addition by 'plus' (op. cit., pp. 25-27). But the anti-Quinean claim that the totality of behavioural dispositions precludes significant conflict over translation and interpretation does not require us to disagree with Wittgenstein on these matters. (In particular, as we saw in the last two sections, opposition to the indeterminacy doctrine does not commit us to the possibility of behavioural or other *analyses* of synonymy etc. at all.) So I see no reasons here for supposing that Wittgenstein's ideas give any support to Quine's.

However, Kripke also urges that my dispositions extend to only a finite number of cases because, for example, some numbers are too big for me to deal with in my lifetime, given my memory, etc. This may be true,[9] and it may be relevant to the points Kripke wants to make about Wittgenstein's views. But it too seems to give no support to the indeterminacy doctrine, as I shall now try to show.

You might at first think that if a scheme of translation is not supported by dispositions which cover infinitely many possible uses of the expression concerned, there must be room for rival translation schemes which fit all the dispositions, yet conflict in that infinite region which lies beyond the reach of all dispositions. So you might think Kripke's points about dispositions actually provide very powerful support for the indeterminacy doctrine. To see why this is wrong it will be helpful to imagine a superficially attractive reply. The reply would be: 'In the region which lies beyond the reach of all dispositions there's no support for translation *at all*. If a particular translation isn't supported by the dispositions it isn't justified in any way. Translation schemes can only cover those regions where behavioural dispositions can, in principle, provide evidence.' Now this particular response would certainly be inadequate. It would simply ignore some of Wittgenstein's most impressive thoughts on the matter. For Wittgenstein's point seems to be precisely that the absence of *this* sort of 'support' or 'evidence' doesn't mean there is an absence of *justification* for taking an expression one way rather than another. It only means that the justification doesn't consist in the presence of this particular sort of evidence (cf. *Philosophical Investigations*, sects. 211, 219). Wittgenstein surely takes a non-realist view of what justifies

[9] But see Blackburn, 1984b, pp. 289-91.

claims about meaning. He is attacking, among other things, the Platonic assumption that if for example 'plus' means addition, then this word must be somehow connected with a certain determinate abstract object, the addition function. And this attack is not confined to views about mathematical language. Wittgenstein is attacking any idea that words are connected with specific entities— 'concepts' or 'meanings'—in a way that either fixes how the words ought to be used on any possible occasion, or in any other way explains how they mean what they do. The considerations we have glanced at in this section suggest that such connections could not possibly exist—even if entities of the right sorts did exist. However, Wittgenstein is by no means suggesting that therefore we are not justified in saying such things as "Plus" means addition'. He is concerned to offer a different way of conceiving of such justification, which does not involve an impossible connection of the word with an abstract object of the sort assumed by certain sorts of realist. If this is anything like a correct indication of what Wittgenstein was saying, his ideas provide no support for the suggestion that the failure of dispositions to extend to infinitely many possible cases would entail Quinean indeterminacy of translation of the relevant linguistic expressions.

You might perhaps object that Quine's point is exactly the same as Wittgenstein's: it's just that Quine chooses a paradoxical way of expressing it. He doesn't after all deny that the homophonic scheme of translation is vitally important, nor recommend using any other. Nor does he deny the utility of translation. But this suggestion ignores certain pertinent considerations. For one thing, unlike Quine, Wittgenstein does not seem to think that what we tend to say about sameness of meaning lacks objectivity—is unscientific, or not about 'matters of fact'—in a special way which marks it off from other sorts of discourse. What he seems above all anxious to convey is that the relevant facts are not of the sorts we tend to expect. In particular they are not facts about current mental states or events, such as images, intentions, intuitions, flashes of insight, awareness of formulas. Nor does Wittgenstein contrast *translation* with other things as Quine does. Nor, as I have said, is there any hint in Wittgenstein that translation is underdetermined by the totality of physically statable facts. Finally, Wittgenstein does not imply that there is no single uniquely correct scheme of translation. On the contrary, he seems to think that if we take account of form of life, then correctness in the use of words, hence meaning and sameness of meaning, are determined. In brief, Wittgenstein seems to think that form of life plus local practices determine meaning and translation, and Quine denies it.[10]

1.12 Quinean indeterminacy, realism, and anti-realism

By denying that there are in general any facts of the matter about relations of sameness of meaning and reference, Quine of course rejects any sort of realism about semantics. But opposition to the indeterminacy doctrine does not commit us to the extreme view which Putnam calls 'metaphysical realism'; nor should we put the doctrine itself into the same slot as Dummett's anti-realism.[11]

As we noticed earlier, Quine sees philosophy as part of the scientific enterprise. It does not have a privileged position and it cannot claim independent authority. So if we are asked *what there is*, the best answer we can give is to say there is whatever our best scientific theory of the world says there is—whatever that theory 'posits' (TDE, pp. 44 f., *WO*, chapter 1, TPT). Even our best theory of the world is subject to correction, but that does not mean we have to be relativists because 'we own and use our beliefs of the moment': from within our current theory 'we can judge truth as earnestly and absolutely as can be' (*WO*, pp. 24 f.). How much of a realist this makes Quine is a hard question, but fortunately there seems no need to pursue it here.[12] The decisive consideration is that he himself has explicitly maintained that the indeterminacy of translation holds even if we adopt a fully realistic position on the entities posited by today's physics. Even if we assume that the laws of physics, and the furniture of the universe as specified in terms of physics, are fixed and definite, there is still room for significantly divergent schemes of translation (1968b, p. 303, FM, TPT). It seems clear that this position can be opposed without having to commit oneself to realism at this level. To oppose it is

[10] Crispin Wright seems to think Wittgenstein's idea is that my meaning X rather than Y is not a matter of fact at all (1980, e.g. pp. 30, 389 ff.). If this interpretation is correct it brings Wittgenstein closer to Quine than I have suggested. Obviously there is much more to be said.

[11] On anti-realism see Dummett, 1976, and the preface and other papers, 1978. On Putnam's ideas on metaphysical realism contrasted with 'internal realism' see his 1981 and the introduction and other papers in his 1983.

[12] One difficulty is to know the sense in which Quine holds that there can be empirically equivalent but mutually incompatible theories of the world: see 6.1. Another is to know whether the indeterminacy would always require the rival translations of a given sentence to have different truth values: see 3.8.

simply to maintain that *if* the totality of physically specifiable truths (or other Quine-acceptable truths) is assumed to be fixed, there is no room for significantly divergent schemes of translation. If that is an acceptable statement of opposition to the indeterminacy thesis, such opposition does not involve commitment to realism about physically posited items. (See 3.1, 9.6.)

These last remarks ought to leave us free to sidestep the current titanic struggles over realism. However, I must say a little more because Putnam has recently enlisted the indeterminacy doctrine— or at any rate the inscrutability thesis—in his attack on what he calls metaphysical realism. Of course his use of the indeterminacy doctrine for this purpose does not imply that he thinks opponents of the former are committed to the latter. Still, let us be clear that they are not so committed.

What Putnam (like Kant) opposes is the idea that we could take a 'God's Eye View': that we could survey on the one hand our theories and ways of talking, and on the other hand naked un-conceptualized Reality, and judge objectively how well the one fitted the other. It should be clear by the end of chapter 3, if not before, that rejection of this variety of metaphysical realism is perfectly compatible with rejection of the indeterminacy thesis. (Indeed, even Putnam thinks that reference is not inscrutable for 'internalist' opponents of metaphysical realism like himself—1981, p. 52.) What Putnam's argument seems to be directed against is the idea that words such as 'rabbit' stand in a special unique 'metaphysically singled out' relation of reference to objects out there in the world, *when these objects are supposed to exist and be individuated independently of conceptual schemes* (1981, pp. 49-55). But rejecting this idea is obviously consistent with also rejecting the indeterminacy doctrine.

Finally, a very brief mention of Dummett's variety of semantic anti-realism. Quine's semantic anti-realism is much more drastic than Dummett's. Baldly, Dummett accepts that we understand all meaningful sentences in such a way that there is no room for significant conflict over translation, and Quine denies it (see 4.10). Quine also denies that the notions of meaning and understanding can serve anything approaching the useful purposes to which Dummett turns them. (See Dummett, 1976, and contrast with Quine's 'Cognitive Meaning'.) Dummettian anti-realists may of course concede that for some pairs of sentences the question whether or not they are synonymous is undecidable. But in such cases they cannot consistently maintain that it is permissible for rival schemes nevertheless to declare that the sentences concerned are (or are not) synonymous.

1.13 The indeterminacy thesis and some current approaches to semantics

We have seen how the indeterminacy thesis threatens attempts to explain meaning and synonymy in terms of the notions of use, of rules and conventions, or of propositional attitudes such as intentions, desires and beliefs (1.3, 1.4). It follows that no attack on it which takes any of these notions for granted ought to be regarded as cogent. However, strong currents in semantic theorizing over the past few decades have treated some or all of these notions as basic: use and rules in much Wittgenstein-inspired theorizing; intentions, desires and beliefs in the work of Grice and his followers; all these notions in the work of Austin and his followers. Evidently, then, the value of this work, so far as it is intended to contribute to setting up a philosophically respectable framework for theorizing about meaning, is challenged by the indeterminacy doctrine.[13] The thesis also impinges on what I take to be the three other main current approaches to semantic theorizing: (*a*) componential analysis (or 'translational semantics'); (*b*) possible worlds semantics; (*c*) Davidson's programme.

(*a*) Componential analysis   Katz's version of this approach, for example, is expressly claimed to be proof against Quinean objections (Katz 1972, xxiii. Cf. 1979, pp. 338 f.). He envisages the possibility of arriving at a single finite set of basic concepts in terms of which any concept of any possible human language could be defined (1972, p. 32). The aim is to be able to provide, for any admissible interpretation of any linguistic expression of any possible human language, a canonical 'semantic representation'. But the indeterminacy thesis would make nonsense of this whole project. If Quine is right, the assignment of semantic representations to expressions could not be carried through in a scientifically respectable way, contrary to its express purpose. For there would be no objective basis for an assignment which corresponded

---

[13] See Romanos for a much fuller and wider-ranging discussion of the implications of Quine's doctrine—though, as I hope will become clear in chapter 12, I think Romanos puts excessive weight on the indeterminacy.

to one permissible translation manual rather than an assignment which corresponded to one of its Quinean rivals. (See 6.2 for what might at first seem to be a way to avoid this conclusion.)

(*b*) The possible worlds approach   A crude example of this approach would be to explicate the meaning of a sentence as a function from possible worlds to truth values. (The inadequacy of this particular example does not affect the point I want to make. For sophistication see Montague 1974, or Lewis, 1970.)

However, even if talk of possible worlds, or of functions from possible worlds to truth values, could be made acceptable to Quineans (a possibility suggested by Quine's paper 'Propositional Objects'), it does not follow that semantic theories employing such notions will automatically become equally acceptable. For any specification, direct or indirect, of the set of possible worlds which such a function takes into the value True for a given sentence will be couched in some language or other. So the specification itself will be subject to the indeterminacy. In this way the indeterminacy thesis threatens to smash the project of possible world semantics as decisively as it would smash that of translational semantics.

(*c*) Davidsonian semantics   The guiding thought here is that a Tarskian truth theory for a language, provided it meets certain constraints, will serve as a theory of meaning or interpretation for that language.[14] The important question of constraints will be discussed in chapter 3, and further at 5.7. Here I merely want to point out that Davidson has always acknowledged that his approach does not provide an a priori basis for ruling out the possibility that two different truth theories might both conform to all the formal and empirical constraints he recognizes and thereby instantiate what looks like Quinean indeterminacy (1967, p. 27, 1974a, pp. 321 f., 1974b, p. 327). However, he thinks that on his approach 'the degree of indeterminacy will . . . be less than Quine contemplates', partly on account of the principle of charity, 'and partly because the uniqueness of quantificational structure is apparently assured if convention T is satisfied'.[15]

I merely note these claims: it would be out of place to investigate them here.

[14] Davidson's original proposals (1967) have been somewhat modified. For more recent statements see his 1976, 1977, and other papers in his 1984.

[15] 1974a, p. 321. Quine queries this reasoning in his Comment (1974, 326–8). See also Kirk (1985).

1.14 Translation manuals

We have seen that Quine tends to state the indeterminacy thesis
in terms of 'schemes of translation' or 'translation manuals'. In
partial explanation he says that a manual for translating between
English and the language of some remote tribe would have 'as its
net yield an infinite *semantic correlation* of sentences: the implicit
specification of an English sentence, or various roughly interchangeable English sentences, for every one of the infinitely many
possible jungle sentences' (*WO*, p. 71). Discussion of this notion,
supplementary to Quine's own remarks about it and about 'analytical hypotheses' (see 2.3) may help to avoid misconceptions.

First a comment on his phrase 'semantic correlation', which
might look slightly inappropriate. Evans remarked that 'A translator states no semantical truths at all' (1975, p. 343), and Davidson
has described translation as 'a purely syntactic notion' (1977, p.
136). Now one point is incontestable: the finished translation manual merely correlates expressions with other expressions—merely
mentions them—and does not use the translated expressions to
link words and things. Moreover, just to know X is a translation
of Y is not to know what X or Y means or refers to. However, there
is evidently an extremely close connection between translation and
semantics more narrowly so called. For suppose we had a rival to
the standard scheme of translation between French and English,
and this rival fitted all the possible evidence in the way envisaged
by Quine (whatever that may be). In particular suppose, if possible,
that this rival manual were to render 'Le photon n'a pas de masse'
by 'Neutrinos have no charge'. Then (given some harmless assumptions) the assumed empirical adequacy of this bizarre manual would
guarantee the empirical adequacy of a scheme of interpretation for
French according to which (*a*) the French term 'photon' was in
some contexts assigned not photons, but neutrinos, as its referents,
and (*b*) 'a de masse' was in some contexts said to be true of x if
and only if x had a charge. The point is that if sentence translation
is indeterminate in Quine's sense, then semantics is subject to the
same indeterminacy when it comes to sentence interpretation; and
(clearly) vice versa. So although a translation manual does not itself
state semantic truths, its justification will be intimately concerned
with semantic truths. Devising a translation manual will not, it
seems, necessarily involve going so far as to devise a theory of
meaning for one of the two languages; but (as we shall see more

clearly in chapter 3) semantic considerations of some sorts will inevitably play a part. So if the correlation of sentences is not itself 'semantic', as Quine puts it, it is at any rate semantically based and justified.

It is crucial that Quine's thesis is supposed to hold for the translation of whole sentences, not just for words or phrases below sentence level. These will be uninterpreted sentences or, let us say, grammatically well-formed sequences of sounds or marks (7.3). There are plenty of examples of apparently conflicting ways of translating words and other sentence parts where the choice between different renderings is underdetermined even by all possible evidence. This goes even for logical expressions. In the French expression 'ne . . . rien', for example, we can correlate 'rien' with 'anything', rendering 'ne' by 'not'; or with 'nothing', in which case we compensate by counting 'ne' as pleonastic.[16] But such examples by no means illustrate the thesis. The two renderings of 'rien' as a sentence part yield equivalent versions ofsentences in which it occurs. Moreover, when 'Rien' by itself is used as a one word sentence, 'Anything' would not normally be a permissible translation.

There is a difficulty, however. Actual translation is *ad hoc*, concerned with individual utterances in context: anything from brief remarks to extended debates in the European Parliament, street signs, instructions on bean tins, scientific texts, haiku, the Bible.[17] So the translator who renders the utterance of sentence *X* by *Y* is not thereby committed to maintaining that *Y* would always be a permissible rendering of *X*. The speaker or writer may have been ignorant or perverse, and the needs of the translation might have precluded merely mirroring such deviations. So one apparent difficulty for the notion of a translation manual is that there seems no justification for assuming that one sentence, or even a set of 'roughly interchangeable' sentences, could even in principle be offered as *the* translation(s) of a given sentence, as Quine's thesis may seem to require.

---

[16] This is an example of Quine's in 'Ontological Relativity'. For a slightly more complicated example see Nancy Tuana, 1981. One good reason for distinguishing Quine's thesis from what is illustrated by such examples is that they do not involve any significant conflict between rival translators over the ascription of beliefs, nor, connectedly, over the translation of whole sentences. See also 7.4.

[17] 'Translation between any two languages always operates, in principle, with respect to contextualized utterances' (Lyons, 1977, p. 643).

We might at first hope to be able to overcome the difficulty by exploiting the notion of context: Y is a permissible rendering of X in contexts of type C. But the trouble is that, just as there is a potential infinity of sentences to be translated (or at any rate we may as well suppose there is), so, for each of these sentences, there is a potential infinity of possible contexts of utterance. And in general there seems no way of actually specifying the subset of contexts in which sentence X might be translatable by sentence Y.

The difficulty would be genuine, I think, if a translation manual had to be a device for providing acceptable renderings of individual utterances in context—if it had to be capable of doing the job of a human translator faced with an actual utterance or text. But there is no reason to assume that Quine does or should conceive of a translation manual in that way. For although practical, or applied, translation is concerned with actual utterances or texts in context, linguists and the rest of us habitually engage also in what might be called *theoretical* or *pure* translation—translation of words, phrases and whole sentences which are not actually being used, and for which no special context of use is envisaged. We even supply pure translations of sentences containing indexicals. For example, we all accept 'He has seen her' as a translation of 'Il l'a vue', just as we accept 'Photons have no mass' as a translation of 'Le photon n'a pas de masse', even when no actual use of any of these sentences is in question, and when the pronouns are not thought of as having been assigned particular references. Discussing pure translations is, after all, one way of improving our grasp of the languages involved, as well as a way of preparing for the tasks of applied translation. And Quine's thesis must be supposed to apply to pure translation, not just to the translation of individual utterances or texts. So I suggest that a Quinean translation manual is best thought of as a manual for pure sentence-translation: a device which gives renderings of sentences without regard to whether or not they are actually used and without regard to context (though there is no reason why it should not note context-dependence in cases where that can be manageably specified).

To say that a Quinean translation manual gives renderings of sentences is not to prejudge the question of determinacy of syntax. The point is that the indeterminacy thesis is supposed to apply to

the translation of sentences even if sentencehood itself is determinate. In fact Quine himself puts no weight on the possibility
that sentencehood is subject to a significant indeterminacy, and
regularly states his thesis in terms of sentences. The roots of the
indeterminacy that concerns him lie elsewhere. (For discussion of
syntax and indeterminacy see chapter 7.)

One more source of uncertainty over the notion of a translation
manual had better be mentioned. Actual translators, though they
may make use of dictionaries and grammars, typically work without
reference to explicitly formulated rules. Certainly they use nothing
that could count as a Quinean translation manual, because no
such thing exists. The nearest approach, I suppose, is computer
programs for machine translation. Notoriously these programs are
still very far from perfect, though to some extent that may be
because they are aimed not at what I am calling 'pure' sentence-
translation, but at the translation of actual texts, where contextual
considerations play a more significant part. However, viewed as
devices for pure translation, perhaps the best of them come within
shouting distance of Quinean translation manuals. Now, mentioning this possibility raises a further question about the nature
of a Quinean translation manual. Does it have to be a set of rules
so explicit as to permit their representation by a computer program
which, when a sentence of one of the relevant pair of languages is
put into it, puts out a sentence (or a set of what it represents as
equivalent sentences) as a translation?[18] Or could it just be a set
of rules usable only by people already familiar with both languages?
Evidently this question in turn raises fundamental questions about
the nature of language and knowledge of language. Is a non-trivial
and fully explicit manual possible? Would a less than explicit
manual reliably produce the same renderings of the same sentences?
We need not attempt to pursue these questions. All that matters
for the present is that a Quinean translation manual must include
some means whereby a potential infinity of sentences of each of
two languages is mapped onto sentences of the other. Thus a
translation manual for languages L_1 and L_2 will generate a pair of
(partial) functions, one taking sentences of L_1 to sentences, or
sets of purportedly equivalent sentences, of L_2, the other taking
sentences of L_2 to those of L_1. (Note that we do not have to
assume that the second function is merely the inverse of the first.)

[18] This is Hellman's ultimate objective (1974).

Further conditions on translation manuals will be discussed in chapter 3.

2

A Case for Indeterminacy

Some people may think they have a single conclusive argument for the indeterminacy thesis. But what is usually offered is not so much a crystalline argument as a heady brew of considerations which, taken together, make the thesis alluring. I shall try to deal with all these considerations in time, but in this chapter I confine attention to Quine's defence of the thesis in *Word and Object*. His discussion there deserves special attention not only because it is in several ways the best and clearest,[1] but because it introduces key ideas which will have to be taken into account later.

2.1 Radical translation and stimulus meaning

In *Word and Object* the indeterminacy doctrine is presented as the inescapable conclusion of an appraisal of the relations between the nature of the possible evidence and the nature of a finished translation manual. Discussion of the case of 'radical' translation helps to make Quine's points vivid. Radical translation is trans-lation from scratch, unaided by interpreters or existing dictionaries or grammars, and unaided even by knowledge of the beliefs, desires, intentions or other propositional attitudes of those whose utterances are to be translated (1.3, 1.4). Towards the end of the chapter he feels able to comment optimistically: 'One has only to reflect on the nature of possible data and methods to appreciate the indeterminacy' (*WO*, p. 72. See 2.9). Let us look more closely at his reasoning.

First, the possible evidence. Speaking of the radical translator Quine asserts that

All the objective data he has to go on are the forces that he sees impinging

---

[1] 'Speaking of Objects' and 'Meaning and Translation' are ancestors of chapter 2 of *Word and Object*. Note that 'The Problem of Meaning in Linguistics', though much earlier, cannot be seen as presenting the indeterminacy thesis. What it does present, very powerfully, is the thesis that where there are conceptual differences between different communities there is no reason to expect uniquely correct translation. That in such cases there is indeed no objective matter to be right or wrong about is surely right: it is thesis X. (See 1.1(*c*) and chapter 10.)

on the native's surfaces and the observable behaviour, vocal and otherwise, of the native. (*Word and Object*, p. 28.)

The alleged gap between these objective data and the linguist's
eventual translation manual is highlighted with the aid of two key
notions: *stimulus meaning*, and *analytical hypotheses*. The first is
intended to highlight the restricted nature of the data, the second
to exhibit the amount of underdetermined theorizing required to
yield the linguist's final product.

The *stimulus meaning* of a given sentence for a speaker at a time
is the ordered pair whose first member is the set of all the stimulations (of any duration up to some convenient short limit or
modulus) which would prompt that speaker's assent to that sentence at that time, and whose second member is the set of all the
stimulations which would prompt his dissent to it at that time.
(The set may, of course, be the empty set.)[2]

Quine is willing to accept the notion of stimulus meaning as
reasonably clear and objective.[3] With its aid he defines certain
other notions. *Occasion* sentences are those such as 'Dog', 'Green',
'It hurts', 'That car is stolen', 'which command assent or dissent
only if queried after an appropriate prompting stimulation' (*WO*,
pp. 35 f.).All other declarative sentences are *standing* sentences,
assent or dissent to which will often be given regardless of current
stimulation, though there is no sharp line between standing sentences and occasion sentences (*WO*, p. 36). *Observation* sentences,
finally, are defined as those occasion sentences whose stimulus
meanings for different speakers do not vary under the influence
of collateral information. Assent to, or dissent from, 'There's a
bachelor', for example, will normally depend on knowledge beyond
what can be gleaned from current stimulation: it is therefore not
an observation sentence. 'There's a cow', in contrast, in spite of
the fact that special knowledge of, say, the habits of cattle-flies
might result in some variations of stimulus-meaning from person
to person, counts as an observation sentence because such variations will be relatively small. It is high in observationality; and

---

[2] To take account of Quine's later elaborations of this doctrine we should regard the
stimulus meaning as an ordered triple, whose third member is the set of all stimulations
which would prompt neither assent nor dissent; but this refinement can be ignored for our
purposes. (Cf. 1970b.)

[3] *WO*, p. 39. But note that he has since urged that even the notions of assent and
dissent, used in defining stimulus meaning, are infected with some degree of indeterminacy,
though it is tolerable (1968b, p. 312).

'Red' is higher still (*WO*, pp. 41, 42, 44. Cf. EN, pp. 86 f., 1970b, pp. 2 f., 5). With the aid of these notions, then, Quine spells out the respects in which, as he claims, our intuitive notions of meaning and synonymy fall short of clarity and objectivity.

2.2 Stimulus synonymy and synonymy

As Quine points out, stimulus meaning will not generally coincide with our intuitive notion of meaning, nor stimulus synonymy (sameness of stimulus meaning) with synonymy, because our dispositions to assent to, or dissent from, a given sentence generally depend heavily on factors other than current stimulation: we draw on other knowledge. This is true even for occasion sentences such as 'That car is stolen'; while dispositions relating to standing sentences will usually be almost wholly independent of current non-verbal stimulation. However, stimulus synonymy for observation sentences gives us something quite close to our ordinary notion of synonymy for those sentences, especially when the degree of observationality is high, as with 'Red'; and 'significant approximation of stimulus meanings' will be an indispensable guide to the radical translator (*WO*, pp. 37, 39, 40).

By going bilingual I become able to tell which pairs of sentences are stimulus synonymous *for me*. I can then translate non-observational occasion sentences just as well as observational ones. Yet collateral information prevents even this 'intrasubjective stimulus synonymy' from being more than an approximation to synonymy as intuitively conceived. Indeed, in many cases it will be a very poor approximation. For example 'This creature has a heart' is intrasubjectively stimulus synonymous with 'This creature has kidneys' for anyone who believes hearts and kidneys always go together. But we should not be inclined to count these sentences as synonymous. And even if we screened off the effects of idiosyncratic information by requiring a candidate pair of sentences to be intrasubjectively stimulus synonymous throughout the entire linguistic community (this is 'socialized' intrasubjective stimulus synonymy) the effects of community wide collateral information would remain. As I have indicated, Quine thinks the whole project of distinguishing a pure knowledge of meanings from universally shared collateral information is illusory (TDE, *WO*, pp. 16, 37–9, 49–51). (This is the 'inextricability thesis', to be discussed in chapter 4.)

Although the results of translating by matching the stimulus meanings of whole sentences will not generally conform to what we expect of synonymy, they are at any rate objectively checkable. Whether two sentences are stimulus synonymous is subject only to the usual inductive uncertainty (*WO*, p. 68). Also objectively checkable is whether a given sentence is 'stimulus analytic' or 'stimulus contradictory', that is, whether it is one to which a person (or in the case of a sentence that is socially stimulus analytic, 'almost everybody' in the community) would assent, if to anything, under any stimulation within the modulus, or whether it is one which commands irreversible dissent (*WO*, pp. 55, 66). But since 'There have been black dogs' falls into the first class, and its contradictory into the second, these classes are very different from the traditionally analytic and contradictory sentences (cf. also EN, p. 86). There is just one further class of expressions—not sentences—which Quine thinks can be translated with an acceptable degree of objectivity: truth-functional connectives such as 'not', 'and', 'or'. These can be translated by testing people's dispositions to assent to or dissent from (short) sentences first singly, then combined by means of the putative truth-functional connective. For example, negation transforms any short sentence to which a person is disposed to assent into one from which they will be disposed to dissent, and vice versa.[4]

These methods do not take the radical translator very far. Standing sentences, which include most expressions of opinion on the world about us, on politics, geography, history, the sciences generally, the character of our friends, etc., do not get translated at all. And even the bilingual translator's renderings of occasion sentences depend on a type of theorizing that goes, Quine thinks, beyond the zone where independent evidence is possible. For in order to be able to produce a version in one language for any one of the potential infinity of translatable sentences of the other, the linguist must segment whole utterances into parts and devise a scheme for matching up sentences on the basis of matching up these parts. In other words, the linguist must have recourse to analytical hypotheses.

---

[4] This simple account has since been modified: 'Existence and Quantification' pp. 104 f., 1968b, p. 314, pp. 316–19, *RR*, pp. 75–8. Nancy Tuana (1981) has shown that Quine is still mistaken about this, since it will always be possible to produce incompatible construals of logical connectives. See n. 15 in chapter 1.

2.3 Analytical hypotheses

Suppose the radical translator has discovered that the jungle people's observation sentence 'Gavagai' is stimulus synonymous with 'Rabbit'. One might think this would amount to establishing that a native term 'gavagai' was translatable by 'rabbit'. To be sure, 'gavagai' may well be translatable by 'rabbit'. But Quine insists we should be mistaken if we assumed this was a necessary consequence of the identity of stimulus meanings between the sentences 'Gavagai' and 'Rabbit'. For without any difference in stimulus meanings, he claims, 'gavagai' could be a word for a whole enduring spatio-temporal object: a rabbit; or for a short temporal segment of such an enduring object: a rabbit-stage; or for any undetached part of a rabbit; or for a part of the spatio-temporally discontinuous aggregate of all living rabbits; or for the recurring universal, rabbithood.

While his readers are still stunned by this profusion, he urges that the whole idea of a term—a word that picks out an object of a certain kind—is, together with the auxiliary apparatus of objective reference (articles, pronouns, singular and plural, copula, identity predicates, etc.) 'provincial to our culture' (*WO*, p. 53). And he maintains—this is the inscrutability of terms—that there is in general *no* objective basis for translating the native's 'gavagai' by 'rabbit' rather than by 'rabbit stage', 'undetached rabbit part', or whatever. These alternative renderings could be made to fit the facts about stimulus meanings, he thinks, 'by compensatorily juggling the translation of numerical identity and associated particles' (*WO*, p. 54). In devising analytical hypotheses the linguist typically aims at matching the functions of the components of a translated whole sentence with the functions of words or phrases in the translating sentence (*WO*, p. 70). But the objective constraints are too sparse to compel the linguist to choose one scheme of analytical hypotheses in preference to another scheme which conflicts with the first; and translation is in general indeterminate.

That, in essentials, completes the case for indeterminacy in *Word and Object*. Before going on to discuss it I will say more about analytical hypotheses.

Any translation manual which is both humanly intelligible and non-trivial is going to have to provide finite means for handling what we had better treat as a potential infinity of possible utterances. The only way this can be done is by systematically analysing actual utterances so that they can be represented as constructed in humanly intelligible patterns from a finite set of elements. It follows that any serious translator must devise schemes for phonetic, phonological, and syntactic analysis. These analyses can certainly be included as one main component of the linguist's analytical hypotheses. However, Quine does not seem to regard this component as giving rise to the sort of indeterminacy he is anxious to explain (see chapter 7). He evidently sees the main, if not the only, scope for his special sort of indeterminacy to lie in whatever else the linguist has to do in order to produce an actual translation manual.

The really significant contribution of a translation manual is to exploit phonetic, phonological and syntactic analyses so as to provide ways of mapping sentences of the one language to sentences of the other. And the only non-trivial way it can do this for a potential infinity of sentences on each side is by correlating sentence-parts with sentence-parts, subject to any number of conditions on context, etc.[5] The hypotheses in accordance with which the linguist makes these part-to-part correlations are the analytical hypotheses which Quine thinks provide scope for the indeterminacy. Note that if syntactic indeterminacies are ignored, as seems reasonable (chapter 7), these part-to-part analytical hypotheses in effect constitute a translation manual in themselves, which is presumably why Quine sometimes writes of the underdetermination of analytical hypotheses as if it were the same thing as the indeterminacy of translation (*WO*, pp. 72, 73, 75).

2.4 *Conditions* $(1)-(4)$ *and* $(1')-(3)$

Summarizing the possible results of the radical translator's use of assent, dissent and stimulus meanings *without* going bilingual, Quine says that (1) observation sentences can be translated; (2) truth functions can be translated; (3) stimulus analytic and stimulus contradictory sentences can be recognized; (4) pairs of intra-subjectively stimulus synonymous sentences can be discovered, though not translated (*WO*, p. 68). If the translator becomes bilingual, (1) is replaced by: (1') all occasion sentences can be translated; and (4) drops out as superfluous (*WO*, p. 71).

It is important not to see (1)-(4), or (1')-(3), as representing

---

[5] *WO*, pp. 69 f.: 'The equational form may be overlaid with supplementary semantic instructions *ad libitum*'.

Quine's list of the objective constraints on translation. What they represent is the results of applying the methods described.[6] Note that becoming bilingual, while it allows the radical translator to produce acceptable versions of many sentences not otherwise translatable, does not guarantee versions that are *uniquely* correct because in effect even a bilingual translator has to construct a scheme of analytical hypotheses, and this scheme is no more open to empirical verification than anyone else's. (1′) merely records that the bilingual translator can produce some translations of occasion sentences; it does not imply that those translations are determinate.[7]

2.5 *Three important theses*

In the case for indeterminacy of translation presented in *Word and Object* three claims seem to carry the most weight:

(A) The holistic 'inextricability' thesis that there is no such thing as pure semantic knowledge, uncontaminated with factual beliefs (2.2);

(B) The thesis that reference is inscrutable (2.3);

(C) The thesis that analytical hypotheses are underdetermined by all possible independent evidence (2.3, 2.4, 2.6, 2.7).

Each of these claims seems to be regarded as giving direct support to the indeterminacy thesis (though we should also note that the indeterminacy thesis is sometimes taken to support (A),[8] and indeed that the three look as if they are mutually supporting). Just what

[6] If you ask 'Why *those* methods?' part of the answer may be that Quine was trying to show the inadequacy of some proposals of Carnap's (see e.g. Gardner 1973, pp. 390 ff.). Another part of the answer may well be that Quine saw no alternative candidates for objectively checkable methods (whatever that may mean: see ch. 3).

[7] (1) seems to imply there is no room for Quinean indeterminacy in the translation of observation sentences; and Quine has committed himself to this claim elsewhere. (*WO*, pp. 42, 76. He is more cautious at EN, p. 89.) That may be so in the case of sentences with the highest possible degree of observationality, such as 'Red'. But it is clearly not so, if Quine himself is right, for sentences like 'Rabbit'—or rather, not in languages such as English. His own reasoning would show that the observation sentence 'Gavagai' could be equally well rendered by 'Rabbit', 'Rabbit-stage' or 'Undetached rabbit part', whose stimulus meanings are 'incontestably identical' (RIT, p. 181), yet which are not synonymous by ordinary standards. Note, however, that in the special case of impoverished languages consisting mainly of one-word observation sentences, translation of these sentences will be determinate even by Quinean criteria—a point that will be exploited in the argument in chapter 11.

[8] See e.g. Grayling, 1982, p. 271.

these claims amount to, and how far they actually do support the indeterminacy thesis, will be investigated in detail: (A) in chapter 4, (B) in chapter 5, and (C) shortly. Meanwhile I want to mention two other considerations which play some part in Quine's discussion of radical translation.

The first was noted in chapter 1. It is that there is no reason to believe the myth of propositions or meanings as 'linguistically neutral' entities (cf. *WO*, p. 76). Now Quine has always said that if it were possible to make clear empirical sense of synonymy, he would have no objections to defining meanings and propositions on that basis (*WO*, pp. 201, 206, 207, 1968b, p. 295, FM, p. 193). His objection is not to meanings and propositions as such: it is to their being construed as somehow independent of language. So in the discussion of analytical hypotheses he exploits the remoteness of the jungle language from the translator's in order to illuminate the claim that, in general, translation between the two can have nothing to be right or wrong about. In particular there are no free-floating meanings which the translator attempts to identify and re-label (*WO*, pp. 76-8). We saw at 1.9 that Quine's opponents can happily concede this. Meanings are not like butterflies; but you don't have to think they are to disagree with him.

The other consideration is the thesis of the underdetermination of our theory of the world by the totality of possible data. In 'On the Reasons for Indeterminacy of Translation' this consideration was offered as 'the real ground' of the indeterminacy doctrine. This approach—'pressing from above'—will be examined in chapter 6.

2.6 Inadequacy of two arguments

The following might at first look like a strong argument for indeterminacy of translation:

1. Construction of a translation manual requires analytical hypotheses.

2. Analytical hypotheses have to be thought up (cf. *WO*, p. 75).

3. Therefore analytical hypotheses are 'not determinate functions of linguistic behaviour' (*WO*, p. 69) (nor, for that matter, of behavioural dispositions in general, nor of all truths that could be stated in terms of physics).

4. Therefore translation is subject to the indeterminacy.

Steps 1 and 2 of this argument may be conceded immediately; but 3 and 4 need examination. 3 may seem to be a valid inference from 2; but the trouble is that 3 is ambiguous. Taken one way it expresses an indisputable truth: no particular scheme of analytical hypotheses is determined in all its details by the relevant behavioural dispositions. This truth is illustrated by the French construction with 'ne' and 'rien' noticed at 1.14. (See also 7.4.) However, if step 3 is interpreted as expressing only this indisputable truth, it does not entail 4. For indeterminacy of translation in the relevant sense is indeterminacy of translation of sentences, whereas step 3 as interpreted above justifies only the unsurprising conclusion that there is indeterminacy in the translation of *some* expressions. So if 3 is to entail 4 in the sense needed here, it must mean that the Quine-acceptable evidence falls so far short of determining the analytical hypotheses that there is room for significant conflict even over the translation of whole sentences. But obviously 2 by itself does not warrant such a strong conclusion.

A rather different approach to Quine's argument, stressing his physicalism, has been noticed by Peter Hylton. The approach is simply to point to the magnitude of the gulf between physics on the one side and linguistics on the other; between the physicalistic conception of members of our species as having dispositions to emit certain sorts of noises in certain sorts of situation, and the idea that sentences can be said to mean the same:

Here the animals, making their noises, there the notion of meaning; the gap between them is surely too wide for any sensible person to suppose it bridgeable. Quine has been much criticised for failing to provide convincing arguments for the indeterminacy of translation. His critics on this score have perhaps failed to appreciate the physicalistic world-view from within which indeterminacy is almost too obvious to require argument. ('Analyticity and the Indeterminacy of Translation', p. 181.)

I find this approach puzzling. Of course I concede that the totality of truths statable in terms of physics (assuming we could contemplate that totality) does not force us to adopt any particular notion of sameness of meaning, or indeed any notion of meaning at all; and it does not force linguists to adopt any particular 'maxims' of translation. But I do not see how this point can be relevant.

Recall an earlier comparison. The totality of truths statable in terms of physics does not compel us to adopt any particular scheme for describing colours, or any particular scheme for talking about the large or small scale contours of things. (We did not have to use such words as 'hilly', 'mountainous', 'rolling', . . . ; 'gnarled', 'smooth', etc.) Yet the failure of physically expressible truths to compel us to adopt one particular scheme of colour or contour description does not imply that it is not a matter of fact whether things actually have such and such colours or contours, for the alternative schemes of description are not mutually exclusive. (The English colour system doesn't imply that other systems are *wrong*.) In contrast, it is a vital feature of the indeterminacy thesis that rival translation manuals are supposed to be mutually exclusive; and this feature makes it natural to conclude that if the thesis is true, translation relations are not matters of fact. Let us agree that the world as given by physics does not force us to adopt any particular scheme of colour concepts, contour concepts, or semantic concepts—how could it? The interesting question is whether, *once we have made our conceptual choices*, the world as given by physics leaves scope for mutually incompatible ways of actually applying our chosen system of concepts. For colours and contours the answer is clearly No. For semantic concepts, the approach under discussion gives us no reason to expect any other answer.

Indeed, that approach seems to be relevant only if the indeterminacy thesis is taken to be no more than one or both of the following: (VI) the thesis that statements about synonymy are not translatable or analysable in Quine-acceptable terms, and (VII) the thesis that different criteria for synonymy can yield conflicting results. We have already seen that neither seems to express Quine's point adequately (1.1(*f*), 1.10), and in the next chapter I shall defend a different interpretation.[9]

2.7 The alleged uncheckability of analytical hypotheses

Quine urges that a linguist could never check one set of analytical hypotheses without taking others for granted. You might suggest that the linguist could *point* to various things and so check whether the word 'gavagai', say, does or does not mean the same as our 'rabbit'. But in pointing to a rabbit, Quine remarks, you are simultaneously pointing to a rabbit-part, to part of the aggregate of all living rabbits, to an instance of the universal rabbithood. Pointing, he concludes, affords no way of telling which interpretation is

[9] There is other evidence that Hylton identifies the indeterminacy thesis with VII: see chapter 1, n. 6.

correct. And if you want to make your inquiries more pointed than pointing can make them—for example by trying to ask a native whether there are two gavagais here or one—you must inevitably make some unchecked assumptions, e.g. about how the Gavagese deal with number and identity. By questioning your informant you may seem to be conforming your original assumptions, when in fact the same questioning would have served just as well to confirm quite different hypotheses. Quine concludes that in principle there is unlimited scope for alternative schemes all consistent with all possible objective evidence. (Notice how holism helps to make this claim palatable: the idea of indefinitely wide scope for adjusting a theory to fit the same evidence is common to both.)

Now this reasoning is a persuasive case for the uncheckability of analytical hypotheses taken singly or in relatively small groups. But does it support the indeterminacy thesis? Here a similar point can be made to one made early in the last section. No reason has been given why the uncheckability of analytical hypotheses taken one by one should imply that the facts leave room for complete systems of analytical hypotheses to conflict significantly at the level of sentence translation. It is not as if Quine had filled in the details of a complete rival scheme of interpretation to the one we should find natural. He suggests that 'rabbit' might be mapped to 'rabbit stage', and 'is the same rabbit' to 'is a stage of the same rabbit as', but he does not spell out whatever additional adjustments would be enough to make the whole eccentric scheme fit the facts. And when an attempt is made to examine what further adjustments would be required, as was made by Evans (1975), the results look unpromising for Quine's doctrine. So only those who are already half in love with the doctrine are likely to be impressed by these suggestions—unless they have further arguments.

3

The Main Thesis

From Quine's point of view the ordinary translator's enterprise is rather like that of a seventeenth century witch-finder, or an eighteenth century chemist trying to isolate phlogiston. They are all looking for what is not really there. However, it seems conceivable that there might have been witchcraft or phlogiston: their non-existence might be just contingent. But if Quine is right there could not possibly have been objective sameness of meaning.[1] So although it is sometimes helpful to spell out what I am calling his non-factuality thesis—that relations of sameness of meaning for sentences are not generally matters of fact—this statement does not bring out what is distinctive in the indeterminacy doctrine. I happen to believe that the totality of possible evidence actually rules out witchcraft and phlogiston. But Quine believes that the totality of possible evidence still leaves room for *conflicting* statements about sentence synonymy—even for exact translations. Consider one of his early statements. 'Manuals for translating one language into another can be set up in divergent ways, all compatible with the totality of speech dispositions, yet incompatible with one another.' (*WO*, p. 27.) What is it for a translation manual to be compatible with speech dispositions or other Quine-acceptable evidence? What is it for two manuals to be incompatible with one another? And what is the Quine-acceptable evidence? By grappling with these questions we shall be able to reach a reasonably clear statement of what can be regarded as the main indeterminacy thesis.

3.1 What evidence must translation manuals fit?

Many critics have objected to Quine's seeming restriction of the independent data to speech dispositions (e.g. Cohen 1962, p. 70, Chomsky 1969, 1975, Dummett 1974a, p. 618). The objection acquires more force if speech dispositions are taken in the narrow sense noticed in 2.4 above: as dispositions to assent to or dissent

---

[1] With the exceptions mentioned in footnote 7 of chapter 2.

from declarative sentences under various stimulations. However, this restriction is often omitted, both in *Word and Object* and later. ('All theoretically possible evidence', *WO*, p. 75; 'all dispositions to behaviour . . . , OR, p. 29 and TPT, p. 23.) More to the point, we could present Quine with a dilemma. If the *totality* of behavioural dispositions actually determined translation, then the claim that something less than that totality failed to determine translation would lose its interest. If on the other hand non-verbal dispositions added nothing relevant, then, while that would be a matter of some interest, it could not be taken for granted. So in that case the indeterminacy thesis might just as well be stated in terms of the totality of all behavioural dispositions, not just those to verbal behaviour. Either way, our requirement that the indeterminacy thesis be both non-trivial and incompatible with semantic objectivism[2] implies that the restriction to verbal behaviour had better be ignored.

But why stop there? Why should behavioural dispositions be the only evidence to be counted as bearing on translation? We know that one otherwise promising set of candidates is ruled out: facts about beliefs, desires, intentions and other propositional attitudes. If for no other reason, these cannot be included because in *Word and Object* it is argued that if they were, translation relations would be facts too. Having argued that the latter are not matters of fact, Quine concludes that the same goes for intentional idioms in general (*WO*, pp. 220 f.)

However, beliefs, wants, intentions and other propositional attitudes are not the only candidates for evidence additional to that about behaviour and dispositions. There is also what goes on inside people's heads, and quite generally whatever is true about physical particles, states and forces in the universe. Since *Word and Object* Quine has made clear that he thinks translation is underdetermined by the totality of such evidence: 'The point about indeterminacy of translation is that it withstands even . . . the whole truth about nature', when this is assumed to be expressible in terms of physical theory (1968b, p. 303). Again:

two translators might develop independent manuals of translation, both of them compatible with all speech behaviour and all dispositions to speech behaviour, and yet one manual would offer translations that the other would reject. . . . I speak as a physicalist in saying there is no fact

[2] See the Introduction.

of the matter. I mean that both manuals are compatible with the fulfilment of just the same physical states by space-time regions. ('Facts of the Matter', p. 193. Cf. TPT, p. 23.)[3]

There is a crucial point of interpretation to settle here. Quine's words may seem to lend themselves to an interpretation according to which 'the fulfilment of just the same physical states by space-time regions' was consistent with any number of significantly different systems of physical theory—different physical laws. On such an interpretation the same *actual* distribution of physical states throughout space-time would be taken to be consistent with physical structures (such as human bodies) being supposed to have any of a wide range of significantly different dispositions. I reject this interpretation for two reasons. First, if different systems of physical laws are assumed to be consistent with space-time regions being in the same 'physical states', it is extremely obscure what constitutes identity of physical state: on good Quinean grounds we should expect such identity to depend on the details of the theory invoked to specify the states. Second, and decisively, this interpretation would trivialize the indeterminacy thesis by assimilating it to the truism that actual behaviour alone, excluding dispositions, does not determine translation ($1.1(a)$). Clearly, therefore, we must take it that the physical evidence includes or implies a system of physical laws, and determines not just actual states but the dispositions of physical structures.

It seems, then, that the indeterminacy thesis is asserted on the basis of two assumptions. The first is that all the relevant evidence about language users will be somehow registered in behavioural dispositions. The second is that *all* empirical evidence will be somehow constituted by evidence statable in terms of physics. (We must assume that physics is well-behaved and does not include, say, propositions in its ontology: see Gardner, 1973, p. 380.)

Given Quine's position that translation is underdetermined even by the totality of physical evidence, the first assumption, that all the relevant evidence will be registered or represented in behavioural dispositions, though by no means obviously true, raises no special problems. Quine reasonably defends the assumption by pointing out that translators take account only of behaviour and not of

---

[3] Quine does of course maintain that physics itself is underdetermined by all possible evidence; but his present claim is stated on the assumption that we adopt a realistic attitude. Cf. 1.12, 1968b, pp. 301 f., and 6.2.

neurological facts; but presumably sceptics would resist this reasoning. (Cf. Friedman, 1975, pp. 363 f.) However, we can legitimately sidestep the assumption by substituting 'totality of physically statable evidence' for 'totality of behaviour and behavioural dispositions' in all statements of the indeterminacy thesis. For if the thesis were to leave open the question whether translation was fully determined by all physically statable evidence it would not support the distinctively Quinean claim that 'there is no fact of the matter'.

The second assumption, that the whole truth about nature is in a way exhausted by the purely physical truths, is of course in a different category. It is a metaphysical doctrine: physicalism (1.7, 1.12). Those who share some version of this doctrine will not regard the assumption as an obstacle to grasping the point of the indeterminacy thesis. Others risk being put off. If the thesis depends on physicalism and you think physicalism is false, why bother with the thesis? However, the thesis can be stated and defended, though at some cost in clarity, without assuming physicalism. For, as we have seen, Quine's main point is a way of putting flesh on the idea that what we take to be translation relations between sentences are not generally matters of fact—any more than things said about witches are generally matters of fact. So we might substitute 'facts' for 'speech dispositions' in the formulation quoted at the beginning of this section, and get: 'Manuals for translating one language into another can be set up in divergent ways, all compatible with the totality of facts, yet incompatible with one another at the level of sentences.' The question whether you believe some facts are not covered by what can be stated in terms of physics therefore seems unimportant from the point of view of the indeterminacy thesis. Even if you think thoughts and feelings, say, involve non-physical entities, you might still think that the *contents* of thoughts and feelings are not matters of fact. If this is correct, commitment to the indeterminacy thesis need not presuppose a commitment to physicalism. The significance of Quine's own physicalism in this connection may therefore be simply that it offers a reasonably firm basis from which to assess his claims about indeterminacy.

I have followed Quine in not explicitly distinguishing epistemological and ontological versions of the indeterminacy thesis, a distinction emphasized by Michael Friedman (1975). Epistem-

ological versions are to the effect that the totality of acceptable
evidence or *data* does not determine translation. Ontological versions are to the effect that the totality of acceptable *truths* or *facts*
does not determine it. The position taken in this section is in line
with Friedman's insistence on the importance of the physi-
calistically based ontological version. In view of the considerations
I have mentioned we could substitute, in statements of the thesis,
'facts' or 'truths' for Quine's words 'evidence' and 'data'.[4]

3.2 Fitting the evidence (I): the 'constraints' approach

So much for the evidence (or facts) which translation manuals have
to fit. But what is it for them to fit that evidence, to be 'compatible'
with it?

One approach would be to specify a set of conditions or constraints, conformity to which was necessary and sufficient for a
translation manual to be counted as fitting the data. (See e.g.
Davidson, 1974a, 1974b, 1975.) The chief difficulty with this
approach is to know what constraints to impose—so it is really the
difficulty of knowing what is the point of thinking up constraints
in the first place. What is it all for? Two broad replies seem
possible. Either (*a*) we are looking for a systematization of the
actual practice of linguists engaged in radical translation[5] ; or else
(*b*) we want a hygienic substitute for that actual practice. But
once these alternatives have been made explicit, the futility of the
'constraints' approach for our purposes emerges starkly.

Alternative (*b*) has in effect already been dismissed. It is equivalent to the project of finding an explication of 'translation' in
terms acceptable to Quine.[6] He himself despairs of it, and I think
his reasoning here is cogent (see e.g. *WO*, pp. 61-7, 201-6). Of

---

[4] Friedman's epistemological version of the thesis takes as the evidence what is in effect
the totality of Quine's 'pegged observation sentences': the true or false standing sentences
which result from joining to each observation sentence expressible in our language each
possible combination of spatio-temporal co-ordinates (see ESW, pp. 316 f.). However, since
this evidence is obviously compatible with infinitely many incompatible ascriptions of
behavioural *dispositions* to people and things, the resulting indeterminacy thesis lacks interest
(cf. 1.1(*a*)). Friedman's suggestions about ontological determination involve a relatively
weak kind of reduction of semantics to physics: each semantic predicate has to correspond
to a set of physical predicates so that the semantic predicate is satisfied (not satisfied) when
and only when one (none) of those physical predicates is satisfied. So far as I can see the
resulting version of the indeterminacy thesis could be understood on the lines to be proposed
in this chapter; but it is hard to be sure because Friedman does not pursue the question of
what would be acceptable as a manual of translation.

[5] For a start on this project, see Hellman 1974.

[6] The following quotation explains explication in Carnap and Quine's sense: 'We do not

course we could arbitrarily fix upon some Quine-acceptable notion that from some points of view was akin to our unreformed notion of translation or sentence synonymy. 'Socialized intrasubjective stimulus synonymy' might be an example (*WO*, pp. 46–51. See 2.2). But, as with this particular example, we have every reason to expect that such a notion would be remote from synonymy in the unreformed sense, so that if it admitted the indeterminacy, that would give us no grounds for thinking our ordinary notion was subject to the indeterminacy too. It would be irrelevant. Even sentences that are stimulus synonymous for nearly everyone are not generally synonymous by ordinary standards; so if fitting the evidence were just a matter of being intrasubjectively stimulus synonymous for nearly everyone, the thesis would be true but without interesting implications for our ordinary notion of synonymy. (Or rather, the thesis would be uninterestingly true if we stayed with our *ordinary* notion of synonymy when it came to judging between rival translation manuals. If we were to apply the ersatz notion instead, of course, the thesis would be trivially false.) So much for alternative (*b*).

But the other alternative does no better. If the aim of thinking up constraints on translation is to do justice to the actual practice of linguists engaging in radical translation, the first difficulty, from our point of view, is to know what constraints to impose on the constraints. After all, one way of doing justice to linguists' actual practice would be to impose the single constraint: 'Sentences are to be admitted as translations of one another if and only if they mean the same'. So presumably we need to say what sort of constraints we are seeking. However, if the constraints we imposed on the choice of constraints were too stringent, we ought to expect that the job could not be done. For example, if we required the constraints to be formulated in terms acceptable to Quine (say in terms of behavioural dispositions, or the extensional language of physics and chemistry), we should be back with the difficulties noted in the last paragraph. There are good reasons for thinking that no set of constraints formulated in those terms could do justice

claim synonymy. We do not claim to make clear and explicit what the users of the unclear expression had unconsciously in mind all along. We do not expose hidden meanings, as the words "analysis" and "explication" would suggest; we supply lacks. We fix on the particular functions of the unclear expression that make it worth troubling about, and then devise a substitute, clear and couched in terms to our liking, that fills those functions' (*WO*, pp. 258-9).

to the actual practice of translators; and if we nevertheless insisted on imposing that condition on the constraints, and then counted conformity to the resulting constraints as defining what it was for a translation manual to fit the evidence, again the indeterminacy thesis would be deprived of all its interest. But what rational basis is there for selecting any other particular set of constraints on the constraints? No doubt the fact that there is no obvious non-arbitrary way to decide helps to explain Quine's thought that there may be no truth of the matter about there being any truth of the matter.[7]

As Quine himself is well aware, linguists engaged in radical translation take account of a whole range of factors, whose relative weights it would be exceedingly hard to assess. But two important and related considerations are worth bearing in mind. One is that the linguists will assume that the resulting translation manual (still assuming the idea of such manuals is not just pie in the sky) will help the user who speaks one of the two languages to get on with speakers of the other—so that by using the translation of a given sentence of the user's own language, the user's purposes are served as well as may be. The other consideration is that linguists expect that the resulting manual will help them understand the motives and explain the behaviour of those whose language they are translating into their own. For, like the rest of us, they assume that the foreigners' behaviour results from their desires and beliefs; and that by discovering comprehensible equivalents for their utterances they will be able to tell what the foreigners' desires and beliefs are. These considerations remind us that our ordinary notions of sameness of meaning and translation are intimately enmeshed in our other ordinary notions such as desire, belief, intention. For that reason we could expect that constraints on translation which did justice to linguists' actual practice could not be formulated in non-intentional terms. But since Quine has acknowledged that if we are permitted to use intentional language we can define synonymy, translation, etc. in its terms, there seems no purpose, from our point of view, in trying to construct an adequate list of constraints on translation. At best such a list would be just a roundabout way of saying what we might have said more directly. (See 9.4 for discussion of the constraints proposed by David Lewis for a rather similar purpose.)

[7] See *Synthese* 27(1974), p. 496.

We might now begin to despair over the problem of explaining the indeterminacy thesis. If fitting the facts cannot be defined by means of a set of constraints or necessary and sufficient conditions, how can it be defined? One idea would be to make a virtue of the impossibility of finding suitably specifiable constraints. We might at first think of simply reformulating the indeterminacy thesis on the following lines.

> V. There is no set of constraints statable in Quine-acceptable terms (physical, dispositional, extensional) which, applied to the totality of Quine-acceptable evidence, determines a uniquely correct scheme of sentence translation between a given pair of languages.

There can be no doubt that Quine would endorse V, nor do I know of any good reason to reject it.[8] However, I do not think it will do as an adequate statement of the indeterminacy thesis because it is too weak. For V is surely consistent with *denial* of the following claim:

> Q. Our ordinary unreconstructed notion of sameness of meaning is such that rival teams of linguists, applying this notion to a given pair of languages but deliberately disregarding all constraints of simplicity and practicality, could produce rival translation manuals which fitted the Quine-acceptable evidence (or facts), yet were mutually incompatible (in the sense that for some pair of sentences, one manual represented them as meaning the same while another implied they did not mean the same).

It is clear that if Q could be established it would show that, contrary to common expectation, sameness of sentence meaning is not a matter of fact. But establishing V would fall far short of establishing that, unless one could also establish that Q followed from V; but I know of no argument which succeeds in doing so. V appears to be compatible even with the most extreme Platonism about meaning: the Platonist need only claim that those constraints which can be formulated in Quine-acceptable terms are insensitive to the facts which determine meaning.[9]

[8] Romanos seems to have something like this interpretation in mind. Cf. the phrase "no objective constraint" (1983, p. 94).

[9] Note that I am using 'Platonism' to refer, not to all varieties of objectivism, but only to those which, like Plato's own, involve some version of the museum myth.

Nor is such Platonism the only possible basis for rejecting Q while accepting V. Compare the case of sameness of colour. We may not be able to find a set of Quine-acceptable constraints which, applied to the Quine-acceptable evidence, yields uniquely correct verdicts on sameness of colour; but it does not follow (does it?) that sameness of colour is not a matter of fact. For it doesn't follow that the *totality* of Quine-acceptable evidence, including evidence about our visual apparatus, doesn't determine uniquely correct answers to questions of the form 'Are these surfaces the same colour?' (subject to normal inductive uncertainty). Similarly, I suggest, if we cannot find a set of Quine-acceptable constraints which yields uniquely correct verdicts on sameness of meaning, it does not follow that sameness of meaning is not a matter of fact (see also 1.9). In other words, V might be true while Q was false.

I conclude that V cannot be accepted as a version of the indeterminacy thesis because, contrary to what Quine has many times expressly denied of the indeterminacy thesis, V is consistent with translation relations being matters of fact. Q has the advantage that it—or rather it together with an argument which actually showed it to be true—would be a *reductio ad absurdum* of the assumption that sameness of meaning is a matter of fact, which seems to be what Quine was aiming at. Q also provides a way of explaining what it is for a translation manual to fit the evidence which does not run into the difficulties we noted earlier. It abandons the 'constraints' approach originally attempted. Instead of looking for a list of explicit conditions by which translators are constrained, we mention conditions by which they must *not* be constrained, and leave the rest to them. Given a candidate translation manual, then, and given an ideal knowledge of all the possible evidence, their task is to consider whether the manual can be made out to fit the evidence by suitably ingenious manipulations of what, in the ordinary sense, speakers of the languages concerned may intelligibly be said to mean by their utterances and potential utterances.

I will now try to support the proposal to use something like Q as an explanation of what it is for a translation manual to fit the evidence.

3.3 *Fitting the evidence (II): linguists as litmus paper*

In spite of the difficulty of specifying conditions necessary and sufficient for empirical adequacy, we can at least expect a high level of agreement among competent linguists over the empirical adequacy of some manuals, e.g. over a French-English manual which rendered 'Il pleut' by 'It's raining'; 'Le photon n'a pas de masse' by 'Photons have no mass'; and otherwise delivered what would be acceptable to French-English bilinguals—common or garden bilinguals, *bien entendu*, not the exotic Quinean variety. So it seems clear that a *sufficient* condition for a translation manual to fit the facts is that a competent linguist—who will of course be capable of acquiring both languages—be disposed to agree that it is acceptable *as* a translation manual for the two languages, having regard to all the possible Quine-acceptable evidence. I think we can be confident this is a sufficient condition for empirical adequacy because otherwise there would be no justification for saying we were talking about translation in anything like its ordinary sense. If what a competent linguist accepts as empirically adequate translation is not to be allowed to count as such for the purpose of the indeterminacy thesis, that thesis lacks interest for philosophy and psychology, and we can turn instead to consider the interesting thesis which results from adopting the above as a sufficient condition for empirical adequacy. But can we go further and count the above condition as not only sufficient, but necessary, for empirical adequacy? Apparently not.

Linguists are likely to reject candidate translation manuals if these are, for example, unmanageably complicated, or if, when compared with other acceptable manuals, they appear to ascribe an implausibly bizarre psychology to the foreigners, or look simply perverse. Conceivably such norms would be enough by themselves to prevent the construction of a pair of manuals that conflicted as envisaged by Quine (a possibility he recognizes: see *WO*, pp. 74 f.). But his point is theoretical; so it would be question-begging to allow either practical difficulties or mere prejudices to disqualify otherwise acceptable manuals. This suggests that our sufficient condition for empirical adequacy might be transformed into one that is also necessary by adding, as in Q in the last section, the proviso that practical difficulties and mere prejudices are to be given no weight. That is, we might say a given translation manual was empirically adequate if and only if a competent linguist who could acquire both languages (note: not *any* competent linguist: that might seem question-begging) and who deliberately disregarded all canons of simplicity and practical convenience, un-

influenced by mere prejudices, was disposed to agree that the
totality of possible evidence would be consistent with its translations of sentences, both between different languages and within
a single language. On the basis of what was said in the last section,
it seems clear that such agreement would depend on there being
an intelligible way of meshing the translation manual in with a
total scheme for ascribing beliefs, desires, intentions, and other
propositional attitudes to speakers of the languages concerned.

Though I think this suggestion is sound, it raises further questions. Phrases like 'simplicity', 'practical convenience' and 'mere
prejudice' are vague, though I do not see how vagueness can be
avoided here. After all, we cannot assume it is possible to find a
really sharp specification of what constitutes an empirically adequate translation manual: that would be question-begging. But
what matters is whether the phrases do any useful work at all. By
discussing certain questions in the following three sections I hope
to show that, understood in the light of these discussions, they are
adequate for their purpose.

3.4 Is finite explicability just a practical constraint?

The radical translator cannot correlate sentences in just any way
that fits his evidence, but must do so in some way that is 'manageably systematic with respect to a manageably limited set of
repeatable speech segments' (*WO*, p. 74). Quine sees this as a
'practical constraint'; but it seems to fuse two distinct constraints,
one of which is not evidently practical. Certainly it is a practical
requirement that the scheme be manageable. But what about the
requirement that the scheme represent utterances as sequences
composed from a finite set of speech segments, or, generalizing,
that the scheme be finitely explicable? (By saying a manual is
finitely explicable I mean that it could be explained to or learnt by
a human being in a finite time, ignoring shortcomings of memory
or intelligence, not that it is specifiable recursively. Perhaps finite
explicability entails recursive specifiability, but if so, that is not
trivial. Conceivably we are so made that a finite period of learning
equips us as, for example, acceptors for a set of grammatical sentences that is not recursive (cf. Matthews, 1979). Fortunately we
need not pursue this question.)

Clearly, if a translation manual for a pair of natural languages is
to be capable of being applied or even grasped by a being with

less than divine intellectual powers, it must be finitely explicable. So, among other things, it must represent the potential infinity of sentences of each language as composed from a finite set of elements. We could not, in general, even discover which sentences were correlated with which if the infinite correlation were not based on a finitely explicable analysis; and a fortiori we could not tell how far such a correlation fitted the facts. So finite explicability is not a constraint from which we could free ourselves even if we wished to. Is it just a consequence of our being unable to apprehend infinite explanations? You do not have to be a constructivist to feel uneasy about the idea of translation manuals that are not finitely explicable. However, I shall not spend time over this issue. It is enough that that idea has not been explained, and indeed threatens to be impossible to explain just because no finite being could tell whether a non-finitely explicable manual fitted the evidence. If Quine's doctrine depended on this idea it would be impenetrably obscure in a way that neither he nor anyone else has suggested. We can therefore treat finite explicability as an objective constraint on translation manuals.

3.5 Rationality and prejudice

Our linguists are to disregard all practical constraints; but they are also to put aside all mere prejudice (see 3.3). But how far are their assumptions about *rationality* mere prejudices? Suppose some candidate translation manual cannot be made to fit the facts except by representing speakers of one or both of the languages concerned as having a bizarre psychology or as remarkably deficient in rationality—as judged by linguists, of course. Is the manual to be disqualified on such grounds? Fortunately there is no need to engage at length in the wider debate on rationality. I think the following considerations will suffice.

First, since we are primarily concerned with translation between actual natural languages,[10] merely to claim that translation between two communities is possible is to impute to them at least a certain minimal level of rationality. For the use of language is a rational activity in the sense that it calls for more or less deliberate action in conformity with certain norms, so that language users are thereby sharply distinguished from non-rational producers of utterances

---

[10] The question of what sorts of languages the indeterminacy thesis is supposed to apply to has rightly not been discussed in the literature. Evidently Quine thinks it holds for all pairs of so-called natural languages; and that is quite enough to be going on with.

such as tape-recorders. Admittedly there is dispute over whether rationality in this sense is a matter of degree; but that dispute is beside the point here. The relevant dispute is not over the distinction between the rational and the *non*-rational, but over that between the rational and the *ir*rational, or rather over degrees of rationality and irrationality—when only beings that count as rational rather than non-rational can also qualify as irrational. We are not taking sides in this dispute if we say (what I take to be beyond serious challenge) that no purported translation manual would be acceptable if it could be made to fit the facts only by representing one or both communities as lacking the qualifications of rational beings: as mouthers of sentence-like sound patterns but not as language-users. (For a related discussion see 7.5 below.) But that does not take us far. The real question is whether a proposed translation manual, acceptable in other respects, must be rejected if it represents the speakers of one or both languages not as non-rational, but as notably irrational, *when compared with a rival manual.* If standards of rationality are objective, then of course there is no problem: people must be represented as being no less, and no more, rational than they really are. But it would be question-begging just to assume they are objective; and if they are not, such principles as that of maximizing ascribed rationality are not going to yield objectively checkable results. To do justice to Quine, therefore, the constructors of translation manuals must not be required to apply such a principle.

That may look like an over generous concession to Quine, but I do not think it is. Consider two sorts of case where a principle of maximizing ascribed rationality might conceivably be invoked. The difference between them is in the degree of irrationality that is ascribed. In the first, a proposed translation manual represents speakers of one or both of the languages as noticeably less rational, by the translators' lights, than the other manual does, yet not as so irrational that we have difficulty understanding how these people manage to live. (For example, it does not represent them as denying the law of non-contradiction, but it does represent them as all committed to the belief that eggs grow on trees.) Now it seems to me that such a case would tend to vindicate Quine's position. One could hardly imagine that determinacy of translation could be restored by brandishing the rationality principle. Someone who takes the rationality principle seriously and proposes to use it in this way must think either (*i*) that degrees of rationality are objective matters of fact and the principle is a heuristic device which helps us to eliminate incorrect translation manuals; or else (*ii*) that degrees of rationality are not matters of fact and the rationality principle is just a partial criterion for the correctness of a translation manual. But on the first assumption (*i*) it must be logically possible that, on occasions, strict application of the rationality principle would lead to the elimination of a manual that was nevertheless *objectively* permissible—simply because as a matter of fact the people in question were not as rational as they were made out to be by one of the rival manuals. To someone making that assumption, then, the rationality principle could not consistently be held to rule out Quinean indeterminacy. Independent considerations would have to be supposed to determine the incorrectness of the manual which ascribed the greater rationality. On the second assumption (*ii*), however (by which degrees of rationality are not reckoned to be matters of fact), no compelling reason is offered why Quine should accept the rationality principle as a constraint on translation manuals. Either way, then, the principle would be powerless against Quine if faced by a case of the sort described.

In the other sort of case, one of the rival manuals, but not the other, represents the members of one or both of the two linguistic communities as grossly irrational. In such extreme cases, by contrast with the first sort, there is every reason to impose a rationality principle: one to the effect that where one manual ascribes this degree of irrationality and the other does not, even though it fits the facts in other respects, the former is to be rejected. For if the only possible cases of Quinean indeterminacy were of this sort, the indeterminacy thesis would be devoid of interest.

Contrary to what is often assumed, then, I conclude that for our purposes there is no useful principle of maximizing ascribed rationality that we can require our competent linguists to apply. The most we can do, without begging the question against Quine, is to ask them to disregard translation manuals that would impute gross irrationality to one of the linguistic communities involved, since the possibility of such manuals lacks interest.

3.6 Fitting the evidence (III): final version

I am arguing that the following can be accepted as an explanation of what it is for a translation manual to fit the evidence.

D. A given translation manual is empirically adequate if and only if a competent linguist who (*i*) could acquire both languages, (*ii*) deliberately ignores all canons of simplicity and practical convenience, and (*iii*) is not influenced by mere prejudice, is disposed to accept that the evidence is consistent with its classifications of pairs or larger sets of sentences as meaning the same.

This may still seem very unsatisfactory. Indeed, you might think that if D is the best that can be done, the indeterminacy thesis fails because it cannot be coherently stated. D uses the phrase 'meaning the same' without explanation (where it might as well have used 'equivalent', 'synonymous', or 'translations'). Moreover the indeterminacy thesis itself implies that no objectively sound definitions of this and related phrases can possibly be given. So it may appear that if D can be satisfactorily explained, the thesis must be false for that reason, while if D cannot be satisfactorily explained, neither can the thesis. But this objection itself rests on a misconception. Clearing it up will help to show why D, or something like it, must be accepted as the best account we can get without begging the question against Quine, and why he can consistently endorse it—even if he might not be altogether happy about it.

In *Words and Objections* he evinced some embarrassment over those formulations in which, for example, he spoke of rival manuals giving versions 'which stand to each other in no plausible sort of equivalence'. In their place he has offered such phrases as 'translations each of which would be excluded by the other system', and 'one translator would reject the other's translation'. (1968b, pp. 296 f. Cf. also the quotation from FM in 3.1.) At first glance, though, these proposals may seem no improvement. Suppose for example that one translator's rendering of a given sentence contained fewer syllables than another's. Obviously that would not be an admissible reason for the one to reject the other's translation. The rejecting manual would be ruled out as impermissible for that reason; otherwise the thesis would be trivially true and philosophically useless. The number of syllables has nothing to do with the sentence's suitability *as a translation* of the given sentence. When Quine says one translator will reject the other's translation, he seems to be making some kind of essential use of the notion of translation. Since this comes from the same tar-barrel as equivalence, the later suggestions may seem strangely to miss the point. However, further consideration shows that this is not so.

Bear in mind that the objection could not be overcome by substituting for equivalence, translation, sameness of meaning and the rest some specially cleaned up series of Quine-acceptable notions, such as intrasubjective stimulus synonymy (3.2). The indeterminacy thesis is about our ordinary unregenerate notions of meaning, synonymy, translation, etc., not about some set of hygienic substitutes. And this remark points the way out of the difficulty. Quine's position is that our ordinary notions of translation, sameness of meaning, etc., as ordinarily used, fall short of the objectivity we are inclined to ascribe to them. We tend to see them as objective because we overlook shared prejudices and the strength of the practical constraints—notably those of convenience and simplicity. Remove these constraints on the activities of translators and—given massive doses of ingenuity, perversity and tenacity—it will be possible to construct rivals to the usual schemes of translation. In accordance with the points noted in 3. 2, some of these rival schemes, however peculiar, will make it possible for speakers of one of the two languages to understand how the beliefs, desires, etc. of speakers of the other are consistent with those schemes, and how those schemes help to make sense of the other speakers. It follows that linguists who consciously eschew the non-objective constraints will be bound to concede that some of these rival schemes are indeed schemes of translation, and that they must be counted as fitting the evidence.

In making these claims about the use by linguists of our ordinary notions of translation, equivalence, synonymy, etc., Quine is obviously not getting tar on his own hands. He is not actually using those notions himself. He is talking *about* them—saying that, contrary to common assumptions, they do not generally mirror matters of fact. We can compare his position with that of Evans-Pritchard investigating the Azande's notion of witchcraft. In pointing out inconsistencies in the tribe's ideas about witches and witchcraft he was obviously neither using these notions himself nor endorsing their objective validity. Similarly Quine, in pointing out what he believes to be the peculiarities of our ordinary notions of meaning, synonymy, etc., is neither using them nor endorsing their validity.

Since D merely summarizes part of the view ascribed to Quine in the last two paragraphs, D seems to be an acceptable statement of his position on empirical adequacy, without being open to the objection raised earlier.

You may feel I have been making heavy weather of this question of fitting the facts. Surely there is a simple test of a proposed translation manual: try it out in the field (a thought we noted in 3.2). Suppose we have devised a manual for Japanese and English. Then let us go to Japan and see how we get on when we use its Japanese versions of whatever English sentences we should have used if the people around us had been speaking English, and its English versions of what they say to us. The suggestion is that our manual fits the evidence (or the facts) if and only if it works and, or, we pass as Japanese speakers.

Now there can be no doubt that a proposed translation manual which passed this test unproblematically must qualify as fitting the facts, and that one which could in no way be represented as passing it must fail to qualify. Otherwise we could not sensibly say we were speaking of manuals of *translation*, and the indeterminacy doctrine would again be trivialized. Nor can there be any doubt that linguists working in accordance with D would have this practical test very much in mind. Some special explanation would be called for if a manual that failed to pass it were nevertheless accepted. Moreover the availability of this simple (or simple-seeming) test helps to show that D is less abstract and mysterious than might appear. However, I doubt if these considerations, though important, imply that D can be dispensed with. For it would be begging the question against Quine to assume that whether or not a translation manual 'works', or whether a person can be counted as speaking such and such a language is always an absolutely straightforward matter of fact, even though he is willing to regard 'general fluency of dialogue' as a criterion for membership of a linguistic community (EN, p. 87).

Someone might fail to pass as a Japanese speaker on account of an unusually eccentric system of beliefs and desires, including, perhaps, a desire to mislead others in certain systematic ways. To avoid any suggestion of begging the question, therefore, it seems best to make explicit, as D does, that all such questions are to be decided by a competent linguist. What if competent linguists disagree? No matter: if just one competent linguist would pass the manual in question, D will count it as empirically adequate, or permissible.

My 'competent linguists' are assumed to be able to acquire both languages. Isn't this parochial and question-begging? It may seem that Quine's point could be appreciated better if we supposed the investigators were from some remote planet, and quite unfamiliar with our ways of thinking and speaking. We should still assume they had access to all the Quine-acceptable evidence, but perhaps we ought not to imagine them being able to acquire the languages between which they had to translate. Looking at the problem in these terms, we may find it easier to grasp the thought that there is unlimited scope for devising rival translation manuals, all compatible with the totality of (austerely specifiable) evidence.[11]

This suggestion, though understandable, is misconceived. For what are these alien beings trying to do? As we have been forced to recognize, the indeterminacy thesis is trivial unless it somehow bears on our ordinary unregenerate notions of meaning and translation. There must be some justification for saying that our investigators' final product is a manual of *translation*, and not just a correlation of sets of sentences arrived at quite independently of our messy ordinary notions. It follows that if the aliens cannot be described as trying to produce a translation manual for the two terrestrial languages they are investigating, their activities, however diverting, are irrelevant. But if they can be described as trying to produce a translation manual, they must count as having, or at least as being capable of using, our notions of translation and sameness of meaning. Now for reasons we noticed earlier, this will not be possible without recognizing that what *our* linguists count as permissible translation manuals are indeed that. But that in turn will not be possible without being capable of learning both languages. For it is not as if radical translators were presented with a purely abstract specification of each of the two languages they had to translate (a syntax and a set of semantic axioms in the style of Davidson, for example) and their task were simply to produce a mapping of the one onto the other subject to some sharply specifiable set of constraints. They do not already know what the languages in question are. They are confronted by native

[11] Such translators would be akin to Blackburn's 'bleak' radical interpreters (1984a, pp. 277–81). But what I am about to say raises doubts about the legitimacy of his contrast between them and their 'homely' counterparts.

speakers, not abstract Davidsonian specifications, and they have to work out any specifications from scratch. Nor, as we noticed in 1.9 and 1.10, does rejection of the indeterminacy thesis require acceptance of the discredited idea that our notions of meaning, reference, etc. are translatable into the austere language of physics. There is just no way for would-be translators to avoid manipulating our ordinary notion of sameness of meaning, together with whatever other notions (e.g. desire, belief, intention, or the like) have to be brought into play in order to manipulate it adequately. And to manipulate these notions adequately for the purpose of testing candidate translation manuals they must be able to catch on to all the behavioural dispositions that are, or could be, possessed by these native speakers (3.3). So the translators must share the same Wittgensteinian 'form of life' as the native speakers (1.11, 10.7). This guarantees that they must be capable of learning to speak their translatees' languages. So no questions are being begged by requiring the linguists who are to be our litmus paper to be capable of acquiring the languages concerned.

To summarize the results of this section, we have the following as our final version of the main indeterminacy thesis:

> I. Our ordinary notion of sameness of meaning is such that rival teams of linguists, applying this notion to a given pair of languages but deliberately disregarding all constraints of simplicity and practicality, could produce rival manuals for sentence translation which fitted all the physically statable evidence (or facts), yet were mutually incompatible.

In the next few sections I shall discuss some further questions about the interpretation of this thesis, and some implications.

3.7 Empirical adequacy and holism

According to Quine's holism, our theory of nature faces the evidence as a whole. (See chapter 4.) So to avoid begging the question we must assume that a translation manual also faces the evidence as a whole. More specifically, a proposed manual of translation might conceivably be empirically inadequate even if there were no specifiable proper subset of Quine-acceptable evidence with which it was in conflict; the conflict would be with the *totality* of evidence. A manual's translations face the tribunal of the evidence not individually but only as a corporate body. (Cf. TDE, p. 41.) Moreover, even if each separate translatability claim relating to each pair of sentences offered as translations of one another were compatible with the totality of the evidence when the rest of the manual was left out of account (because of the possibility of compensating adjustments) the manual as a whole might still conflict with the evidence. The incompatibility would hold between the totality of the evidence and the totality of the manual. By the same token, neither Quine nor anyone else who accepts this holistic position needs to be able to specify the actual constraints on translation. It is a matter of a whole scheme of translation meeting a complex totality of conditions. (Of course this does not preclude specifying the *kinds* of conditions that matter.) The points about empirical adequacy in the last section must be read with Quinean holism in mind.

3.8 Translation and truth values

One clear implication of the interpretation of the indeterminacy thesis adopted here is that for translation manuals to be empirically adequate, it is not enough that translated and translating sentences be both true, both false, or both without truth value. One variant on this idea is that the only condition to be met is that as far as possible sentences held true by speakers of the one language should also be held true by speakers of the other. Another variant is that in each possible world, translated and translating sentences should have the same truth values.

It should be clear that none of these suggestions is adequate. They all make the indeterminacy thesis either trivially true or trivially false. If we judge 'conflict' between rival manuals by our ordinary standards of sameness of meaning, then it is trivial that merely preserving sameness of truth value—even in all possible worlds—permits countless sentences to be 'translated' by sentences that do not mean the same. For example '2 + 2 = 4', '3 + 3 = 6' and 'The square root of 2 is not a rational number' share the same truth value, are held true by (virtually) everyone who understands them, and retain the same truth value in all possible worlds. But no one would say they meant the same by ordinary standards. So if the indeterminacy thesis were merely that there can be this sort of conflict if the only constraint is the preservation of sameness of truth value in all possible worlds (thesis VIII), it is trivially true, and has no interesting implications. Similarly, for the same reasons, if the only constraint were to maximize agreement in what sentences are held true or false. The same points hold even if we confine ourselves to the translation of more straightforwardly factual truths. For example 'There are three rabbits in the garden' is truth-functionally equivalent to 'The number of rabbits in the garden is the cube root of 27'—and that in every possible world. Of course one could suggest that our ordinary standards of sameness of meaning ought not to be applied here: we ought to be consistent and apply the same standards when judging whether two translation manuals conflict as the ones we apply when judging whether they meet the conditions on empirical adequacy (cf. 1.1(*e*)). But then we shall have no possible indeterminacy. If truth-functional equivalence is sufficient for sameness of meaning across the board, it guarantees that no pair of manuals can conflict, and the indeterminacy thesis is trivially false. Clearly, then, the thesis is interesting only if it is kept sharply distinct from thesis VIII.[12]

Quine has maintained that in some cases the rival manuals might offer, as their versions of a given sentence, sentences with *different* truth values. The sentences might even be 'patently' contrary in truth value (*WO*, pp. 73 f.; cf. also Quine, 1974b). And indeed, since material equivalence, or sameness of truth value, is one sort of equivalence, this view appears actually to be entailed by those formulations of the indeterminacy thesis according to which the sentences stand to each other 'in no plausible sort of equivalence however loose'. However, it is important to recognize that this extreme claim is a sort of optional extra. It is not entailed by the account of incompatibility of translation manuals to be offered in section 3.11, and it is not required in order to guarantee the interest or importance of the thesis. This point needs to be noted because there has been a tendency to assume that a demonstration of the impossibility of the different truth values case would be a refutation of the indeterminacy thesis itself.[13] It should be clear that the indeterminacy thesis would remain extremely significant even if, for example, it were restricted to pairs of logically or conceptually

[12] Bechtel has suggested that for Quine 'all that is involved in an adequate translation is a mapping from one set of linguistic entities onto another that preserves the truth value assignments to the observation sentences' (1980, p. 316). But this cannot be right. It again makes the indeterminacy thesis trivially true, since e.g. it would let us switch round '1 + 1 = 2' and '2 + 2 = 4'. It also ignores what Quine says about other constraints, e.g. the matching of stimulus analytic and stimulus contradictory sentences. See 2.2, and 2.4.

[13] See Dummett's criticisms, especially those discussed at 9.6 below.

necessary truths and falsehoods (as non-Quineans would shame-lessly put it), or to pairs of contingent sentences that necessarily shared the same truth value. Imagine there could be two empirically adequate translation manuals which offered, say, 'There is no greatest prime' and 'Any integer is uniquely decomposable into primes' as their respective versions of some foreign sentence; or for some other sentence, 'There are just four cows in that field' and 'The number of cows in that field is the minimum number of colours needed to colour a simply connected surface divided into areas, no two areas with a common boundary to be the same colour'. If such manuals were empirically adequate, that would be profoundly interesting. So the interest of the indeterminacy thesis does not depend on its requiring the possibility that two empirically adequate translations have different truth values.

I do not think it follows from this that the indeterminacy thesis must be taken to require pairs of rival translating sentences to be bound together by logical or conceptual necessity. However, this assertion might be challenged. You might suppose that if a pair of actually true sentences differed in meaning, and their truth values were not analytically linked, then it must be possible for their truth values to have differed from one another, hence for the two translation manuals in question to have remained empirically adequate even if the world had been different in ways corres-ponding to the different truth values of the sentences. But this objection overlooks the fact that Quine rejects the idea of a sharp distinction between analytic necessity on the one hand, and physi-cal necessity on the other (see e.g. TDE, 1970a, p. 100). And if there is no sharp distinction, then what non-Quineans would call non-logical and non-conceptual factors might still make it im-possible that the two sentences should have differed in truth value. Suppose for example the two sentences were 'All rabbits have hearts' and 'All rabbits have kidneys'. Quine could insist that these sentences could not differ in truth value, yet without conceding that the impossibility was logical or conceptual.

3.9 *Translating observation sentences*

In general radical translators must render observation sentences, if at all, by observation sentences that are as nearly as possible stimulus synonymous. Indeed they must begin their work by doing so, since these sentences 'afford our only entry to a language' (EN,

p. 89). At any rate that, roughly, is Quine's own view, and in this section I want to show that it is also implied by the interpretation of the indeterminacy thesis advocated here. (See SO, p. 4, *WO*, pp. 29, 32, EN, pp. 88 f., RIT, pp. 179 f., NNK, p. 74, FM, pp. 179, 180.)

As we have seen, he maintains that observationality is a matter of degree. Even a one word observation sentence like 'Rabbit' may have slightly different stimulus meanings for different people on account of differences in collateral information (*WO*, p. 37, 2.2). It follows that when observation sentences with lower levels of observationality are being translated, the requirement to maximize the matching of stimulus meanings will be liable to increasing competition from other constraints. However, the question that concerns me (because some of my later arguments will depend on how it is answered) is whether it could ever be permissible to infringe the general requirement—even when there is no gain in overall simplicity, practical convenience, etc.[14] Suppose the observation sentences of the two languages concerned had stimulus meanings that matched perfectly. Suppose also that there was a 'standard' translation manual which not only respected this fact, but produced ideal matches between all sentences at all higher levels of theoreticity too. In these circumstances, could a translation manual which flouted the general requirement to maximize the matching of stimulus meanings in the translation of observation sentences nevertheless be permissible (empirically adequate)?

As far as I can see, any argument for the ultra-Quinean idea that such a manual could be permissible would have to rely on Quine's holism (see 3.7 and the next chapter). The thought would be that in principle we could compensate for any such eccentric renderings of observation sentences by radical adjustments elsewhere in the manual. An example may make this suggestion look less wildly implausible than at first appears: perhaps we could render the natives' one-word observation sentence 'Gavagai' by 'Linguist'. To make sense of this decision we should have to credit the natives with a bizarre system of beliefs, for example, by representing them as endowing the creatures we call rabbits with remarkable intelligence and paranormal powers (they can record

---

[14] This last clause explains the qualification 'in general' at the beginning of this section. It also, I believe, avoids what might otherwise have appeared to be a counter-example described by Paul Churchland, 1979, pp.64 f.

their data and theories by remote psychic action). Now as a sentence, our expression 'Linguist' is so far from being stimulus-synonymous with the foreigners' 'Gavagai' that it is not an observation sentence at all. Yet it might seem that by ascribing sufficiently strange beliefs to the foreigners we could make this rendering fit in with the rest of our manual. The universal prevalence of bizarre beliefs among the native population would seem to explain how a sentence could work like an observation sentence while not being translated by an observation sentence of our own language. But is this really feasible? I think it appears to be so only so long as we disregard other dispositions than current dispositions to respond to patterns of sensory stimulations. Consider first what would happen if the foreigners were to be relieved of their delusions. If 'Linguist' were really a permissible rendering of 'Gavagai', then they would have second order dispositions which, if they were to lose their delusions, would result in their ceasing to produce that utterance on sight of rabbits. (See Appendix B on second order dispositions.) Then that utterance would cease to be an observation sentence. But it is a question of Quine-acceptable fact whether or not the foreigners have such second-order dispositions. If they lack them, our non-standard manual is not permissible. But they will lack them, for by definition their (first-and second-order) dispositions with respect to 'Gavagai' exactly match our own with respect to 'Rabbit'. Were this not so, we should be back splashing about in the shallows with inexact translation. For this reason alone it appears that our non-standard scheme will not after all be permissible.

A similar difficulty faces our non-standard scheme as soon as we consider whether that scheme allows, even in principle, for there to be a handful of Gavagese whose systems of belief are more normal than those our non-standard manual requires us to impute to the bulk of the population. For presumably, if 'Linguist' were a permissible translation of 'Gavagai', such more normal individuals would not be disposed to utter 'Gavagai' on sight of rabbits, nor would they let their children or other learners of Gavagese treat that sentence as an observation sentence connected with rabbits in the way described. By definition, however, all Gavagese (this side of schizophrenia) are disposed to assent to 'Gavagai' on sight of rabbits, and lack any tendency to prevent children or other learners from copying them in this respect.

These points about the particular example we have been discussing do not of course settle the matter. But they do illustrate a vital general consideration. This is that if you render an observation sentence by a non-observation sentence (or even by a less highly observational observation sentence), you cannot claim to be giving, as your translation, a sentence which 'performs the same sort of functions' in the translating language as the translated sentence performs in its language. The difference in degree of observationality marks a difference in function even by objective (or Quine-acceptable) standards. (In 'Epistemology Naturalized' he even says 'The observation sentence . . . has an empirical content all its own and wears it on its sleeve' (EN, p. 89).) The lower the level of observationality, the less closely the sentence is linked causally to certain types of stimulation of the sensory receptors, and the more scope there is for other parts of the web of belief to inhibit the tendency to give a reliable response to the sentence when it is uttered under given patterns of stimulation. But this is just to say that according to our ordinary notion of sameness of meaning—closely enmeshed as it is with ideas of sameness of use and function—the answer to the question raised in the second paragraph of this section must be No. Given that two languages are so similar that the stimulus meanings of their observation sentences are exactly matched, and there is an ideally straightforward scheme of translation for all other sentences too, a rival manual which flouted the requirement to maximize the matching of stimulus meanings would not be empirically adequate.[15] To dramatise this point, notice that someone who used such a manual in the hope of simulating the behaviour of a speaker of the foreign language would fail: there would be a relevant non-trivial difference in dispositions, and any competent linguist would count this as a failure to speak the language.

3.10 'Exact translation'

In chapter 1 I pointed out that if the indeterminacy thesis depended only on the familiar point that *inexact* translations of a given sentence may be non-equivalent, we could love it and leave

---

[15] It is entirely consistent with this point, of course, to maintain that two stimulus synonymous observation sentences might not be synonymous. See 2.2. The point made above is not to be confused with a principle of charity: maximize agreement on what sentences are held true. *Pace* Davidson (1974, 1975) it seems we can get translation started without such a principle. (See McGinn, 1977 for criticism of Davidson on this.)

it in exchange for the challenging thesis that empirically adequate translation manuals might give non-equivalent yet exact translations of the same sentence (1.1(*d*)). But the notion of exact translation is not itself exact, and I want to explain how my use of it is to be understood.

Presumably exactness of translation is a matter of degree, with the complete coincidence of homophonic translation—translation of each sentence by itself—as a limit. If so, that limit will be approached from several different directions, since there are several dimensions along which exactness might be sought. Depending on their predominant purposes and interests, different translators will give priority to maximizing different kinds of exactness. In rendering the names of plants, for example, translation for scientific purposes will aim at the literal meaning regardless of the relative familiarity or cultural significance of species to speakers of the translating language. In other cases literalness can have ludicrous results because, as we noticed in 1.1(*f*), exactness of literal equivalence by no means entails exactness of cultural equivalence. But this again is a familiar point. Quinean indeterminacy would be a trivial thing if it depended on the fact that the constructors of different translation manuals may have divergent purposes and priorities. Not only would it be trivial. It would be quite useless for Quine because it would be consistent with the most extreme Platonism about meaning. For Platonists can easily agree that when translators have different purposes they will want to associate sentences with different Platonic meanings. If we are not to misrepresent the indeterminacy thesis, therefore, we must assume our translators share the same purposes and priorities, whatever these may be. In view of the points that were made in 1.1(*b*), it seems best to assume that these purposes and priorities are scientific. The translators are to be supposed to be aiming at exact literal synonymy—whatever that means exactly.

The same considerations as earlier forced us to have recourse to the judgement of competent linguists also compel us now to leave them to decide whether a given translation should be counted as exact. For we have to pick a course between two opposed hazards: trivializing the indeterminacy thesis, and begging the question. Trivialization results from constraints that are too liberal; question-begging from imposing constraints that Quine could not happily endorse. To lay down rigid conditions for what may be counted as exact translation would be unacceptable when the objective validity of such conditions is one of the questions at issue; yet we must avoid making the thesis depend on the truism that inexact translations can conflict. Since it is our ordinary notions of translation and meaning that are under attack, the only appropriate solution seems to be to let competent linguists decide—provided they eschew prejudice and ignore the constraints of simplicity and practicality.[16]

3.11 *Incompatibility between translation manuals*

The indeterminacy thesis is that two empirically adequate translation manuals might yet be mutually incompatible. What sort of incompatibility is in question?

We have seen that Quinean indeterminacy requires conflict at the level of *sentences* (1.11). Obviously the sort of conflict that matters most concerns which sentences are said to mean the same, whether they belong to the same or different languages. Explicitly or implicitly a translation manual classifies sentences or sets of sentences as meaning the same—as synonymous. So presumably we can take it that two manuals conflict in the way that matters if their respective synonymy classifications of sentences are logically incompatible; so that when one licenses the claim that a given pair of sentences are synonymous, the other licenses the claim that they are not. (Notice how we avoid any implication that synonymy relations are objective matters of fact.)

Stronger interpretations might be suggested, of course. One would be to say the manuals were incompatible only if some sentences were rendered by sentences counted as logically incompatible by at least one manual. But that seems an excessive burden to foist on to Quine. For we have seen that the thesis remains profoundly disturbing even if the translating sentences are counted by at least one manual as not meaning the same—even if they share the same truth value. If the conflict between rival

---

[16] Although the possibility of non-equivalent rough translations does not by itself constitute a significant indeterminacy, it remains conceivable that there should be significant conflict even over rough translation. If one translation manual counts X as a rough rendering of Z, while rejecting another manual's claim that Y translated Z just as well, that would be a genuine conflict between the two manuals, and—if both manuals were empirically adequate—would exemplify the indeterminacy thesis just as decisively as conflict over exact translation. However, Quine is clearly committed to its not being the *only* possible sort of conflict because he holds that the domestic indeterminacy thesis is his main thesis (see 3.13 and chapter 10).

manuals were less than this, however, the resulting thesis would clearly lack interest.

3.12 The relativistic thesis

Quine makes several remarks to the effect that statements of synonymy make sense only relative to a scheme of translation. (Cf. e.g. *WO*, pp. 75, 221.) But this relativistic thesis (IV) must not be misunderstood. At first you might connect it with the fact that acceleration, for example, cannot be specified except relatively to a frame of reference. (Such comparisons seem to be encouraged at OR, pp. 48–55.) So you might think he was committing himself to regarding statements of the form 'X means the same as Y relative to **M**' as scientifically acceptable. But there is a striking disanalogy between the scientific cases and that of translation. The concepts of physics are acceptable to Quinean naturalism; but meaning and translation are not (TDE, *WO*, p. 75, OR, TM, MVD, and 1.7). Quine's acceptance of the relativistic thesis must therefore not be taken to commit him to more than that there *are* schemes of translation, and that it is a question of fact whether X is correlated with Y according to a given scheme. The relativistic thesis does not commit him to regarding the notions of translation and sameness of meaning, even when thus relativized, as acceptable.[17] It amounts to no more than accepting that it is a fact that sentences of the form 'X means the same as Y' occur in schemes of translation. We cannot properly call Quine a relativist about meaning. He is not a relativist: he is a semantic nihilist.

A few more comments on the relativistic thesis. It is clearly not just a special case of the truism that any statement has to be understood in terms of the theory, or 'loose total fabric of quasi-theories', from within which it is made. I am happy to endorse this truism, but it clearly does not commit me to maintaining that synonymy statements have to be relativized to translation manuals. I think statements such as "Le photon n'a pas de masse" means the same as "Photons have no mass"' make sense well enough as they stand. I may be wrong about that, but at least it seems entirely consistent with holding that such statements are made from within a loose theory in which phrases like 'means the same' have a place.

Nor is the relativistic thesis to be read as just a way of putting

[17] So he is not open to the objections raised by Field (1975) and Davidson (1979), both of whom point out that it would be inconsistent for him to treat relative reference as a well-defined notion.

the incontestable point that statements of synonymy presuppose some agreement on their context and purposes. (See the example in *n*.5, 1.1(*f*).) I am assuming we are concerned with 'pure' translation (1.14), and with sameness of what is roughly indicated by 'literal meaning' (1.1(*b*)). Again, this point is quite consistent with rejection of the idea that, when context and purpose have been agreed on, there is a further need to agree on which translation manual our synonymy statements are to be taken to be relativized to.

So the relativistic thesis is not to be regarded as a misleading statement of those obvious points. It means that no synonymy statement makes good *Quinean* sense unless it has the form '*X* means the same as *Y* relative to (or 'according to') manual **M**'. And the point of the phrase 'relative to **M**', clearly, is that if Quine is right about the indeterminacy there will not generally be any uniquely correct statements of the form '*X* means the same as *Y*'. So when we understand it correctly, the relativistic thesis IV turns out to be logically equivalent to the indeterminacy thesis itself. The indeterminacy thesis commits you to the relativistic thesis, and the relativistic thesis commits you to the indeterminacy thesis.

3.13 The domestic thesis

In *Word and Object* Quine said:

> The infinite totality of sentences of any given speaker's language can be so permuted, or mapped onto itself, that (*a*) the totality of the speaker's dispositions to verbal behaviour remains invariant, and yet (*b*) the mapping is no mere correlation of sentences with *equivalent* sentences, . . . (p. 27).

Such a permutation could be used to represent other speakers of your language as using its sentences with different meanings from those you yourself give them. So we have the possibility of an 'impractical joke': given enough perversity and ingenuity we could devise a permutation that would 'attribute unimagined views to our compatriot, while conforming to all his dispositions to verbal response to all possible stimulations' (*WO*, p. 78). It is a striking fact that Quine himself sees the indeterminacy of 'radical' translation, which typically concerns a pair of languages unlike in syntax and conceptual scheme, as just a way of putting the domestic thesis 'less abstractly and more realistically' (*WO*, p. 27. Cf. OR, pp. 46 f., *RR*, p. 83). If we may take this at face value it means that the general thesis stands or falls with the intralinguistic version, in which case the task of opposing the general thesis is much simplified. This is worth bearing in mind. In chapter 10 I shall return to consider this point of Quine's more closely, and to give it support.

3.14 Domestic indeterminacy and individual interpretation

The domestic version of the indeterminacy thesis helps to bring out the thoroughly radical nature of the doctrine. To the extent that an empirically adequate permutation can be applied to other speakers of our own language, the question of what beliefs, wants, intentions, etc. their utterances express is not one of fact; so that in general it is not a matter of fact what beliefs, wants, etc. people have (1.3 and 1.4, *WO*, p. 221). It is important not to confuse this radical doctrine with the far less disturbing claim that in some *individual* cases there may be no answer to the question of what a person means, believes, etc. A Quinean permutation for English, say, would apply to *any* English speaker on any occasion: it would not have to lie in wait for unusual circumstances. The point is worth noting because people sometimes assume that the latter claim is the same as, or at any rate lends support to, the full-strength indeterminacy thesis.[18]

Consider a case sketched by Dennett. He imagines a reputable art critic, Sam, who praises and promotes his son's mediocre paintings, and goes to his grave insisting on his son's genuine talent. Now, has Sam been suffering from self-deception, or has he been deliberately disguising his true beliefs out of loyalty? Dennett suggests that conceivably there might be absolutely no objective evidence to decide the issue—not even evidence detectable in the minute details of Sam's brain. In that case, he urges, there would be no fact of the matter as to which interpretation of Sam's state of mind was correct.[19] Assuming for the moment that such cases are genuinely possible, it is clear that their existence is consistent not only with translation generally being determinate in the way the indeterminacy thesis denies, but with psychological interpretations of individuals generally being determinate. For such

---

[18] Indeed Quine himself sometimes gives the impression of implying this, e.g. in *WO*, p. 46, where he says: 'We will construe a neighbour's word heterophonically now and again if thereby we see our way to making his message less absurd'. My point is that this obvious good sense has no tendency to support domestic indeterminacy.

[19] Dennett 1978, pp. 37 f. and 49.

cases depend for their intelligibility on our being able to tell whether, for example, a person is self-deceived or just pretending their son has talent. So they are consistent with its being a question of fact what one means by what one says.

There is, however, an interesting lack of clarity about the story of Sam the critic. It emerges when we ask whether he has a propensity to acquire all the dispositions that would be appropriate for each of the incompatible beliefs ascribed to him by the two interpretations. A man who merely said for public consumption that his son was a talented artist, while believing the contrary, would surely be disposed to give something like *silent* assent to the sentence 'Your son has no artistic talent'. The self-deceiver would presumably not have just those dispositions. These points are hardly conclusive. But I think they put the onus back on defenders of the possibility alleged by Dennett, and they also remind us of some of the Quine-acceptable evidence that bears on questions of interpretation. If even occasional cases where individual psychological interpretations are indeterminate prove hard to describe convincingly, the vastly more radical nature of the indeterminacy thesis demands powerful arguments indeed. In the next part (chapters 4–8) I shall examine in turn each of the main arguments for it. (In case anyone thinks the interpretation of the indeterminacy thesis offered here makes it easy to refute, they might care to glance at chapter 9.)

Part II

The Case for Quine's Doctrine

In general, progress in philosophy is not made by having better and better hunches about the final outcome of a philosophical enquiry, but by deeper analysis of the arguments and counter-arguments that bring us towards that outcome. . . . As we advance, the path twists and turns; by taking a few steps along it, one may find oneself facing in the opposite direction to where the path will eventually terminate. . . .

DUMMETT

4

Holism and Inextricability

The unit of empirical significance is the whole of science. ('Two Dogmas of Empiricism', p. 42.)

This famous slogan sums up—at some cost in clarity—Quine's linguistic and epistemological holism. In this chapter my overall aim is to show that this holism, contrary to what he suggests, gives no support to the indeterminacy thesis. It will be necessary to distinguish and explain two different holistic claims: the Duhem-Quine thesis and the inextricability thesis. In pursuit of this aim I shall discuss some arguments for and against them.

4.1 The Duhem-Quine thesis and the indeterminacy thesis

Let us follow precedent and call this the *Duhem-Quine thesis*:

> Our statements about the external world face the tribunal of experience not individually but only as a corporate body (TDE, p. 41).

The thesis may also be viewed from a different angle:

> A statement about the world does not always or normally have a separable fund of empirical consequences that it can call its own (EN, p. 82).

An experience may conflict with a whole theory or system of beliefs, but it does not determine just which beliefs must be revised. The complex interconnections among the statements or beliefs composing the theory ensure that there is an indefinitely wide range of ways of accommodating the recalcitrant experience (TDE sec. 6, *WO*, pp. 17-21, EN, pp. 79, 82, ESW, pp. 313-15).

The Duhem-Quine thesis is surely attractive. So if it could somehow be shown to support the indeterminacy thesis, that would be a powerful reason for accepting the latter. And at first glance you might think it did support the indeterminacy thesis. After all, manuals of translation are theories of a kind, so perhaps the indeterminacy thesis can be seen as a direct application of the Duhem–Quine thesis. However, there are at least two reasons why this attempt at direct application fails. One is that the Duhem–Quine thesis relates only to the accommodation of theories to limited bodies of evidence. It says only that the evidence we actually have, or shall get, cannot force us to revise our theory in any particular way, hence that two different theories could fit the same finite body of evidence. But, as we noticed in 1.1(*a*), the indeterminacy is supposed to hold in the teeth of the totality of possible evidence, not just in the teeth of whatever evidence we may happen to have. Nor does the Duhem–Quine thesis go so far as to say, nor does it seem to imply, that two different theories could fit all the *dispositional* facts (see 3.1).

Another reason why the Duhem–Quine thesis cannot be seen as giving direct support to the indeterminacy thesis is that the latter is supposed to withstand 'the whole truth about nature' (3.1), while the former gives us no licence to assume that conflicting theories of translation are compatible with that all-encompassing totality—any more than it would entitle us to assume that conflicting (not just different) theories of geometrical optics, for example, might be compatible with the whole truth about nature.

However, in 'Epistemology Naturalized' (1969) Quine has appealed to the Duhem–Quine thesis as 'the crucial consideration' behind his argument in that essay for the indeterminacy of translation (EN, p. 82).

4.2 *The argument in 'Epistemology Naturalized'*

The other vital premiss Quine uses in this essay is the Peircean doctrine that the meaning of a sentence turns purely on what would count as evidence for its truth. For reasons I shall give, I do not understand the argument here, but in outline it seems to go as follows:

(1) Two sentences or theories have the same 'empirical' meaning if but only if they have the same empirical evidence (the Peircean doctrine).

(2) But theoretical sentences 'have their evidence not as single sentences but only as larger blocks of theory' (EN, pp. 80 f. The Duhem–Quine thesis).

(3) Therefore, for any pair of languages, if we take a theory

stated in the sentences of one of the languages, there will be no justification for pairing off sentences of the other as translations of those theoretical sentences, 'except as these correlations make the translation of the theory as a whole come out right'. Any translations of the sentences will be as correct as any other, 'so long as the net empirical implications of the theory as a whole are preserved in translating. But it is to be expected that many different ways of translating the component sentences, essentially different individually, would deliver the same empirical implications for the theory as a whole; deviations in the translation of one component sentence could be compensated for in the translation of another component sentence' (EN, p. 80).

One difficulty with the reasoning here is this. Steps (1) and (2) do not appear to entail that translation between single theoretical sentences is subject to the indeterminacy. Instead they appear to entail that such translation is impossible. For if two items mean the same only if they share the same evidence (1), and no single theoretical sentence has any evidence (2), then no single theoretical sentence means the same as any other. Thus the premises of the argument appear to entail something actually inconsistent with the putative conclusion (3). (You might suggest that one way for all the sentences to have the same evidence would be for them all to have no evidence, so that they all meant the same for that reason. But this suggestion makes nonsense of the idea of 'compensation' in (3).) However, Quine can hardly have overlooked this point because, in the paragraph immediately before the one quoted, he explicitly states that 'the component statements simply do not have empirical meanings by Peirce's standard' (EN, p. 79). Moreover, in the paragraph on which I have based step (3), he is talking about what he calls 'ordinary unphilosophical translation, such as from English into Arunta or Chinese' (EN, p. 80). So you might suggest that the inconsistency is only apparent: the impossibility of translating single theoretical sentences à la Peirce, which follows from (1) and (2), is not to be taken to entail the impossibility of pairing them off by 'ordinary unphilosophical translation'.

But this suggestion will not save the argument. If ordinary unphilosophical translation is essentially different from Peircean translation, why should the Peircean premiss (2) be supposed to have any bearing on the question of indeterminacy of translation, which, as we saw in the last chapter, is concerned with ordinary unphilosophical translation? If these are different sorts of translation, then (1) and (2) provide no reason for supposing that the only justification for pairing off theoretical sentences as 'ordinary unphilosophical translations' of one another is whether they make the Peircean translation of the theory as a whole come out right. If the indeterminacy is not of Peircean translation, but of ordinary unphilosophical translation, then whether or not it is subject to the indeterminacy must surely be decided by reference to its own standards, whatever they may be, and not to Peirce's. (Or should we take Quine's point to be merely that Peircean standards of synonymy, when combined with the Duhem–Quine thesis, fail to determine synonymy *as judged by ordinary standards*? If so we can concede that thesis immediately, and move on to consider the interesting thesis whose features we investigated in the last chapter.) I conclude that if 'translation' is used univocally throughout the argument (1)–(3), the conclusion is inconsistent with the premisses; while if it is not used univocally, the argument is at best incomplete.

As Christopher Boorse has pointed out, Quine here disregards the defensible suggestion that it is not only the empirical implications of a theory, but its internal structure, that should be taken into account when attempting to translate it (1975). By ignoring this consideration the present argument simply begs the question. Clearly, the argument falls far short of establishing the indeterminacy thesis, even if premisses (1) and (2) are both accepted.

4.3 Inextricability

The Duhem–Quine thesis has always been associated with claims about linguistic and factual contributions to the truth of statements. The dogma of reductionism, which implies that it is 'significant in general to speak of the confirmation and infirmation of a statement', is 'at root identical' with the dogma that there are analytic statements, 'vacuously confirmed, *ipso facto*, come what may' (TDE, p. 41). So 'it is nonsense . . . to speak of a linguistic component and a factual component in the truth of any individual statement' (TDE, p. 42). Dispositions to be prompted by stimulations to assent to and dissent from sentences 'may be impure in the sense of including worldly knowledge, but they contain it in a solution which there is no precipitating' (*WO*, p. 39). Here it will be useful to isolate the following *inextricability thesis*:

> There is no such thing as pure semantic knowledge. What might be thought of as that sort of knowledge is inextricably merged with what people would like to call non-linguistic beliefs.[1]

It seems that in *Word and Object* the alleged inextricability of semantic and factual knowledge is regarded as contributing to the indeterminacy of translation. Not that Quine spells out what that contribution is: all the emphasis is on the underdetermination of analytical hypotheses. But at any rate some points relating to the inextricability thesis are clearly seen as preparing the ground for the indeterminacy thesis. (Notably the inextricability is invoked to rebut the idea that socialized intrasubjective stimulus synonymy is an adequate reconstruction of our intuitive notion of sentence synyonymy—*WO*, pp. 62, 66). This gives us reason enough to discuss the inextricability thesis. We should also take note of Dummett's claim that 'unless reinforced by the inextricability thesis, the indeterminacy thesis is quite implausible' (1974a, p. 395).

In addition you might well think that the inextricability thesis is itself inextricable from the indeterminacy thesis. For if there is no such thing as knowledge of meanings unmixed with beliefs about the world—if there is no 'fact of the matter' as to what constitutes semantic knowledge as contrasted with factual beliefs— then presumably the totality of Quine-acceptable facts permits significantly divergent schemes for assigning meanings to sentences. So it appears that for meanings to be inextricable just *is* for interpretation, hence translation, to be indeterminate in Quine's sense. In fact this line of thought is defective, as we shall see later. But it may still help to reinforce the idea that inextricability supports indeterminacy. Since the inextricability thesis looks a good deal more plausible than the indeterminacy thesis, an examination of their relations is clearly necessary.

---

[1] Although this is my own formulation, the quotations just given leave no doubt about Quine's commitment to the thesis. The name 'inextricability thesis' comes from Dummett (1974a, p. 365).

4.4 Reasons for inextricability (1): the Duhem–Quine thesis

The Duhem–Quine thesis does not seem to provide any *immediate* justification for the inextricability thesis. There is no obvious reason why someone who held that semantic knowledge was distinct from non-linguistic knowledge should not also follow Quine in holding that one's system of beliefs about the world faces experience as a whole. Even a rigid analytic–synthetic distinction is compatible with there being an indefinitely wide range of ways of accommodating one's empirical beliefs to a given recalcitrant experience. (Indeed this appears to have been Duhem's own position: 1914/1954, pp. 205, 292 f.) So the idea of the underdetermined revisability of theories does not look like an immediate threat to semantic theorizing. However, it does pose an indirect challenge to semantic theorizing, and so may seem to provide a corresponding justification for the inextricability thesis. The challenge comes from the idea that *all* the sentences a person holds true belong to a single system—a single complex instrument for anticipating the stimulation of one's surfaces (TDE, pp. 42 f., *WO*, p. 12).

Why is this a challenge? Firstly because the interconnectedness of all sentences seems to leave the semantic theorist with no objective basis for distinguishing a class of analytic or meaning-constitutive sentences, held true solely on account of a grasp of their meanings. In Quine's picture the traditionally analytic sentences, together with logical and mathematical truths and high-level physical laws, are all interconnected in various ways with the more obviously empirical sentences of the system. For this reason it is in his view conceivable, if unlikely, that bizarre patterns of experience on the one hand, or pressure for unusual types of theoretical simplicity on the other, should result in such radical upheavals in a person's system that even some 'analytic' sentences were given up. In this way the interconnections foil the semantic theorist's attempts to draw a non-arbitrary analytic–synthetic distinction. Of course there is still room for people to entertain *theories* about what words or sentences mean. Indeed our adherence to such theories can be allowed to explain some of our behaviour, e.g. our responses to special questionnaires devised by semantic theorists. But in Quine's view the prevalence of such theories no more justifies the supposition that there really is such a thing as pure knowledge of meanings than the ancient prevalence of theories about witchcraft justifies our supposing that there really used to be witches.

Acceptance of Quine's views on the interconnectedness of all the sentences in a system seems, then, to require acceptance of his view that there is no subset of stimulus-analytic sentences which represents a pure knowledge of meanings. However, someone might be willing to accept this view while denying the inextricability thesis itself. One might still insist that there is a pure knowledge of meanings, distinct from empirical beliefs, even if that knowledge cannot be adequately represented by stimulus-analytic sentences which belong to the language. Knowledge of meanings, though practical, may be conceded to be in principle capable of representation in propositional form (cf. Dummett 1976, p. 69). But no one has actually managed to carry through such a representation for any natural language; and even if it were to be done, we can easily imagine that its sentences would fall far short of stimulus analyticity. Besides, a community with (practical) knowledge of the meanings of the expressions of their language might still lack the linguistic means to represent that knowledge propositionally. At least this suggestion is not obviously absurd.

However, Quinean holism challenges this suggestion too. It does so by offering to *replace* the idea of an objectively distinct semantic competence by that of a single complicated instrument for dealing with the world, an instrument capable of being regarded as, or manifested by, a complex of behavioural dispositions. The idea is that there is no need to introduce the notion of pure semantic knowledge in order to describe or explain the workings of this instrument. Instead we need refer only to the physical structure of the human nervous system and our capacity to acquire dispositions to respond diversely to various patterns of sound under various patterns of sensory stimulation (cf. e.g. EN, MVD). If you accept this view there may seem little point in rejecting the inextricability thesis. All the same, it is not as if Quine, or indeed any psychologist or philosopher, had actually managed to spell out a theory which successfully explained the use of language along these lines. He has simply offered us a picture. Those who find the picture congenial will tend to accept the inextricability thesis, but it is not clear that they will be right to do so. The picture will be discussed further when we come to examine Dummett's objections to inextricability. For the present we must conclude that the argument from the Duhem–Quine thesis is less than overwhelming.[2]

4.5 Reasons for inextricability (II): Quine's reductionist assumption

In spite of his attack on reductionism in 'Two Dogmas', Quine imposes, both there and in _Word and Object_, a condition on acceptable accounts of meaning and synonymy which can hardly be justified except on the basis of a fairly strong reductionist assumption. Of course he does not demand that meaning be defined in terms of experiences, for that is one of the views he attacks. But he does require synonymy to be defined 'in terms relating to linguistic behaviour' (TDE, p. 24); and in _Word and Object_ he takes this condition in a very restrictive sense by assuming, in effect, that knowledge of meanings would have to be defined in terms of dispositions to assent to or dissent from sentences under various patterns of stimulation. If this assumption is accepted, it combines with a familiar and uncontentious point to make the inextricability thesis seem inescapable.

The familiar point is that if we consider the problem of radical interpretation we cannot in general discover what people's utterances mean independently of discovering what they believe (nor, indeed, independently of what they want, intend, etc.; but let us focus on beliefs). Even assuming we know when people are making sincere assertions, what they assert depends on what they believe; but we cannot tell what they believe without knowing what they mean. So our interpretative theory must yield beliefs and meanings together. (See Davidson, 1974a.) So if the only acceptable way to characterize meaning and knowledge of meaning is in terms of dispositions to assent to or dissent from sentences under various patterns of stimulation, and if we are not allowed to assume we know what beliefs are held, in general it will be impossible to characterize pure semantic knowledge. For no dispositions will be guaranteed to represent semantic knowledge pure and simple. On those assumptions, therefore, the whole idea of such knowledge is idle. (see _WO_, pp. 38 f.).

---

[2] The argument against holism which Katz gives (1979, p. 341) is unsound. He assumes that the necessity by which a Quinean belief system 'must' be revised in the face of a recalcitrant experience is logical. But that assumption is gratuitous: the necessity need be no more than practical. The individual needs to be able to operate successfully in the world, so needs to maintain a reasonably workable system. Not revising the system in the face of experience would tend to make it unworkable, hence the (practical) necessity for revisions.

In section 9 of *Word and Object*, having explained the notion of
stimulus meaning, Quine shows, given the reductionist assumption,
that there is no way to pick out those stimulations that would
prompt assent to the queried sentence 'Gavagai?' just on the
strength of an understanding of 'Gavagai' and unaided by collateral information, e.g. by memories of recent sightings of rabbits
in the neighbourhood, by observation and knowledge of the ways
of rabbit-flies, or by verbal hints from others. He goes on to urge
that the trouble is more widespread: it is that 'we have made no
general experimental sense of a distinction between what goes into
a native's learning to apply an expression and what goes into his
learning supplementary matters about the objects concerned' (*WO*,
p. 38). There is no 'evident criterion' whereby to strip away the
effects of such socially shared information as that about the rabbit-
fly or a bystander's language, and leave just the meaning of 'Gavagai'. He then puts the difficulty in more general terms. Suppose
A were said to be the class of just those stimulations each of
whichwould prompt assent to a sentence *S* in the absence of
collateral information. And suppose a further class of stimulations,
A', were said to prompt assent to *S* partly on account of certain
widely shared collateral information *C*. He suggests that we could
equally well describe the same situation by saying that on acquiring
C the *meaning* of *S* is implicitly changed, so that members of *A'*
now suffice outright, just like members of *A*.

We might have supposed there would be a difference between
the case where, having learnt to say 'Gavagai' on sighting a rabbit-
fly, we left the meaning of that sentence unchanged, and the case
where our acquisition of the new disposition resulted in 'Gavagai'
coming to mean 'Rabbit or rabbit-fly'. But on Quine's account this
distinction is illusory. 'What we objectively have is just an evolving
adjustment to nature, reflected in an evolving set of dispositions
to be prompted by stimulations to assent to or dissent from sentences'; and in general there is no objective basis for distinguishing
the contributions respectively made to those dispositions by semantic knowledge and knowledge of non-linguistic facts. The dispositions contain 'worldly knowledge', but 'in a solution which
there is no precipitating' (*WO*, pp. 38 f.).

Quine's reductionist assumption is of course consistent with the
heavy behaviouristic bias of his discussions in *Word and Object*.
But he offers no independent justification for it. Nor does he apply

it to theories in general. On the contrary he recognizes that 'posits', such as molecules or photons, can be unavoidable (except at the cost of equally artificial expedients: see *WO*, p. 22). So is it just behaviouristic prejudice which leads him to take for granted that any specification of knowledge of synonymy and knowledge of meanings must be in terms of dispositions to assent to or dissent from sentences under various stimulations?

He can reasonably challenge opponents to suggest alternative terms for specifying knowledge of meanings, terms which make as 'clear empirical sense' as is made, in his view, by talk of dispositions and stimulations. But this challenge is blunted by the objection already hinted at. The requirement that talk of semantic knowledge be actually *reduced* to behavioural terms is unjustifiably strong. Why insist that knowledge of meanings be reducible to behavioural terms when there is universal agreement that talk of quarks, photons, etc. cannot be reduced to talk of instrument readings or bubble-chamber photographs? Unless the indeterminacy thesis is presupposed, the reductionist assumption lacks justification even by his own lights, and can hardly be taken to vindicate the inextricability thesis.

4.6 Reasons for inextricability (III): Change of meaning or change of theory?

The third main consideration which seems to support the inextricability thesis is that when a scientific law is revised, there is in general no point in inquiring whether what has occurred is a change of meaning or a change of theory (*WO*, p. 57). Quine refers approvingly to Putnam's 'The Analytic and the Synthetic', where Putnam employs the notion of a 'law-cluster concept'. A theoretical expression, such as 'photon' or 'rest mass', will generally lack a clearly defined stimulus meaning, constant from person to person. This is a trait it shares with such words as 'bachelor'. But whereas 'bachelor''s utility in communication depends almost exclusively on its connection with 'unmarried man', that of a theoretical expression is likely to be based on its role in a whole cluster of laws. The result is that while giving up 'bachelor''s link with 'unmarried man' would make the word virtually useless, giving up one of the cluster of laws in which a law-cluster word occurs need not even be felt to involve a change of meaning. Special cases of this point are those in which the word in question purports to refer to an object of some kind. In such cases we cannot sensibly distinguish knowing what these objects are and knowing what the theory says about them. We cannot for example first learn what quarks are, then learn what to say about them. (Admittedly Quine's view, like Putnam's, would allow us to learn what quarks are without learning *exactly* what a particular theory says about them. We might learn about quarks from theory *A* and thereby be equipped to talk about quarks in connection with theory *B*, without knowing exactly what theory *B* said about them, provided the differences between *A* and *B* were not too great. But that does not significantly affect his claim, since one can reasonably say that knowing what quarks are, or understanding the word 'quark', does not require knowing everything there is to know about them.)

These points are at least persuasive. Theoretical expressions surely cannot be explained except by explaining the relevant parts of the theories in which they occur, and this cannot be done without conveying what those theories are. It does seem to be nonsensical to suggest that knowing the meaning of a theoretical expression (in the sense of an expression which derives its whole use in the language from its use in scientific theories) is distinct from knowing bits of the theories in which it is embedded. In the case of such theoretical expressions, at least, the idea of a 'pure' knowledge of meanings is hard to sustain. And certainly the idea of an analytic-synthetic dichotomy for theoretical sentences seems absurdly inappropriate.

4.7 *Generalizing from the case of theoretical expressions*

Quinean holism allows no principled distinction between, on the one hand, what anyone would count as a theory (e.g. quantum mechanics, or the theory of evolution) and on the other hand that 'loose total fabric of quasi-theories' (*WO*, p. 24) which is incorporated in ordinary talk about ordinary things, whose origins are lost in the mists of time and which we imbibe with our mother's milk. So Quinean holists will regard the points noted in the last section as establishing the inextricability thesis in its full generality. But of course opponents of Quinean holism would regard that as a question-begging leap.

The objection will be that there is a reasonably well defined gap between ordinary language and theories of sorts which illustrate the points we have been discussing—theories such as quantum mechanics or special relativity. Suppose, for example, that John and Jane both speak English, and John shares all Jane's beliefs except that while she knows a lot of quantum mechanics, he is ignorant of this theory. Obviously Jane understands many sentences that John does not, and for that reason one might suggest that they do not speak exactly the same language. Yet it appears that there is a part of English they do share: the common part which excludes quantum mechanics. Are Quinean holists committed to the view that although John and Jane both understand the sentences of this common part of English, they somehow do not understand them in quite the same ways, so that they cannot strictly be said to speak the same language even when quantum mechanics is left out of account? I do not see how such an extreme holism could be defended, either empirically or on general theoretical grounds. But I will not pursue the issue here. For our purposes it is enough to notice that if defence of the inextricability thesis depended on this extreme holism, the defence would be curiously unpersuasive. If on the other hand this assumption is not made, then the argument for inextricability sketched in the last section raises no serious problem for the semantic theorist. For theories in the narrow sense occupy a relatively small part of the total linguistic resources of most language users—indeed many communities are wholly without such theories—and the semantics of such theories can be regarded as a special case.

However, perhaps an argument like the one in the last section can be based on examples drawn from less elevated regions of discourse.

4.8 Dog theory and quark theory

Take the case of 'dog', which is not a theoretical expression in the narrow sense. Typically the child picks up an understanding of this word by actually encountering dogs in various circumstances, with or without appropriate remarks from others; by seeing pictures of dogs with or without commentaries; by hearing stories about dogs; and—not least—by learning other words, such as 'cat', 'horse', 'cow', 'wolf', which help it to catch on to the boundaries of application of 'dog'. Evidently the child cannot get through these phases of learning without acquiring a fair amount of factual information about dogs—weakness for bones, sense of smell, where Fido lives and barks, and so on. Now, is there any good reason to suppose that knowing what 'dog' means is something in principle distinguishable from having a whole cluster of more or less factual beliefs about dogs? In other words, is there any relevant difference between this case and that of 'quark'?

Well, you can point to a dog but not to a quark. But is that relevant? After all, we had to learn what *kind* of thing people were pointing to when we heard them say things like 'Look at the doggie', pointing. Admittedly, observation sentences including the word 'dog' serve to introduce that word far more directly than 'quark' could possibly be introduced, which is partly why dog theory, if it is a theory, is so much easier to pick up than particle physics. Still, is that a reason for thinking that knowledge of the meaning of 'dog' can be separated from more factual beliefs about dogs, as knowledge of the meaning of 'quark' cannot be separated from knowledge of what the theory says about quarks?

I do not see how the observability of dogs can be supposed to block the Quinean argument, once we concede, as I think we must, that pointing alone cannot determine what 'dog' means. (It is not as if the observability of dogs tended to make the claim that there are analytic sentences beginning 'All dogs are . . . ' more plausible than the corresponding claim for quarks.) If this is correct, the scientific illustrations are by no means the only plausible illustrations of the inextricability thesis (though there remains quite a strong objection still to be considered: see 4.11).

4.9 Relevance of the Kripke-Putnam theory of natural kind words

Support for the inextricability might also be looked for from another direction: the ideas of Kripke and Putnam. According to Putnam's theory of natural kind words, understanding such words requires knowledge of 'stereotypes'. For example, in the case of 'rabbit' it requires knowing that rabbits are typically supposed to be small, shy, furry animals with long ears, small, fluffy, white tails, and prominent front teeth. But stereotypes do not support *analytic* truths. If for example having long furry ears belongs to the stereotype of 'rabbit', we may not legitimately conclude it is analytically true that all rabbits have long furry ears.

Now at first glance it may seem that these ideas have a bearing on our discussion of inextricability. If we attend to Putnam's insistence that stereotypes do not support analytic truths, and his inclusion of a term's extension in what he has called its 'meaning vector' (1975b), he may appear to be thereby committed to the inextricability doctrine. If, however, we note that knowledge of stereotypes can be separated from other items of knowledge, and also that a person can know how to speak a language without knowing the extensions of its natural-kind terms, his position may appear quite consistent with rejection of the inextricability thesis.

Putnamian proponents of inextricability could point out that stereotypes contain 'factual' items and do not support analytic claims, and further that the boundary of the stereotype is not sharp. On the other hand Putnamian opponents of inextricability could stress both that a stereotype could well include purportedly factual information which was false, and that to know what the stereotype is is not to accept it. The case of tropical peoples who refused to believe bona fide accounts of snow is relevant. They knew the stereotype as well as the rest of us, and could indeed refer to snow if ever their incredulity abated. So their knowledge of the meaning of this word would be sharply distinct from actual factual beliefs about relevant non-linguistic facts. I conclude that even if Putnam's views on natural kind words are accepted, they do not necessarily commit us to the inextricability thesis.

4.10 *Dummett's arguments against inextricability*

Now for some objections to the inextricability thesis. First, Dummett's attack on it in his wider critique of Quine's philosophy of language.

The main weight of Dummett's attack on the inextricability doctrine is carried by the notion of justifying, or giving reasons for, assertions. He assumes we acquire practices of giving and seeking reasons for assertions as 'an integral part of what we learn when we learn to use language' (1973, p. 614. Cf. 1974a, pp. 370-2). He urges that it is fundamental to the use we learn for a sentence whether or not we treat it as a stopping point in the search for justification. Reports of observation are one kind of stopping point, and 'another are sentences which we take as constitutive of meaning' (1973, p. 619). Basic logical laws, and 'many problematic assertions of the kind discussed by philosophers', are offered as examples (1973, p. 620).

In a language of a sort to which the inextricability doctrine applied, Dummett holds, there would be no such sentences. All stimulus-analytic sentences would be treated indiscriminately as not requiring justification; and that shows how remote Quine's picture is from language as we use it. According to Dummett, language-learning as it actually is involves learning what justifications are required for sentences of different kinds. Children learn how to question not only idiosyncratic beliefs, but commonly agreed beliefs as well. But on Quine's model, language-learning 'could only be indoctrination' (1973, p. 622). Children could never learn how to criticize accepted beliefs because they could never tell which revisions could intelligibly be proposed, or what the significance of any revision would be. Once we take account of the established practice governing the justification of statements, 'there is no obstacle to distinguishing, among generally accepted statements, between those which are treated as requiring no further justification and those a request for the justification of which is acknowledged as legitimate' (1973, pp. 622 f.). It follows that if the inextricability doctrine holds at all, it holds, at most, on empirical grounds. But a language in which it did hold would be an odd thing, not only for the reasons mentioned but because once a sentence became stimulus-analytic there would be no way in which it could be revised (1973, p. 623. Cf. 1974a, p. 392).

Now Quineans could accept a number of these points. Giving and requesting reasons for assertions is indeed part of the ordinary use of language, and acquiring these practices is indeed an integral part of language-learning. In learning to use a given sentence we learn whether or not it may be treated as a stopping point in the search for justification: Quine's observation sentences are one example of such stopping points. And without such sentences as 'Bachelors are unmarried men' words such as 'bachelor' have no utility in communication (*WO*, p. 56, also 4.6). But what Quineans cannot consistently accept is that there is a reasonably well defined class of sentences that we take as 'constitutive of meaning'. They cannot accept that any adequate model of existing natural languages requires a *dichotomy*—even if its exact boundaries are hard to determine in practice—between sentences constitutive of meaning and other sentences.

The word 'dichotomy' needs emphasis because if Quine can consistently concede that some sentences may be regarded as having a lot more to do with (what we think of as) meaning than others, he is not open to Dummett's criticisms. And in fact Dummett's arguments fail to show why Quine should not be able to concede this.

In *Word and Object* Quine says we learn such words as 'bachelor' and 'brother' only by their respective associations with other words. If for example the link between 'bachelor' and 'unmarried man' were to be severed, the word would be left with 'no evident social determination, hence no utility in communication', because it lacks a community wide stimulus meaning. That is why we regard 'unmarried man' as 'semantically anchoring "bachelor"'' (*WO*, p. 56). Later he points out that dropping a logical law would involve a devastatingly widespread revision of the truth values of sentences incorporating the logical particles thereby affected, with the result that we should not know how to use those particles: we feel there would be a loss of meaning here for much the same reason as in the case of 'bachelor' (*WO*, p. 60, cf. pp. 66 f.). He does not elaborate these remarks in *Word and Object*. (But cf. *RR*, especially pp. 79 f., and NNK, p. 78.) But I think they could be expanded so as to provide him with a way between the horns of the dilemma Dummett offers him: accept some more traditional doctrine of meaning, or else be left with a grotesquely deficient model of language. For our purposes it will be enough to point towards the possibility of such a middle way: we do not have to attempt to work our way along it.

This middle way would exploit two plausible considerations. First, although the connections between the sentences of a Quinean sentence-system are multifarious, certain connections have comparatively little, certain others comparatively much, to do with preserving the *utility in communication* of some of the expressions which figure in them. Second, it is a *matter of degree* how far a given set of intersentential connections tends to preserve the communicational utility of the incorporated expressions. For example English speakers have dispositions which ensure that normally, if and only if they are disposed to assent to/dissent from a sentence of the form '—— is a bachelor' they are also disposed to assent to/dissent from the corresponding sentence of the form '—— is a married man'. The links between these sentences, as will be universally agreed, have a lot to do with preserving the communicational utility of 'bachelor'. The utility of 'unmarried' and 'man', on the other hand, depends very little, if at all, on these particular links, and much more on their extensively ramified links with other words and things.[3] On this account, sentences such as 'All bachelors are unmarried men' will be stimulus analytic because they are easily recognized by English speakers as representing intersentential links of the sort illustrated.

These are mere suggestions, but they do seem to promise a basis for a Quinean reply to Dummett's criticisms.

According to the middle way, stimulus analytic sentences will vary in the degree to which the intersentential connections they encapsulate or represent tend to preserve the communicative utility of expressions occurring in the connected sentences. They will also vary in the extent to which the fact that they perform this function is recognized. The role of 'Bachelors are unmarried men' is pretty obvious. The role of 'Whoever can see can perceive' is perhaps less immediately recognized as that of representing links between 'see' and 'perceive' which help to preserve the communicational utility of both words. So this sentence, or one where the links are more complex, such as, perhaps, 'Whoever can perform an action can remember', could well be held, even by Quineans, to *approach* Dummett's conception of sentences constitutive of meaning, with the significant reservation that no sentence is *wholly* constitutive of meaning. In contrast, 'There have been black dogs', while stimulus analytic in most English speaking communities, would be recognized quite widely as *not* representing the sorts of intersentential connection on which the utility of its components depends. For that reason it would not be treated as standing in no need of justification.

Dummett realizes, of course, that the vagueness of the boundaries to the class of sentences constitutive of meaning exposes him to the charge of obscurity (1973, p. 620). But notice that the pro-Quinean reply to Dummett advocated here rests on quite dif-

---

[3] There is no reason why Quine should strive to make the notion of communicational utility precise. He need only concede that this notion, which I suppose we can all use in a rough and ready way, can be given some objective foundation in our behavioural dispositions and their tendencies to facilitate our dealings with one another. (Churchland's notion of "semantic importance" is essentially the same. His discussion, pp.51-63, seems wholly consistent with what is suggested here.) The notion seems to be coextensive with that of meaningfulness or significance, and neither Dummett nor anyone else, so far as I know, has argued that Quine is not entitled to presuppose it. True, Dummett actually quotes from the remarks of Quine's on which the present suggestion for a middle way is based, and comments: 'New social determination is, of course, but old meaning writ large' (1973, p. 612. See also 1974a, p. 360). My point is that it is but old *meaningfulness* writ large. The difference is crucial.

ferent grounds. For the middle way both supplies an explanation of the vagueness of those alleged boundaries and shows how, in spite of the vagueness, Quineans can consistently concede that there are reasons for our feeling that some stimulus analytic sentences have a lot more to do with meaning than others, without conceding that any sentences (apart, perhaps, from those like 'Bachelors are unmarried men') are wholly constitutive of meaning.

Emphasizing these features of the middle way, then, it seems Quineans can dispose of Dummett's other critical points. Learning a language that fitted Quine's model need not be indoctrination because the child could perfectly well learn which stimulus analytic sentences represented intersentential links strongly supportive of communicational utility, and which did not. Admittedly there would be many intermediate sentences about which the child would be left uncertain; but since that goes for mature philosophers too, it is hardly an objection. And since children and others could learn to recognize the difference in question, the middle way thereby shows how a sentence once admitted to the archives of stimulus analyticity might later be re-evaluated. (Dummett's charge that Quine's model provides no mechanism for such re-evaluations may, however, be partly based on his interpretation of Quine's decision to treat language as a complex of dispositions. On Dummett's interpretation there is a single set of linguistic dispositions possession of which is necessary and sufficient for speaking the language in question (1974, pp. 360 ff.). But Quine need not accept this interpretation and would do well to reject it for reasons given in Appendix B, so I think we may ignore this feature of Dummett's critique.)

I do not claim that a Quinean model of language developed in terms of the middle way roughly indicated here would necessarily be superior to the Fregean model with which Dummett unfavourably compares it. More would have to be said before we could sensibly decide between them. But it does appear to be a natural, attractive option for Quineans. Since Dummett has given no reasons against it, his arguments against the inextricability thesis are inconclusive.

4.11 An objection to the arguments for the inextricability thesis

The inextricability thesis is to the effect that there is no such thing as a pure knowledge of meanings unmixed with beliefs (or knowledge) about what we tend to call non-linguistic facts. But there is an objection to the reasoning of sections 4.6–4.8, reasoning which was based on the seeming absurdity of distinguishing between knowing the meanings of theoretical expressions and knowing bits of the theories in which they are embedded.

The objection is that it has not been shown that a knowledge of the meanings of theoretical expressions is inextricable from factual beliefs, but at most that it is inextricable from *knowledge of what the theory says*. After all, we can know what a theory says without actually accepting it. I know what the phlogiston theory says, hence understand the theoretical term 'phlogiston', without accepting the phlogiston theory; so my knowledge of the meaning of the theoretical term *can* be separated from my beliefs about the world. Understanding the expressions of a theory may be conceded to be inseparable from knowing what the theory says, but knowing what the theory says is always in principle separable from actually endorsing it.

There is not likely to be disagreement over this point. True, it has been suggested that no unbeliever can properly understand the word 'God'. But even if the suggestion were conceded to have some plausibility for that special case, it could not be generalized without absurdity. It would have the plainly absurd consequence that when Einstein rejected Newtonian mechanics he thereby manifested, not his profound insight into that theory, but a failure even to understand it. Granted the point, then, what should we do about it?

Even if we assume, not unreasonably, that the members of a given linguistic community will normally use words in sentences actually held true in the community, that does not dispose of the difficulty. For one thing, two or more conflicting theories may be accepted by different groups within the same community, and both theories may be actively discussed throughout it. So although in such cases every theoretical expression in use would belong to some accepted theory, many of the utterances in which these expressions occurred would be used to make statements *against* the relevant theories, by people who rejected them. Moreover, even if all members of the community shared the same theory, we have seen that their knowledge of what that theory says, and with it their knowledge of the meanings of its expressions, would not necessarily desert them if, as is always possible, they were to desert it. And, of course, all this goes for 'dog' just as well as it goes for 'quark'.

It might now appear sensible, at first sight, to revise the inextricability thesis so that instead of denying that there is such a thing as pure semantic knowledge unmixed with factual knowledge or beliefs, it says only that there is no such thing as a pure semantic knowledge unmixed with knowledge of just which supposedly factual beliefs *would* have to be held by uncritical users of the expressions in question. But the revised version would be useless for Quinean purposes.

Suppose you accepted a straightforward truth-conditions account of knowledge of meaning, that is, you held that knowing the meaning of a given declarative factual sentence consisted in knowing what conditions must be satisfied for that sentence to be true. Then you would readily agree that there is no such thing as a knowledge of the meaning of the sentence unmixed with a knowledge of what factual beliefs would have to be held by uncritical users of the sentence. But you would not regard that as a reason for rejecting the idea of a pure semantic knowledge. On the contrary, you would regard it as a partial explanation of the nature of such knowledge. Nor would an anti-realist find anything to complain of in the inextricability thesis if it were to be revised on the lines suggested. If knowing the meaning of a sentence consists in knowing its assertibility conditions, that knowledge will not generally be separable from knowledge of what factual beliefs must be held by sincere users of the sentence. But this view is entirely consistent with maintaining that there is pure semantic knowledge: such knowledge will simply be knowledge of assertibility conditions. So the proposed revision would destroy the inextricability thesis.

The objection I have been discussing is directed against the arguments of sections 4.6-4.8, rather than against the inextricability thesis itself. Since the arguments of those sections are the only ones that looked better than mildly appealing, it seems to me that the thesis remains at best unproven. But I shall not pursue the issue. The question of the theory's truth is not crucial for our purposes, at any rate if what I am about to say is right.

4.12 The inextricability thesis does not support the indeterminacy thesis

Even if the inextricability thesis is true, does it in any way support the indeterminacy thesis? I remarked earlier that the two theses might be supposed to be virtually indistinguishable. Let us begin by looking more closely at that idea.

The thought is that if there is no such thing as a pure knowledge of meaning, the Quine-acceptable facts cannot possibly determine translation uniquely: to suppose they did so would be to suppose that there was sameness of meaning, hence that there were meanings, hence that there was pure knowledge of meanings. (For not even Quine would deny that whatever was determined by facts acceptable to him would itself be a matter of fact: see 1.9. We need not worry about Quinean ultras, who might insist that all statements of fact must be *translatable* into Quine-acceptable terms: see 1.10.)

But there is a *non sequitur* here. True, whatever is uniquely determined by the Quine-acceptable facts must be reckoned a matter of fact too. So if translations are so determined, questions of translation are questions of fact. It follows immediately that in that case questions of sameness of meaning are matters of fact; and therefore—assuming, as Quine might, that statements of sameness of meaning can be represented by sentences to which a person may be disposed to assent—that there is such a thing as a pure knowledge of sameness of meaning. But it does not follow that there is such a thing as a pure knowledge of meaning. It is a platitude, after all, that we may know *that* a given pair of sentences mean the same without knowing *what* they mean: knowledge of sameness of meaning is not at all the same as knowledge of meaning. And since the argument assumes that knowledge of sameness of meaning entails knowledge of meaning, it fails.

There is a plausible reply. If there is no such thing as a pure knowledge of meaning, how is knowledge of sameness of meaning possible? What is it knowledge *of?* Surely the project of translation presupposes there is a pure knowledge of meaning, and indeed purports to represent, in its way, just that knowledge? This objection rests on an equivocation. We may indeed say that translation aims to represent the meanings of sentences in one language by correlating those sentences with sentences of another language. We may say this because we may say that a person's knowledge of a given language involves knowledge of the meanings of its sentences. But we are not also entitled to assume that this knowledge constitutes a pure knowledge of meanings *in the sense in question here*. Knowing the meanings of the sentences of a language need involve no more than knowing how to use and interpret them; and this knowledge may well not have an objectively distinct component, 'pure' semantic knowledge. That there is such a pure component is a piece of disputed theory; but that there is such a thing as knowing how to use the sentences of a language is not disputed even by Quine. So the objection fails.

The above not only shows that the two theses are distinct. It also helps to show that the inextricability thesis does not entail, and does not even provide support for, the indeterminacy thesis. At first you might think this absurd. What is the inextricability thesis if not the rejection of just such objective relations of synonymy as determinacy of translation would imply? But, as I briefly indicated earlier, there is a significant misrepresentation here. The inextricability thesis is not to the effect that there are no objective relations of synonymy. It is to the effect that there are no pure semantic facts, and no pure semantic knowledge. It is one thing to say two expressions mean the same, quite another to say their synonymy holds in virtue of a special class of pure semantic facts. A translation manual's claims about sameness of meaning have only to be consistent with the *totality* of facts (3.1); there is no need for the manual to go further and attempt to extract pure semantic facts, even if that were possible. It seems clear that someone who maintained, with Quine, that the contributions made by convention and factual knowledge to the use of expressions cannot be disentangled could quite consistently maintain that nevertheless the use of expressions is enough to determine synonymy and translation. The appearance of inconsistency arises from that slippery word 'meaning'. But by now we are surely not going to insist that talk of *sameness* of meaning commits us to the existence of meanings as items about which special semantic knowledge is possible (which is not, of course, to deny that it allows us conveniently to speak of meanings as, say, sets of synonymous expressions).

I have been arguing that the inextricability thesis does not entail the indeterminacy thesis. But we still need to consider the possibility that it lends support to the indeterminacy thesis without actually entailing it. As noted earlier, Dummett suggests that the indeterminacy thesis is 'quite implausible' unless reinforced by the inextricability thesis. He thinks the latter is required in order to legitimize the passage, in Quine's argument in 'On the Reasons for Indeterminacy of Translation', from the underdetermination of theory to the indeterminacy of translation. In particular he thinks the inextricability thesis is required in order to prevent the transition to the indeterminacy thesis from being stopped by an argument based on a certain plausible assumption. This assumption is that if two different theories can be empirically equivalent, then a compatibility relation between observation sentences and theory must be definable. Dummett argues that if such a relation is definable there will be no room for indeterminacy of translation of theories; but he acknowledges that the assumption conflicts with the inextricability thesis. Now there is no doubt that the inextricability thesis can be effectively invoked against certain objections to the indeterminacy thesis, and vice versa. In that indirect fashion the two theses can be said to reinforce one another, and nothing I have to say could upset that claim. However, the loose and indirect sort of reinforcement which that implies is hardly important if, as I shall argue later, Quine's argument in 'On the Reasons' can be blocked without assuming the falsity of the inextricability thesis (chapter 6). Reinforcement is not available from that particular direction.

So far as I can see, there is only one other angle from which the inextricability thesis might be said to give support to the indeterminacy thesis. We saw earlier that knowledge of sameness of meaning cannot depend *logically* on the existence of a pure knowledge of meanings (which of course does not exist if the inextricability thesis is true). But someone might argue that such knowledge would have given the project of translation something to be right or wrong about in a uniquely decisive way: translation would have been right or wrong *about meanings*. For example a pure knowledge of the meanings of sentences in two languages would have invested a bilingual with just the kind of authority the indeterminacy thesis denies. If there is no such thing as a pure knowledge of meanings, choice of an alternative objective control on schemes of translation might be thought to be arbitrary, in which case, it may seem, indeterminacy must prevail. This is not a watertight a priori argument from inextricability to indeterminacy because it does not exclude the logical possibility of alternative objective controls on translation. But it does face opponents of indeterminacy with the task of explaining why there should be such alternative controls, and what they are.

It will help us to assess this line of thought if we consider the sorts of case that seem to support the inextricability thesis most strongly: sentences from highly developed scientific theories. Take for example the French sentence 'Le photon n'a pas de masse', and assume the inextricability thesis does hold in such cases. Now, is it reasonable to say that here the non-existence of a pure knowledge of meanings deprives translation of non-arbitrary objective controls? It seems clear that the notion of a pure knowledge of meanings is superfluous here. We can get along very well with two other related notions: the notion of knowledge of a theory, and the notion of knowledge of the structure of a theory. Knowledge of a theory is no more (though no less) problematic than knowledge of a language, and requires no special comment at this point. As to what may be counted as the 'structure' of a developed scientific theory, that is not of course a trivial question; but fortunately there is no need to pursue it. All we need to notice is the following two points: (1) There cannot be exact translation between the French physicist's theory and the English physicist's theory unless the two theories can be regarded, by those who know both, as having more or less the same structure;[4] and (2) It is not an arbitrary aim of translation to ensure that as far as possible sentences of one theory are mapped onto sentences of the other so that each member of a pair of correlated sentences occupies what can be regarded, by those who know both theories, as the same position in their respective structures. Of course the Quinean will insist that there is no unique mapping of that sort, in which case a theory's structure is perhaps not an objective matter of fact (see 9.3). But that is beside the present point, which is simply to meet the objection that translation is *arbitrary* unless a pure knowledge of meanings is presupposed.

For there can be no serious doubt that if a given scheme of translation does succeed in respecting the intuitions about theoretical structure of those who know the translated theories—as the

---

[4] Recall that the indeterminacy thesis must not be taken to be exemplified merely by conflicts over inexact translation (1.2).

scheme which maps 'Le photon n'a pas de masse' onto 'Photons have no mass' certainly does—then that scheme of translation is permissible, it fits the facts. Nor can the aim of reflecting structural isomorphism be regarded as an arbitrary control on translation. To be sure, this aim does not by itself guarantee that there is a unique scheme for translation between the two theories. The point is only that the common assumption that such a unique scheme must exist if exact translation is possible at all is not undermined by the fact that one cannot know, for example, what photons are without knowing what the theory says about them. Knowing the theory is not a matter of merely knowing 'meanings'; but that is no reason to think there is scope for significant disagreement over the *translation* of theories. The indeterminacy thesis requires a separate defence, and the inextricability thesis seems not to constitute such a defence.

5

'Pressing from Below'

Quine has distinguished two ways of supporting his doctrine of the indeterminacy of translation so as to 'maximize its scope'. One, 'pressing from above', depends on his thesis of the underdetermination of our theory of nature by all possible observations, and will be examined in the next chapter. The other consists of 'pressing whatever arguments for indeterminacy of translation can be based on the inscrutability of terms' (RIT, p. 183). Many philosophers today regard this approach as very effective, if not conclusive. However, in this chapter I shall try to show that pressing from below fails because no good reasons have so far been given for the inscrutability of terms. Or rather, no good reasons have been given for the right sort of inscrutability of terms. For it is an unfortunate fact that in discussions of these matters this phrase has been used in significantly different ways. So as well as examining the arguments, I shall have to try to clarify the thesis. Let me emphasize that here I shall not be directly attacking the thesis itself, but only the arguments for it.

5.1 Inscrutability
Commenting on the famous 'gavagai' example, Quine has described it as 'at best an example only of the inscrutability of terms, not of the indeterminacy of translation of sentences'. But what is the inscrutability of terms? Allegedly, two empirically adequate translation manuals might render a term of one language by different terms of another—for example, 'gavagai' by 'rabbit' or 'rabbit stage'—so that the translating terms would not even be true of the same things. (See *WO*, p. 51, OR, pp. 30-5, RIT, p. 182.) So it seems that the inscrutability thesis (at any rate the strong inscrutability thesis: see 5.4 below) is the Quinean doctrine of indeterminacy applied to terms instead of to whole sentences. And just as the indeterminacy thesis for whole sentences implies that what we pre-theoretically take to be relations of synonymy and translation are not generally matters of fact, so the strong in-

scrutability thesis implies that what we pre-theoretically[1] take to be relations of reference or denotation are not generally matters of fact (cf. OR, pp. 34 f., 37 f., TPT, pp. 19–22).

Put like that, the inscrutability thesis may seem on the one hand as clear as the general indeterminacy thesis for sentences—that is, reasonably clear—but just as problematic. And you will probably also be inclined to think the inscrutability thesis entails the indeterminacy thesis. Unfortunately things are not so simple. For Quine himself thinks the inscrutability thesis is unproblematic—there is 'little room for debate over it'—yet he does not think it entails indeterminacy of sentence translation (RIT, p. 182).

5.2 The Japanese example

The claim that there is little room for debate over the inscrutability of terms is backed up by an example from real life—the Japanese classifier example set out in 'Ontological Relativity' (OR, pp. 35–9). We are told that the Japanese expressions known as classifiers can be construed in either of two ways. They can be construed as a device for forming different styles of numerals: by attaching one classifier to the numeral corresponding to '5' you get a style of '5' suitable for counting slim things such as pencils; and so on for each different classifier. Alternatively the classifiers can be construed as forming part of the term—the term for 'oxen', 'chopsticks', etc.— rather like English 'pieces of', 'sticks of', or as in the present example, 'head of'. So we have a Japanese phrase consisting of a sequence of words $x\ y\ z$, where x 'is in effect the neutral numeral "5"', y 'is a classifier of the animal kind', and z 'corresponds in some fashion to "ox"'. Now on the first approach to translating this Japanese expression z, the phrase $x\ y$ constitutes a numeral suitable for counting animals, and z is construed as the *individuative* term 'ox'. So the whole phrase is rendered by 'five oxen'. On the second approach z is construed as a *mass* term, and the result of attaching y to it is a 'composite individuative term', y z, in effect 'head of cattle'. Again the whole phrase comes out as 'five oxen'. Yet the two construals, though compensatory adjustments ensure the same net results for the phrase as a whole, are in remarkable contrast: as an *individuative* term z is true of

[1] The qualification 'pre-theoretically' is vital here, as with the main indeterminacy thesis, since on some theories it is unproblematic that reference is not a matter of fact. Of course even our untutored notion of reference belongs to a theory of a kind—our ordinary folk semantical theory. But this rough and ready 'theory' is pre-theoretical in my sense.

each bovine; as a *mass* term it denotes 'the unindividuated totality of beef on the hoof' (OR, p. 37). Thus the two construals assign vastly different references to the same expression. There is, however, 'no question of right or wrong' between these two accounts. The question is 'undecided by the totality of verbal dispositions. It is indeterminate in principle; there is no fact of the matter' (OR, p. 38).

If Quine himself had not actually labelled this as a specimen of referential inscrutability I should have argued that it was not. But the label is, after all, his own; so I will simply point out how strikingly this example differs from what we had been led to expect. To say that it shows that the inscrutability of terms need not always entail indeterminacy of sentence translation is an understatement. It shows that some cases of the inscrutability of reference have nothing to do with strong inscrutability at all.

To see what I am getting at, suppose there is a language other than Japanese but with a stock of classifiers and associated syntax exactly matching the Japanese. The idea is that in those areas relevant to the translation of the Japanese phrase $x\ y\ z$ this other language—I am told Korean fits the description—can be regarded as syntactically and semantically isomorphic to Japanese. (There is no need for more detail: the points I am going to make will be clear enough on this basis.) Korean, I understand, has a numeral a which is in effect the neutral numeral '5'; a classifier b of the animal kind; and an expression c which corresponds in some fashion to 'ox'. So one very natural way to translate $x\ y\ z$ into Korean (though we must not assume it is the only permissible way) will be by $a\ b\ c$.

The first thing to be said about this example, given that the Japanese example must be accepted as *an* illustration of the inscrutability of reference, is that it shows that such 'weak' inscrutability may depend entirely on one of the two languages having resources which the other lacks.[2] So the most Quine can say on the basis of the Japanese example is that the reference of z, the Japanese 'ox' expression, is inscrutable *relative to English*. For relative to Korean the reference of z is not inscrutable at all: its reference is exactly the same as that of Korean c.

Now you might perhaps object that Quine's point is that *his*

---

[2] The same point is made by Hartry Field (1975, p. 396). But I am not happy with Field's description of what I am calling strong inscrutability as just a more extreme version. As I hope will be clear, I regard strong and weak inscrutability as entirely different in kind.

questions about reference are phrased in English—what questions a Korean might ask are beside the point—and there is no determinate answer to his questions when they are applied to a language syntactically and semantically divergent from English in the way illustrated. I have two replies to this objection. First, while I certainly agree that it would be wrong to say either that the Japanese expression *z*, as it occurs in *x y z*, 'really is' an individuative term, or that it 'really is' a mass term—there is certainly no fact of the matter about that, and indeed I wonder if anyone has ever assumed otherwise—the word 'inscrutability' is oddly infelicitous. It is not as if the Japanese were up to something that English speakers could not detect. We can see perfectly well what they are about with their use of *z*. It's just that we don't seem to have the equipment for doing exactly the same sort of thing in our own language. *Neither* of the two pieces of English linguistic machinery which come closest to doing the same thing can be said to reproduce what the Japanese 'really' do.[3] So to say that *z* really is a mass term or really is an individuative term would misrepresent the situation much as we should misrepresent the nature of the Greek aulos if we insisted it was really a clarinet or really an oboe (see 1.1(*c*)). (Perhaps the expressions 'mass term' and 'individuative term' need to be supplemented by something like 'classifier-linked term'.)

Complaints about the use of the word 'inscrutability' are of secondary importance, however. The present objection to my approach is that the Korean parallel is irrelevant because Quine is talking only about questions about reference that can be easily formulated in English. And my second, main, reply to this objection is that if it is correct, then this sort of inscrutability still has nothing to do with Quinean indeterminacy. For, to repeat, Quinean indeterminacy is of interest only if it is not just a matter of inequivalent *rough* translations; and surely it is clear that the Japanese expression *z* can only by translated into English roughly. One cannot say the facts are consistent both with translating it *exactly* by 'ox' and with translating it *exactly* by 'beef on the hoof'—or both with saying it has exactly the same reference as 'ox'

[3] People sometimes suggest that the issue might be settled by studying the verbal dispositions of native Japanese speakers who know English. But of course this misses the point. If dispositions or other facts could settle the matter, Quine would simply seek, or invent, a different example. His claim is that there can be divergent construals that fit *all* the facts.

and with saying it has exactly the same reference as 'beef on the hoof'. To justify such claims Japanese syntax would have had to differ from what it actually is in just those respects that, as things are, make both these expressions acceptable as rough equivalents for z. On the one hand Japanese would have had to lack the classifier construction, and on the other hand it would have had to possess something analogous to the devices English has for distinguishing the 'mass' use of a term from the 'individuative' use. If anyone doubts these assertions, I think a glance at the Korean parallel will settle the matter. Korean does provide an exact translation of z (the 'ox' expression), namely c. For c has (or we can suppose it has) exactly the same role in Korean as z has in Japanese.[4] Each of the English expressions 'ox' and 'beef on the hoof', by contrast, has only *roughly* the same role as z. So these cannot be anything but rough equivalents for z, and can illustrate only weak inscrutability of reference.

I had better stress that I am not defining the difference between strong and weak inscrutability in terms of 'rough' versus 'exact' translation. The essential difference is that weak inscrutability depends on one language having syntactic or semantic resources which the other lacks, while strong inscrutability does not. Indeed, strong inscrutability is supposed to exist even within a single language—a point which by itself is enough to show the irrelevance to it of the Japanese example. Differing thus radically, the entailments of the two theses are different too. Weak inscrutability fits those remarks of Quine that were mentioned at the end of the last section: there is little room for debate over it, and it does not entail indeterminacy of sentence translation (if only because it involves only rough translation). Strong inscrutability, however, gives the lie to both remarks. It is highly debatable, and it does seem to entail indeterminacy of sentence translation.

That weak inscrutability exists is undeniable. (Compare common or garden indeterminacy of sense and reference: 1.1(d).) But it goes no way at all to support the strong inscrutability thesis.[5] Indeed,

---

[4] To avoid irrelevant quibbles we must take this to mean that it is consistent with the facts to say that z and c have exactly the same roles in their respective languages.

[5] Weak inscrutability is consistent even with the museum myth and the mental archery myth (1.9). For exponents of these myths need not maintain that either an English speaker's museum or stock of referential arrows coincides exactly with those of a Japanese speaker, so they can happily accept that Japanese z does not have exactly the same meaning or reference as either 'ox' or 'beef on the hoof'.

there can clearly be no objection to a *single* translation manual for Japanese and English offering *both* 'ox' and 'beef on the hoof' as rough equivalents to the 'ox' expression z. Strong inscrutability, in contrast, would here require a permissible manual which rendered z by 'ox' and actually *ruled out* the rendering 'beef on the hoof'. But evidently weak inscrutability provides no justification for supposing it would be possible to devise the compensatory adjustments that would be necessary to bring such a manual into line with the facts. That such adjustments could be made is just as problematic as the indeterminacy thesis itself. From now on, therefore, I shall ignore the Japanese example, and weak inscrutability in general, and concentrate on strong inscrutability.

5.3 Quine's arguments for strong inscrutability

So far we have considered no arguments for strong inscrutability beyond the inconclusive ones offered in chapter 2 of *Word and Object*. It is time to look at Quine's other attempts to defend his doctrine.

The *locus classicus* is 'Ontological Relativity' (OR) of 1968. (Some important ideas are collected in 'Ontological Reduction and the World of Numbers' of 1964. But this earlier work, though it occasionally appears to treat cases of reduction and explication as if they were cases of translation, does not carry the suggestion that apparent references to the objects of a reduced theory could be interpreted as references to the objects of the reducing theory.)

In 'Ontological Relativity' Quine points out that sometimes we use words like 'alpha' and 'green' as concrete general terms, as in 'That is an alpha', 'Your eyes are green'; sometimes as abstract singular terms, as in 'Alpha is a letter', 'Green is a colour'. Evidently the words are taken to have very different references in these different uses; and although we can remove any ambiguity about a given use of one of them by seeing, for example, whether it takes a definite or indefinite article, or a plural ending, or stands as a singular subject, such checking depends on 'our special English apparatus of individuation', which itself, he asserts, is subject to indeterminacy of translation. He concludes that this an example of the inscrutability of reference (OR, pp. 38–41).

The notable thing about this example is that the inscrutability is made to depend on the alleged indeterminacy of translation of the English apparatus of individuation (OR, pp. 35, 45; cf. *WO*,

p. 35), when this indeterminacy thesis itself has not been supported
by any considerations over and above the inadequate ones noted in
chapter 2 above. Evidently this variety of referential inscrutability,
unlike that of the Japanese example, would be strong. But since
Quine's presentation of this variety *presupposes* indeterminacy of
translation, it hardly supports the case for indeterminacy.
However, he moves on to consider a series of examples which do
not appear to presuppose indeterminacy of translation for the
apparatus of individuation. He says:

The inscrutability of reference runs deep, and it persists in a subtle form
even if we accept identity and the rest of the apparatus of individuation
as fixed and settled; even, indeed, if we forsake translation and think only
of English. ('Ontological Relativity', p. 41.)

First he invites us to consider just what are the expressions of
first-order proof theory. Unlike single signs, they cannot safely be
taken to be sets of actual inscriptions. One possibility is to construe
them as sequences of signs; alternatively both primitive signs and
longer expressions can be construed as Gödel numbers. That leads
to the question of what the natural numbers themselves are.
Frege's, Zermelo's, and von Neumann's accounts in terms of sets
are incompatible but equally correct. (See the next section.)
    Are these cases, as they stand, meant to illustrate inscrutability
of reference? Quine does not say so here. They seem to be intended
to show only that 'there is no clear difference between *specifying* a
universe of discourse . . . and *reducing* that universe to some other'
(OR, p. 43). I find his examples unpersuasive even in that role,
however, since there seems no particular reason to count them as
specifying rather than explicating items in the respective object-
theories. For it is quite natural to say I can specify the universe of
discourse of proof theory (protosyntax), to use Quine's example,
by saying just that it consists of such and such primitive symbols
and strings of those symbols—and leaving it at that. (See any
textbook.) Quine's claim that there is no clear difference between
specifying and reducing seems to follow only if you refuse to accept
this natural and generally accepted sort of specification and insist
instead on what would more illuminatingly be called an explication.
His proof theorist, or protosyntactician, is 'thoughtful' just because
he is not content with proof theory but tries his hand at ontology.
According to Quine this Hamlet-like figure starts sensibly enough

by listing his primitive symbols and explaining concatenation. But then he falls to brooding over what on earth he is talking about. Now Quine has so far given us no reason for supposing there is a real problem here. Why must there be *any* answer to the question of what this individual is talking about, over and above the simple one: symbols and strings of symbols? It is not as if the protosyntactician could only have specified the items in question if he had actually asked himself whether they were sequences or Gödel numbers or. . . . Of course you *can* ask such questions. But if you do, what good reason is there to expect there will always be an answer? Quine does not say; and in fact he gives us no reason to assume that specification must be like explication. So he can hardly claim to have produced persuasive illustrations of the claim that there is no clear difference between specifying a universe of discourse and reducing it to some other. It would have been even less justifiable, therefore, if he had claimed that these cases illustrated strong inscrutability of reference.

Quine goes on to make certain claims about the possibility of constructing rivals to homophonic translation. Instead of relying on the homophonic scheme we could 'systematically reconstrue our neighbour's apparent references to rabbits as really references to rabbit stages, and his apparent references to formulas as really references to Gödel numbers and vice versa' (OR, p. 47). Unfortunately he does not explain in any detail how this could be reconciled to the facts: there is just the claim that it *could* be done by means of cunning compensatory adjustments to our translations of our neighbour's 'various connecting predicates'. You might at first suggest that the Löwenheim–Skolem theorem went at least some way towards vindicating these claims. For it shows that we can preserve the same assignments of truth values to sentences while reinterpreting the predicates of the language and taking its terms to refer to any number of quite different sets of things from those to which they are assigned by any 'standard' interpretation. Certainly 'The true sentences stay true under all such changes' (FM, p. 190). But we saw in 3.8 that if that were the only constraint on translation, the indeterminacy thesis would be trivial. (However, see 5.5–5.7 below.)

Nor do I find Quine any more persuasive on this issue in 'Things and Their Place in Theories' (1981). There is a claim that by means of a suitable function (what Quine calls a 'proxy function') we can

'reinterpret' references to one set of objects as references to another
set of objects. There is a further claim that in some cases (e.g.
reinterpreting numbers as certain sets, physical objects as certain
place-times, place-times as sets of quadruples of numbers, mental
states as certain bodily states) the result is that 'verbal behaviour
proceeds undisturbed, warranted by the same observations as before and elicited by the same observations'. And then—hey pre-
sto!—'the conclusion I draw is the inscrutability of reference'
(TPT, p. 18 f.). Of course there would be no difficulty in filling
this gap in the reasoning if we could simply assume indeterminacy
of sentence translation. But the present question is whether these
arguments themselves, either directly or via any support they may
give to the doctrine of strong referential inscrutability, support
the indeterminacy thesis. I think they do not, as I shall now
explain.

5.4 Why Quine's arguments fall short

Consider first the example of reinterpreting numbers by sets. Zermelo represents each natural number n as the set whose sole member
is n's predecessor, while von Neumann represents n as the set
whose members are all the natural numbers less than n, zero being
represented by the null set in both accounts. Now, the natural
conclusion to draw from the availability of these mutually incompatible reinterpretations would be that our ordinary use of
numerals is subject, not to strong referential inscrutability, but
to *common or garden indeterminacy of reference*—the analogue of
common or garden indeterminacy of sense (1.1(*d*)). This ordinary
sort of indeterminacy consists in the fact that the use of a word
often, if not always, fails to determine the answers to some questions about its application. Is the number 3 a member of 5? Well,
you can treat it as such without bumping against any solidly established linguistic practice to the contrary. On the other hand
our pre-theoretical intuitions may suggest the contrary. Whether
or not 3 is a member of 5 seems simply to be indeterminate. But this
sort of indeterminacy should give no encouragement to partisans of
Quinean indeterminacy, whether of translation or of reference.

This everyday sort of indeterminacy of reference does not support the thesis of the indeterminacy of translation, as we have
already noted, because any adequate translation of 'four' had better
reproduce the same indeterminacy—as does French 'quatre', for

example. Nor does this common or garden indeterminacy of reference support the strong inscrutability thesis because it does not entitle us to conclude that the facts are consistent with taking our ordinary use of number-words in *either* of the two conflicting ways envisaged. The very fact that our ordinary use of '4' is consistent with Zermelo's explication and also with von Neumann's is enough to show that neither of these explications can permissibly be said to coincide exactly with our ordinary use. In other words, the facts about our ordinary use of number words enable us to reject the suggestion that, for all we know, we might have been using them to refer to Zermelo's sets, or might have been using them to refer to von Neumann's. At any rate the facts that linguists and others would normally take into account would enable us to reject that suggestion. One such fact is that—prior to theorizing—we are not disposed to assent to '2 is a member of 4', which is true for von Neumann's scheme but not for Zermelo's, and also not disposed to assent to '3 is a member of 4 but not of 5', which is true for Zermelo's but not for von Neumann's. Since nothing Quine says in the train of reasoning noted in the last section shows that such facts may not properly be taken into account,[6] that reasoning fails, at least for this particular example.

His other examples do no better. The fact that people are disposed to assent to ' "Rabbit" refers to rabbits and not to rabbit stages' is prima facie evidence that 'rabbit' refers to rabbits and not to rabbit stages; for that sentence deals with a matter on which we should normally expect the speakers of a language to have authority. (Certainly Quinean theorizing may lead us to doubt that authority, as we shall see at 5.7. But the present question is whether that theorizing is well founded.) And we have already noted that Quine does no more than gesture towards the complex and extensive compensatory adjustments that could allegedly be made to accommodate the eccentric interpretation of 'rabbit' as referring to rabbit stages. Similar points can be made about his other alleged examples of strong inscrutability: the considerations he adduces are just too weak to carry persuasion.

There *is* common or garden indeterminacy of both sense and reference; and these indeterminacies leave room for the useful practices of reduction and explication. Indeed they leave room

---

[6] Indeed he himself implies that such facts go against the suggestion that these cases exemplify indeterminacy: 1968b, 296, RIT, p. 183.

for free choices between incompatible candidate reductions and explications. Sometimes it seems as if Quine is not, after all, aiming to do more than reinforce these widely acceptable points. As long as there are people who assume that sense and reference are *not* subject to these non-Quinean indeterminacies, Quine's remarks (like Wittgenstein's) are salutary. They are also a salutary warning against the related Platonizing assumption that if it makes sense to say that such and such a word (e.g. 'number') refers at all, then there must be some fully determinate class of objects that it denotes. The trouble is that his strong inscrutability thesis goes far beyond these points. When it does, his arguments are powerless to support it, as I have tried to show.

Of course these considerations do not *refute* the doctrine of strong referential inscrutability. But perhaps they do show that Quine has not established it or even—when it is distinguished from weak inscrutability—made it plausible. However, the discussion has been taken further, in ways that have led some people to believe that the indeterminacy and inscrutability theses have now actually been proved. In the following sections I shall examine the arguments put forward in later discussions.

5.5 The permutation theorem

The central idea in these further arguments is to exploit the notion of a permutation, or one-to-one mapping onto itself, of all the individuals in the universe. If the only constraint on our interpretations of referring expressions is that we get the right assignments of truth values to all sentences, then it seems that by means of such a permutation we can ensure that any bizarre assignments of references to terms are balanced by exactly compensating assignments of extensions to predicates. For example, we normally take it that the name 'London' refers to London, and 'Mt. Everest' to Mt. Everest. But now apply to this standard interpretative theory the permutation **P** which maps London onto Mt. Everest, Mt. Everest onto the Moon, the Moon onto London, and everything else onto itself. Then we get a bizarre interpretation according to which 'London' refers to Mt. Everest, 'Mt. Everest' to the Moon, and 'the Moon' to London, but which otherwise agrees with the standard interpretation in its assignment of people, places and things to names. You might protest that this bizarre assignment of references is obviously incorrect, at any rate if we are right about the truth values of certain sentences. For example, we all accept that the following sentence is true: 'London is a city'. But it appears that our bizarre scheme of reference would make this sentence come out false, since Mt. Everest is not a city. However, the protest is premature. For the idea is that we compensate for our bizarre scheme of reference by reinterpreting predicates with the aid of the permutation P and its inverse, P^{-1}. Standardly we should say that the predicate 'is a city' was true of x if and only if x was a city. But suppose that on our bizarre interpretation of predicates we say that the predicate 'is a city' is true of x if and only if $P^{-1}(x)$ is a city, that is, if whatever is mapped onto x by P is a city. The effect of combining this bizarre interpretation of that predicate with the bizarre scheme of reference is to ensure that those two sentences both keep the value True. It is important to see just how this works. In a statement made by means of the sentence 'London is a city', the predicate 'is a city' is applied to whatever is referred to by the name 'London'. Now on the standard interpretation that item is London, so that, since on the standard interpretation that predicate is true of it if and only if it is a city, our sentence comes out true on this interpretation. On the bizarre interpretation 'London' refers to Mt. Everest; but on the other hand the predicate is true of that item on the bizarre interpretation if and only if P^{-1}(Mt. Everest) is a city. So, since P^{-1}(Mt. Everest) is London, the sentence comes out true again.

Using the techniques of possible world semantics and model theory, Putnam has generalized these points to show that, given any 'sensible' interpretation I of a language L, there are other interpretations of L which disagree with I as dramatically as you like, but make the same sentences come out true as I does—in every possible world.[7] However, that is not the point at issue in this chapter. What we want to know is whether the permutation theorem, by itself or with further supporting argument, establishes the indeterminacy of translation or the strong inscrutability of reference. I shall argue that it does not. (My reasons do not depend on the details of Putnam's proof.)

[7] For Putnam's full statement of his proof see 1981, pp. 217 f. (And 1980.) There are complications when it comes to extending the theorem to a language with indexicals and other features whose explication in terms of possible worlds is contentious; but Wallace, who seems to have initiated the use of permutations for this purpose, shows how indexicals could be handled, and, as he says, it seems unlikely that the argument will go through for the central cases and fail over these other difficulties. (1979, p. 308.)

5.6 Does the permutation theorem support Quine's theses?

We know that the relative simplicity of rival schemes of translation or interpretation is to be discounted when deciding whether such schemes are permissible. So you might think that, given Putnam's version of the permutation theorem, not much supplementary argument would be required in order to prove both the inscrutability thesis and the indeterminacy thesis. Indeed, more than one writer has assumed that the permutation theorem requires very little supplementation indeed in order to prove these theses. (See Davidson, 1979.) I shall argue that that is not so, and that the permutation theorem gives Quine's theses no support at all.

It is essential to bear in mind that Quine's theses must be taken to hold for our untutored notions of reference and sameness of meaning. His point, both as it bears on the meaning of whole sentences and as it bears on reference, is that *these* ordinary unreconstructed notions lack the sort of objectivity we are inclined to ascribe to them (chapter 3). Now it has been suggested that we know all there is to know about reference and satisfaction 'when we know how they operate to characterize truth'.[8] According to this proposal, *any* intension-fixing relation for a given language L which gets the right truth values for all sentences of L for all possible worlds counts as a relation of reference for L. But whatever the merits of this proposal as a step towards better ways of doing semantics, it does nothing to support the inscrutability thesis, even though, by Putnam's version of the permutation theorem, it would allow rival schemes of 'reference' for a language to diverge in grotesque ways. For this proposal deliberately disregards those features of our untutored conception of reference in virtue of which we typically assume, for example, that you cannot refer to or talk about something like the Eiffel tower unless you, or at any rate someone you are linguistically associated with, is in some sort of causal relation with the Eiffel tower, for example, has climbed it or seen it.[9] (The causal connection might be very

[8] Davidson, 1977 and also 1979, Wallace, 1979, Evans, 1982, p. 42, and the references (!) there to Frege and Russell.

[9] I doubt if anyone would seriously challenge the assumption that this is a feature of our ordinary conception of reference, at least as it concerns ordinary things like shoes and ships and sealing wax. Cf. Putnam: 'One cannot refer to certain kinds of things, e.g. *trees*, if one has no causal interaction at all with them' (1981, p. 16). He later correctly points out that a causal link is not sufficient, nor even necessary in every case. But he does nothing to refute the assumption in question here. I do not assume that a causal connection holds in

indirect, as in cases where what is referred to is posited at a high theoretical level, e.g black holes or the Big Bang.) And the permutation theorem is quite compatible with the claim that when this additional constraint is taken into account, reference is determinate.

It is not accidental that our ordinary notion of reference requires there to be appropriate causal links between whatever a term refers to and our use of that term. The rationale is that our use of words to refer to things helps us—in many cases at least—in our non-verbal dealings with those things. Our use of the word 'potato' helps us deal with potatoes in its way just as forks and sacks, in their different ways, help us deal with potatoes. Similarly, *mutatis mutandis*, for the proper names of people and places. This point is reinforced when we consider the possibility of massive atom-for-atom reduplication in the universe, with, for example, a Twin Earth embedded in a Twin Solar System.[10] We could preserve the truth values of all sentences in all possible worlds even if, for every possible world which included Twin Earth, 'London' were taken to refer to Twin London and vice versa, and similarly for all other names. But because we require reference to be a relation which links verbal 'aboutness' to non-verbal aboutness, the suggestion that 'London' might refer to Twin London would not fit our ordinary notion of reference. For further reinforcement consider this passage from Kingsley Amis's *One Fat Englishman*.[11]

Roger watched Helene while she chatted to her husband and to Macher's girl, accepted a towel from Grace and moved round the pool to within a few yards of him, . . . He was just rehearsing mentally the casualness with which he would get up and walk over and ask her how she had enjoyed her swim when Macher said: 'Some girl, that'. 'Girl?' Roger went through the motions of noticing he was not alone. 'What girl?' 'Not Suzanne Klein, the girl I brought. You haven't noticed her. The other girl. The blonde. The Dane. The professor's wife. Mrs Bang. Helene. That girl.' He pointed. 'Oh yes, I think I see which one you're referring to.'

every case of reference, nor does my later argument require it to do so. We can in a sense refer to numbers, for example, but that does not imply we are causally linked to numbers. We can also exploit references to things with which we do have causal links to secure reference to things with which we do not, as Putnam's example of 'extraterrestrials' shows.

[10] The possibility of massive reduplication in this connection is discussed by Strawson (1959, pp. 20 ff).

[11] Penguin Books, p. 24.

This nicely illustrates the intimate links we suppose to exist between the ways bits of language refer to, or are about, people or things, and the ways bits of non-verbal behaviour are directed at, or relate specially to, people or things. I take it that reflection on the sort of situation that is described will convince anyone that our ordinary notion does require the existence of such links. Since the attempt to use the permutation theorem on behalf of the inscrutability thesis appears to flout this requirement, I think the attempt fails. However, there are ways in which it may seem that this objection could be met.

5.7 Reference and causation

The point about causation has been noted in discussions of the permutation theorem; but it has been dismissed. The most serious reason seems to be this.[12] Suppose we think C is an appropriate causal relation between word and object. Then we may have a theory according to which we use the word 'Quine' to refer to Quine if and only if our use of the word 'Quine' stands in relation C to Quine. But suppose we have a certain permutation P of the universe.[13] Then the following theory will fit all the facts just as well as the first: the word 'Quine' refers to P(Quine) if and only if the word 'Quine' stands in a certain different causal relation C' to P(Quine), where x stands in C' to y if and only if x stands in C to $P^{-1}(y)$. Clearly the two theories will be empirically equivalent. Davidson, arguing in this vein, concludes that no causal or other 'physicalistic' analysis of reference 'will affect our argument for the inscrutability of reference, at least as long as we allow that a satisfactory theory is one that yields an acceptable explanation of verbal behaviour and dispositions' (1979, p. 16).

This last clause of Davidson's is puzzling. Read at face value it

---

[12] I had better distinguish the causal objection from two quite different claims I do not want to defend at all. These are (a) that reference can be adequately *defined* in terms of some causal relation; (b) that reference is some relation (causal or other) definable in terms of *physics*. I do not accept either (a) or (b). (See McGinn, 1981 for reasons.) All I am saying is that our ordinary notion of reference—the one which is needed if the inscrutability thesis is to be both interesting and useful to defenders of the indeterminacy thesis—is one which requires certain sorts of causal links in at least many cases. This claim is entirely compatible with the claim that there is no sharp way to specify the causal link, and the claim that in some cases—even some cases where the referents are physical objects (leaving numbers aside)—there is no such causal connection.

[13] To adapt what follows to Putnam's version of the permutation theorem, substitute for the single permutation P a set of permutations of (possible) individuals for each possible world.

seems to give the game away. For it seems to imply that the sole constraint on interpretations is that they yield acceptable explanations of verbal behaviour and dispositions. And this in turn seems to imply that any intension-fixing relation for a given language L which yields the right truth values for all sentences of L for all possible worlds can be counted as a relation of reference for L. Now we know the permutation theorem shows that reference in *that* very liberal sense is indeed inscrutable. But if that is all Quine's inscrutability thesis adds up to we can leave it at once and proceed to examine a much more interesting and, indeed, unsettling thesis: the thesis explained earlier in this chapter, according to which reference as ordinarily understood is subject to the indeterminacy. The reasons for fixing on this thesis are parallel to those given in chapter 3 for the corresponding thesis with respect to sentence synonymy. I shall therefore ignore Davidson's last clause, and assume from now on that a 'satisfactory theory' has got to be a theory of reference which conforms to our ordinary conditions on reference, including the causal requirement under consideration. Roughly and vaguely, this requirement—the *Connection* condition—is that in general, or at least in many cases, an expression x refers to a certain item y only if (*i*) the use of x stands in an appropriate sort of causal relation to y; (*ii*) the use of x facilitates non-verbal dealings with y. I do not pretend to be able to make this Connection condition any sharper; but so far as I can see it does not have to be. For all I am aiming to do is show that something like this condition is required by our ordinary conception of reference. If that is correct, mere preservation of truth values in all possible worlds is not the only constraint. (Bear in mind I am not suggesting the Connection condition is a *sufficient* condition for reference.)

These last remarks might appear not to dispose of the reply that any causal relation deemed appropriate for reference can be mapped, by means of a permutation, onto a different causal relation which preserves all the right relationships between words and things, and fits all the facts if the 'sensible' relation fits the facts. My reason for rejecting this reply is that it overlooks the point that the Connection condition is supposed to be a further *constraint* on anything purporting to be an account of our ordinary notion of reference. Since it is a constraint it cannot be attacked on the ground that it would be vulnerable to the permutation theorem if that were assumed to satisfy all the appropriate constraints. This point is explained by Y in the following dialogue with X, a proponent of the inscrutability thesis.

(1) X: The permutation theorem shows that reference is inscrutable.

(2) Y: No. For reasons we have noticed, we are concerned only with the ordinary notion of reference. And as the Amis passage helps to remind us, this ordinary notion of reference imposes conformity to the Connection condition, at least for cases like 'rabbit', 'shoe', 'ship', 'sealing wax'. There must be appropriate causal links between the use of an expression and whatever it refers to, and there must be intimate links between linguistic and non-linguistic aboutness. But the bizarre interpretations which result from applying arbitrary permutations to interpretations which satisfy the Connection condition do not themselves satisfy that condition. For remember that the permutation theorem imposes no constraints whatever on what the permutation may be. We can choose an entirely arbitrary mapping of objects to objects, for example of the set of people onto a subset of stars. Suppose, then, we arbitrarily choose such a permutation P, and that by applying P to our sensible scheme of reference for English (according to which the name 'Quine' refers to Quine), we get a scheme under which 'Quine' refers to a very remote star, invisible to the naked eye. It is clear that our use of the word 'Quine' has nothing to do with that remote star, and in no way helps us in our non-verbal dealings (if any) with it. Since such bizarre interpretations fail to meet the Connection condition, which is a constraint on our ordinary notion of reference, they give no support to the inscrutability thesis.

(3) X: By what right can you or anyone else claim to know *what* the 'ordinary notion of reference' does or does not involve? Since all the 'normal' causal relations C between the word 'Quine' and Quine are paralleled by relations C' between 'Quine' and the star, the *objective* evidence—behavioural dispositions, brain states, anything you like—is entirely consistent with English speakers other than yourself regarding not C, but the (to you bizarre) relations C' as essential for reference. So your conception of 'the ordinary notion of reference' is a piece of fiction, without objective support.

(4) *Y*: You seem to have overlooked the fact that English speakers are disposed to assent to sentences such as ' "Quine" refers to Quine', and to dissent from the sentence ' "Quine" refers to a remote star'. You will of course concede that it *is* a fact that we have these dispositions. So how do you account for it, except by agreeing that there is an ordinary notion of reference, and that according to it the expression 'Quine' refers to Quine? (Cf. Field, 1975, p. 379.) Remember we're considering arguments for the inscrutability and indeterminacy theses; so you can't use either thesis as a premiss in your attempts to overcome the point about causal connections.

(5) *X*: You're missing the point. I don't have to appeal to either the inscrutability thesis or the indeterminacy thesis to deal with what you've just been saying. It's true that all English speakers are disposed to assent to sentences such as ' "Quine" refers to Quine'. But how do you know how to interpret them? The permutation theorem shows that the occurrence of 'Quine' at the end of that sentence doesn't have to be taken to be referring to Quine. You yourself are begging the question if you assume it does. For it could be taken to refer to the remote star.[14]

To make this point vivid I'll borrow an idea Putnam ascribes to Robert Nozick. You think your word 'Quine' refers to Quine, your 'rabbit' to rabbits, your 'cause' to whatever you think causes are, 'refer' to whatever you think reference is. O.K., suppose that's so. Suppose God has arranged things so that when a *man* uses these words they refer to one set of things in each case. But by the same token God has also arranged that when a *woman* uses the same words, they refer to a completely different set of things in each case. So 'Quine' spoken by a woman refers to something quite different—let it be a certain star—from what it refers to when a man is speaking; 'rabbit' used by a woman denotes tin cans, 'refer' used by a woman denotes a correspondingly different relation— one that could be got by means of suitable permutations of the sets of (possible) objects in all possible worlds—and so on. (Cf. Putnam, 1983: ix-xi.) Nothing you say rules out this possibility.

---

[14] *X*'s reply to (4) has to be along these lines. It would not do merely to say (as suggested on behalf of conventionalists by Hartry Field) that nevertheless it's merely a *convention* that we apply 'reference' to the relation supposedly picked out by such sentences as ' "Quine" refers to Quine'. Why should anyone deny that it is a convention? After all, it's a convention that we apply 'cat' to cats.

So my reply to your last remark is: just imagine it had been made by a woman under the system I've just described! You might as well accept that the whole notion of 'scrutable' reference is misconceived.

(6) *Y*: I see why you think I'm missing the point. But really you're the one who's missing it. In fact you're missing it in two distinct ways.

The first is this. The position Putnam and Nozick are attacking with the help of the example you've just given is not the one I'm defending. They're attacking a certain metaphysical doctrine, which Putnam calls 'metaphysical realism' (see 1.12). The characteristic feature of this position, at any rate the feature he attacks with the argument you've been pressing, is hard to put clearly, but perhaps this will do: There is a single correlation (of 'reference') between words and things, which is (*a*) set up by our use of words, yet (*b*) such that reality is divided up into things and kinds independently of our conceptualizing. But I'm not attempting to defend this position. No doubt Quine's indeterminacy theses go against metaphysical realism in Putnam's sense. But it would vastly detract from their interest if we construed them only as expressions of opposition to that special variety of metaphysical realism. One crucial consideration is that a translation manual and a scheme of reference are both purely verbal items. A translation manual correlates sentences with sentences, a scheme of reference correlates quoted words, or names for words, with words in use (e.g. it will include sentences like ' "Rabbit" refers to rabbits'). That being so, both men and women speakers of English accept (in the sense that matters here: they are disposed to assent to it) the *same* scheme of reference for English. For they both accept the 'sensible' scheme which includes ' "Rabbit" refers to rabbits', ' "Quine" refers to Quine'. And the question at issue is whether a rival to this scheme could fit the Quine-acceptable facts (other than the fact that this scheme is universally accepted). If such a rival scheme *were* permissible, then certainly we could use it to represent others as using our shared word 'rabbit' to refer to things other than rabbits. But by opposing the Quinean claim that there could be such a rival scheme I'm clearly not committing myself to clause (*b*) of metaphysical realism.

The other way you're missing the point is even more serious. You keep accusing me of begging the question. My counter-charge is that you're doing the same. You keep ignoring my objection that you ought to have included the Connection condition *as a constraint* on schemes of reference. Instead of replying to this objection you reproach me with illegitimately assuming a prior, determinate, grasp of the references of 'refer' and 'cause' (your (3) and (5)). But you can't legitimately raise this sort of objection.

You start by claiming that the only constraint on schemes of reference for a language L is that they preserve the right truth values for all sentences of L in all possible worlds. The permutation theorem then shows that there will be any number of mutually incompatible schemes of reference which all satisfy this constraint (cf. 5.5). You conclude that reference is inscrutable. I then object that you ought to have imposed a further constraint: the Connection condition. And you reply that I cannot legitimately assume I know what 'refer' or 'cause' refer to—they have indeterminate reference—and that I therefore have no right to insist on the Connection condition. But this is blatant question-begging. If it were legitimate, I could make an exactly similar objection to your own choice of a constraint. What's sauce for the goose is sauce for the gander. If I can't assume I know what 'cause' and 'refer' refer to, you can't assume you know what 'true' and 'sentence' refer to, and therefore you have no right to insist on your own favoured constraint. (Indeed, if you're consistent you ought to allow me to object that you can't tell whether any of your own 'schemes of reference' for L actually does preserve truth values, so you can't even prove the permutation theorem, since according to you the predicate 'preserves truth values' must lack determinate reference just as much as 'refers' and 'causes'.) But plainly such objections to the choice of constraints would not be legitimate. This is because the choice of constraints is prior to any conclusions we might draw from considering the sort of theories which turn out to satisfy the constraints. You're saying, in effect: 'If we apply *these* constraints—and what others could there be?—we get inscrutability'. Clearly, then, the constraints must be understood to be due to be operated in accordance with normal practice, and so in accordance with what we should ordinarily count as fitting our use of words like 'true' and 'sentence'. But I'm saying: 'If we take into account this *further* constraint—the Connection condition—we don't get inscrutability—or at any rate your argument no longer looks as if it shows that we do'. So my proposal to include the Connection condition among the constraints on schemes of reference can't be criticised for begging the question. Your replies so far have been misconceived.

(7) *X*: Look, suppose Putnam uses a set of permutations to construct a rival to the 'sensible' scheme of reference for English. And suppose someone else, perhaps an alien from Alpha Centauri, considers these two rival schemes. Obviously the alien will see that Putnam's two schemes are different from one another. But will this creature also be able to tell what, objectively, are the extensions of the words Putnam uses in his schemes? (Cf. Davidson, 1979, p. 14) No, because by the permutation theorem all the possible evidence will be consistent with any number of mutually incompatible interpretations of Putnam's schemes. 'The interpreter of the schemer will . . . be able to tell that the schemer's schemes are different from one another, but he will not be able to pick out a unique correct way of matching the schemer's words and objects. It follows that the schemer cannot have used words that determined a unique scheme. Reference remains inscrutable.' (Davidson 1979, p. 16.)

(8) *Y*: I interpret this as your resignation. You must know you're not entitled to *assume* that the interpreter of the scheme won't be able to pick out a unique correct way of matching the schemer's words and objects. To assume that would be to assume the inscrutability thesis itself, or at least to assume that schemes of reference are not constrained by the Connection condition. So you're just begging the question.

(9) *X*: No, you're just being parochial. The Alpha Centauran might have what seemed to us to be bizarre ideas about causation, yet there would be no way we could prove him/her/it wrong.

(10) *Y*: To be capable of being counted as having what seemed to us bizarre ideas about causation, your Alpha Centauran couldn't be very much different, intellectually, from one of us—might as well *be* one of us. (Philosophically useful stories about what extraterrestrials might conceivably think have to be about what might *conceivably* be *thought*.) Otherwise why say this creature's ideas were about causation at all? But then any disagreements between us would have to be treated like disagreements between human beings. So the alienness of your Alpha Centauran friend leaves things just as they were. The fact is that once the Connection condition is accepted as a constraint on our ordinary notion of

reference—the only one that concerns us—the permutation theorem can be seen not to support the inscrutability thesis.

Here the dialogue can stop. The thought that our ordinary
notion of reference imposes something like the Connection condition seems to be accepted by Quine, and even by Putnam when
he is not expounding his ideas about inscrutability. (Quine's acceptance of this point no doubt helps to explain both his requirement that there should be agreement in stimulus meaning
between sentences offered as translations of one another, and also
why his alternatives to rendering 'gavagai' by 'rabbit' are other
rabbit-related terms, rather than, as Putnam claims they should be,
anything else whatever (Putnam, 1981, p. 35. See also 3.9). The
same thing also no doubt helps to explain why Quine thinks the
scope for the indeterminacy increases as the level of theoreticity
rises. Without the Connection constraint the permutation theorem
would allow the indeterminacy to be introduced at any level of
observationality or theoreticity whatever.) Of course the Connection condition together with the fixing of truth values in all
possible worlds cannot be assumed to refute the inscrutability
thesis. But so far as I can see it blocks any attempt to enlist the
permutation theorem in support of the inscrutability thesis.

5.8 Ontological relativity

It seems conceivable that there should be inscrutability of reference
even if there were no scope for disagreement about ontology. The
'gavagai' example suggests as much, since even if the perverse
translation manual mapped that expression onto 'undetached rabbit
part' rather than 'rabbit', nothing in Quine's argument implies that
the manual could not ascribe the translator's own ontology to
the natives. Some other native expression might be mapped onto
'rabbit', and similarly throughout. Consideration of the permutation theorem suggests the same conclusion. Even if that theorem had succeeded in establishing the inscrutability thesis, the
theorem's proof presupposes that we already know what individuals exist—and even what possible individuals there are in
each possible world—so that again the rival schemes of interpretation will not differ in the ontologies they ascribe to speakers
of the language in question. So inscrutability of reference does not
seem to entail any particular conclusions about ontology. However,
from our point of view that is irrelevant. What interests us is

whether there are any considerations about ontology which provide independent support for the inscrutability thesis. So far as I can see there are none; but to be confident of this we must look at the doctrine of 'ontological relativity'.

As presented in the eponymous essay, the doctrine of ontological relativity seems to be that answers to questions about ontology, like answers to questions about position and velocity, require a kind of relativization. 'Reference is nonsense except relative to a coordinate system' (OR, p. 48); 'It makes no sense to say what the objects of a theory are, beyond saying how to interpret or re-interpret that theory in another' (OR, p. 50). I say the doctrine 'seems' to be to this effect because there is an interpretation of these quotations which makes it trivially true—and when one attempts to distinguish Quine's actual position from the trivial truth, the doctrine threatens to become very obscure.

The trivial truth is that you cannot explain what the objects of a theory are, or what such and such expressions refer to, except by means of some language. Since you cannot say anything except in some language, Quine presumably means more than that. One thing he seems to mean is that you cannot explain what the objects of a theory are except by using some theory of your own: there is no theory-independent standpoint. 'We must speak from within a theory' (TPT, p. 22). But 'theory' in Quinese is a very broad term indeed, embracing our 'loose total fabric of quasi-theories' (WO, p. 24). To speak a language at all is in his sense to speak from within a theory. Even observation sentences are to some extent theory-laden (1979b). Certainly this liberal use of 'theory' is some-times criticized; but given that liberal use, the doctrine is un-remarkable. If that is all there is to ontological relativity, it clearly does nothing to support the doctrine of the inscrutability of ref-erence, much less indeterminacy of translation, and we can leave it here and now. However, when Quine speaks of ontological rela-tivity he seems to mean more than that we cannot say anything except from within some theory. And the extra component seems to be the (strong) inscrutability of reference itself.

Given strong inscrutability of reference, it will not be a question of fact what is referred to by the terms of a theory. The most that can be said is that its terms have such and such references relative to (i.e. *according* to) a certain interpretation (3.9). (If that is so, of course, there will always be room to question the references and ontological commitments of what Quine calls the 'background theory'—the theory in terms of which the references of the terms in the object theory are interpreted (OR, pp. 48-53). See below.)

Can ontological relativity be analysed, then, simply as the conjunction of (*a*) the platitude that statements about ontology or reference have to be made from within some theory or other, with (*b*) the doctrine that reference is (strongly) inscrutable? That would be worth knowing, and is obviously consistent with what Quine says. It also clearly implies that ontological relativity yields no independent argument for inscrutability of reference. However, the simplification must not be at Quine's expense; and it does not quite seem to do justice to some of his remarks about 'relativizing to a background theory'.

If you want to explain what a certain word refers to, pointing alone is not enough because in pointing to a rabbit you are thereby pointing to a rabbit-part, etc. (*WO*, pp. 52 f., OR, p. 32, and 2.12 above). So you must use some language or other in your explanation. That is the platitude. But if reference is inscrutable there will always be room to question the references of terms in the explanation itself: 'When we ask, "Does 'rabbit' really refer to rabbits?" someone can counter with the question: "Refer to rabbits in what sense of 'rabbits'?" thus launching a regress;. . . .' (OR, p. 48 f.)[15] Quine compares these questions with questions about position and velocity. They too can be answered only relative to a given coordinate system, about which it will always be possible to raise further questions—about the position of its origin and the orientation of its axes—which in turn can be answered in terms of different coordinate systems. But just as the regress of these questions is in practice ended by 'something like' pointing, so 'we end the regress of background languages, in discussions of reference, by acquiescing in our mother tongue and taking its words at face value' (loc. cit.).

Now this last phrase is unfortunate. If there really is such a thing as 'taking words at face value' Quine's whole discussion is mistaken. For in that case our ordinary terms are hard currency, not endlessly bouncing chains of I.O.U.'s.[16] The answer to 'What sense of "rabbit"?' would be 'The sense in which we take the word

[15] Cf. Wittgenstein: 'Every interpretation, together with what is being interpreted, hangs in the air; the former cannot give the latter any support.'—*Phil. Inv.*, section 198.

[16] Rosenberg uses this happy metaphor, 1974, pp. 54 f.

at face value'—and no troublesome regress could get started. And this straight answer would explode inscrutability of reference as well as ontological relativity. For if there really is such a thing as taking words at face value, distinct from merely *using* them, then obviously face value reference *is* reference, and reference is determinate—'scrutable'. It would therefore be inconsistent for Quine to regard taking words at face value as something over and above merely using them in the ordinary way. It would commit him to regarding reference as a matter of fact. However, there is no evident reason for him to accept that particular account of taking words at face value. It seems enough for his purposes to regard it as simply using the words of the language in the ordinary way, without continuing to press questions about what its expressions refer to. (His more recent metaphor is hardly more helpful: 'Staying aboard our own language and not rocking the boat' (TPT, p. 20).)

Quine's analogy with spatio-temporal coordinate systems has been attacked as incoherent. Field has objected that the notion of a general term denoting a set relative to a given translation manual 'does not seem to make any sense' (Field, 1974: 206). Field points out that Quine cannot consistently define such predicates as 'Term F of theory T_1 denotes x relative to theory T_2'. For in order to define such predicates we should have to establish a relation between one or other of the two theories and x (and no object other than x); and that is ruled out by the indeterminacy thesis (op. cit. p.208). See also Davidson, 1979.) However, there seems no reason why Quine should need to be able to define such predicates (3.9). If he accepts that interpretation he is in trouble for the reasons Field and Davidson spell out. But we need not suppose he intends to invoke a mysterious relation of 'relative reference'. We can simply take him to be trying to epitomize the following doctrine: that no more can be involved in assigning references to terms than can be done by *saying*, perhaps in some other language, what those terms refer to; that the facts leave such interpretations underdetermined; and that even when a particular assignment of the object theory's terms to the background theory's terms has been fixed, that interpretation itself is also subject to the indeterminacy.

It now seems clear that the case for ontological relativity is no more, and no less, than the case for strong inscrutability of reference. That is a useful simplification, which seems to be confirmed by Quine's remark that the inscrutability of terms is 'the substance of ontological relativity' (RIT, p. 183). I conclude that ontological relativity gives no support to the inscrutability thesis.

5.9 Does strong inscrutability entail indeterminacy of sentence translation?

I have been trying to show that 'pressing from below' fails to give the indeterminacy thesis any independent support. We have seen that although there is certainly weak inscrutability of reference, it does nothing to support the doctrine of the indeterminacy of translation of whole sentences. We have also seen that none of the arguments so far produced does anything to support the strong inscrutability thesis, assuming the indeterminacy thesis itself may not be presupposed. Pressing from below appears to be a more ambitious enterprise than may at first have appeared. However, in the light of Quine's remark that 'the inscrutability of terms need not always bring indeterminacy of sentence translation in its train' (RIT, p. 182), you may have been wondering whether sections 5.3 to 5.7 were necessary. In fact they were. That remark of Quine's is strictly correct in view of his confusing use of 'inscrutability' to embrace the weak variety exemplified by the Japanese case as well as the strong variety putatively illustrated by *gavagai*. However, the strong variety does appear to entail indeterminacy of sentence translation.

Suppose sentence translation to be determinate. Then if Quine is right to regard the general indeterminacy thesis as just a way of making the domestic thesis vivid (on which see chapter 10), there is no indeterminacy in the domestic case. It follows that English sentences such as ' "Rabbit" refers to rabbits', ' "Beef on the hoof" refers to beef on the hoof' are determinately translatable. But now, all English speakers will be disposed to assent to all such sentences—or at any rate they will be disposed to do so in all cases where they are disposed to assent to the corresponding existential sentences 'There are rabbits', 'There is beef on the hoof', etc. So, by the assumption that translation of all these sentences is determinate, English speakers cannot be represented as meaning by them anything other than what they are taken to mean by their (determinate) homophonic translations. In particular it will not be permissible to interpret ' "Rabbit" refers to rabbits' as meaning that 'rabbit' refers to rabbit stages. Such anti-homophonic interpretations would be permissible only if translation of those sentences were subject to the indeterminacy, contrary to our assumption. Now, might it still be permissible, in spite of these facts, to interpret 'rabbit' as referring not to rabbits but to rabbit-stages? Not according to our ordinary notion of reference. For if sentence translation is determinate, we shall not be able to represent English speakers as *believing* that 'rabbit' refers to anything but rabbits, or as *intending* to use that word to refer to those creatures. The same reasoning will prevent any English speaker from supposing that others believe 'rabbit' refers to anything but rabbits, or intend to use the word to pick out anything but rabbits. It seems, then, that if there is strong referential inscrutability there will also be indeterminacy of translation. So if translation is *not* subject to the indeterminacy, as I shall argue in chapters 10 and 11, neither is reference.[17]

---

[17] Michael Levin has offered a different argument purporting to show that inscrutability entails indeterminacy of sentence translation (1979, p. 25). Unfortunately his argument fails because it depends on the assumption that anyone who maintained that the translation of terms might be indeterminate while the translation of whole sentences was determinate would concede that in that case translation of those sentence-parts that were *not* terms would also be determinate—a concession he shows to be inconsistent. But there is no reason to expect that concession to be made. As the Japanese example shows, if you choose to translate a term *t* by *t′* rather than by *t″*, you must make compensating adjustments to your translations of other sentence-parts. Levin's argument would work if maintaining that sentence translation is determinate necessarily involved maintaining that the translation of *open* sentences was also determinate. But this is not obvious, nor does Levin attempt to prove it.

6

'Pressing from Above'

In *Word and Object* 'pressing from below' seemed dominant. But in 'On the Reasons for Indeterminacy of Translation' (1970) Quine is anxious to correct what he sees as a misapprehension: 'The real ground of the doctrine of indeterminacy of translation is very different', he insists (RIT, p. 178, cf. 182), and sets out the argument he dubs 'pressing from above'. This argument depends on his doctrine of the underdetermination of our theory of nature.

6.1 Underdetermination of theory

As stated in 'On the Reasons', the underdetermination thesis is a platitude. Suppose we take all the observation sentences of our language, consider all the further sentences that result from applying to each a possible date and position, and then let the truth values of all these 'pegged observation sentences' (not themselves observation sentences, of course) be determined by all past and future events in the world, observable though mostly unobserved. Then the thesis is simply that 'physical theory is underdetermined even by all these truths' (RIT, p. 179). Since no account is taken of what would have been observable if things had been arranged differently (e.g. as a result of experiments) this thesis can hardly be denied. In the article 'On Empirically Equivalent Systems of the World' (1975) the underdetermination thesis has been significantly revised. Now it is to the effect that our theory of the world is underdetermined by the totality of true 'observation conditionals'. (The antecedent of such a sentence is a conjunction of pegged observation sentences, and its consequent is a pegged observation sentence.) However, we need not discuss the merits of this or other versions of the underdetermination thesis as such. Our concern is whether, assuming it to be true, it supports the indeterminacy thesis.

Before we examine Quine's argument there are three obscurities to be noted: (*i*) What is it for two theories to be not just different but incompatible? (*ii*) Does underdetermination of the sort Quine's argument envisages require the possibility of rival theories that are not just different but incompatible? (*iii*) What is it for theories to be different?

(*i*) Quine explicitly asserts that physical theories can be 'logically incompatible and empirically equivalent' (RIT, pp. 179, 181, ESW, p. 322). But what is it for two theories to be incompatible? It cannot be just that one contains the negation of a sentence of the other. That might reflect no more than simple equivocation, as when one theory uses 'force' where the other uses 'energy', and vice versa. Similarly, any apparent differences in the objects quantified over by the two theories might reflect no more than different choices of words. Of course there would be no difficulty if we had an acceptable notion of meaning, but if we did we should not be where we are now. Perhaps this difficulty could be handled analogously to the one about the incompatibility of translation manuals: two theories would be incompatible if competent experts would count them as such. However, I am not concerned to produce a satisfactory formulation of the main doctrine, but simply to say enough about it to be able to show why it does not support the indeterminacy thesis.

(*ii*) Quite apart from the question of how incompatibility between theories is to be understood, we may wonder whether Quine's argument really needs incompatibility rather than mere difference. As we shall see, mere difference between theories would be enough for his present purpose, even though he seems to have independent reasons for maintaining the stronger thesis. (Of course the point that two empirically adequate physical theories might be just different is uncontentious.)[1]

(*iii*) Still, what is it for two physical theories to be genuinely different, even if not incompatible? As Quine is aware, if merely verbal differences were admitted, or differences that could be construed as the result of some other simple transformation of one theory, the underdetermination thesis would be useless for the purposes of the present argument because it would trivialize the indeterminacy thesis too. Since writing 'On the Reasons' he has proposed quite an attractive answer to this question, but I defer

---

[1] Though it is worth noting that in 'Empirical Content' he at last proposes that all apparent conflicts can be resolved: 'Both theories can be admitted . . . as true descriptions of one and the same world in different terms' (1981b, p. 30)—a remarkable trivialization of the underdetermination doctrine.

discussion of it because it appears to threaten his main argument (6.8). The question of the identity and difference of theories remains obscure, and makes the underdetermination thesis correspondingly hard to assess.

6.2 Indeterminacy of translation not a special case of the underdetermination of theory

Quine does not regard the indeterminacy of translation as just a special case of the underdetermination of theory (RIT, p. 180, 1979b, p. 66), nor is his present argument to that effect. However, some critics have found the distinction obscure. Chomsky, faced with Quine's attempts to meet his criticisms, has continued to insist that the indeterminacy of translation 'amounts to nothing more than the observation that empirical theories are underdetermined by evidence' (1975, p. 182; cf. 1980, pp. 258 n.26), and Rorty has argued that the indeterminacy thesis is simply a matter of the underdetermination of theory 'turning up where we did not expect to find it' (1972, p. 450; cf. 1980, pp. 193-209. Cf. also Putnam, 1974.) These objections must be taken seriously. I start with Chomsky's.

He complains that Quine has failed to show that linguistics generally, and theories of translation in particular, are underdetermined by the evidence in a way that physics is not:

> It is quite certain that serious hypotheses concerning a native speaker's knowledge of English . . . will 'go beyond the evidence'. . . . Since they go beyond mere summary of data, it will be the case that there are competing assumptions consistent with the data. But why should all of this occasion any surprise or concern? ('Quine's Empirical Assumptions', p. 67.)

In reply Quine concedes that linguistics and theories of translation are like physics in being underdetermined by all possible data, but insists that the indeterminacy of translation is 'additional'. The question is whether he succeeds in making good this claim.

His case depends on a claim about the special status of physics: 'Theory in physics is the ultimate parameter. There is no legitimate first philosophy, higher or firmer than physics, to which to appeal over physicists' heads (1968b, p. 303).' This claim will be discussed shortly, but first let us see how he puts it to work. His idea is that although physics is underdetermined, we can for present purposes regard current physics as fixed, and imagine the appropriate truth

values assigned to all sentences couched in terms of current physics. The set of all those physical sentences to which the value True
is assigned will then represent 'the whole truth about nature' (in a
sense to be explained). What makes the indeterminacy of translation 'additional' is that it withstands this whole truth about
nature: 'there is no fact of the matter even to *within* the acknowledged underdetermination of a theory of nature' (1968b,
p. 303). In concluding his reply to Chomsky he repeats the plausible claim that when someone asks a linguist 'What did the native
say?', the expectation is that this question has an English answer
which is objectively right even if we forget that natural knowledge
generally is underdetermined. So he thinks Chomsky has missed
the point.

Chomsky retorts that he has been given no reason to doubt that
the theory of translation is 'part of the theory of nature, hence
underdetermined by evidence only as physics is' (Chomsky, 1975,
p. 183). The various versions of the indeterminacy thesis 'amount
to no more than an unargued claim that the study of language faces
some problem over and above the familiar underdetermination of
nontrivial theory by evidence' (op. cit., pp. 196 f.). However, I
think it will become clear that Chomsky has failed to do justice to
Quine's chief contention.

Evidently the verdict depends on the significance of Quine's
claim that theories of translation are not only underdetermined
as physics is underdetermined, but underdetermined even *by* the
totality of truths expressible in terms of physics. At the very least
this claim seems to give a sense to the idea that the indeterminacy
of translation is not just parallel to the underdetermination of
physics, but 'additional'. Chomsky never seems to address this
claim directly: he turns aside to note the inadequacy, or lack, of
arguments for it (cf. 1975: 183–5, 187). But although Quine's
arguments for the indeterminacy are weak, that is not to the point
here. What matters is whether the thesis of the underdetermination
of sentence translation by the totality of truths expressible in terms
of physics is significantly different from, and more interesting and
important than, the thesis that all theories are underdetermined by
observables. Could Chomsky reasonably say that even *if* translation
at sentence level is underdetermined by the totality of truths expressible in terms of physics, that should not occasion any surprise
or concern?

A comparison may help. It is generally assumed that chemical phenomena are explicable in terms of physics, and that the entities and properties dealt with by chemistry involve nothing over and above those describable in terms of physics. Taking this for granted, and assuming we ignore the underdetermination of physics itself, chemical truths are determined in the relevant sense by the totality of truths expressible in terms of physics. (Quine's physicalism implies that he would accept this: cf. *WO*, pp. 234-6, 264 f., FM.) This does not mean that the *concepts* of chemistry, as well as the truths statable in terms of these concepts, are also somehow generated by the totality of physically statable truths. No doubt there is scope for workable chemical conceptual schemes other than the one used on earth today. The point is that for any given chemical theory, together with its associated terms and concepts, the set of all physically statable truths determines just which chemical sentences are true. (Otherwise there would presumably be gaps in our physics.) Not that this wholly undermines the autonomy of chemistry as a science. Chemical concepts, the form of chemical theories, and chemistry's methods of inquiry will be guided by the needs of chemists, not by those of physicists. Now, it is at any rate conceivable that the relations between physics on the one hand, and psychology and linguistics on the other, should in some important respects resemble those between physics and chemistry. In particular it is conceivable that, for any adequate psychological or linguistic theory, the following should hold: (*a*) psychological and linguistic concepts, theories and methods are largely autonomous, i.e. developed and applied largely without regard to the details of physics; (*b*) given the theory to be employed (e.g. given an abstract 'theory of translation' which specifies the concepts that will be used in particular schemes of translation), the truths statable in terms of that theory are determined by the set of all truths statable in terms of physics.

I expect that many, perhaps most, psychologists and linguists uninfluenced by Quine would be ready not only to agree that it is conceivable that both (*a*) and (*b*) should hold, but to commit themselves to their truth, once they realized, via (*a*), that it does not involve commitment to the translatability of psychological or linguistic statements into physical ones (1.10). So, since Quine's claim is that (*b*) is in fact false, I should expect that claim to occasion considerable surprise and concern among psychologists

and linguists. At least it should now be clear how the underdetermination thesis is distinct from the indeterminacy thesis.

However, Rorty takes up Chomsky's point and argues, in effect,
that Chomsky is right but perhaps the talk of a 'parallel but
additional' indeterminacy is just a picturesque way of insisting, in
the teeth of ancient prejudices, that even our ideas about what
people mean are subject to the underdetermination of our theory
of nature. It is just that this underdetermination turns up where
we did not expect to find it (Rorty, 1972, p. 450). But I think
Rorty's discussion is seriously defective.

He rightly points out that Quine implies there *is* a 'legitimate
first philosophy, higher and firmer' than *linguistics*, to which to
appeal over linguists' heads; and goes on to say 'of course Quine
cannot mean this'. The point of this remark, it emerges, is not that
Rorty is unaware that Quine really does think that physics is a
'higher and firmer' theory than linguistics; but that in Rorty's view
Quine's account does nothing to explain how linguistics differs
from other sciences (Chomsky's complaint). He concedes to Quine
that even if we knew all about the elementary particles we should
still have a free choice between 'tied' translation manuals, but
insists that we should have the same choice between tied chemical
and biological theories: 'There is nothing special about the case of
linguistics' (1972, p. 452. Cf. 1980, pp. 202 f.). And here, I think,
he has gone astray.

Bear in mind that for Quine's purposes 'tied' translation manuals
have to be not just different but non-trivially incompatible at the
level of sentence translation.[2] One of them must say or imply
something about sentence synonymy which another contradicts.
So in order for Rorty's claim that there is nothing special about
the case of linguistics to hold, the totality of facts about elementary
particles must be compatible with two chemical theories (for example) which are not just different but non-trivially incompatible.
Now I think I understand how two incompatible chemical theories
might still be compatible with the totality of *observables*. Nor do I
have any difficulty conceiving of two chemical theories that used
different *concepts* being compatible with the totality of facts about

[2] In the last section I remarked that Quine's present argument requires only that there
could be empirically adequate but different, not necessarily also incompatible, theories of
nature. Clearly he still needs to maintain that empirically equivalent translation manuals
could be incompatible. (See 3.11.)

the distribution and states of elementary particles. But how could two non-trivially incompatible chemical theories both be compatible with the same totality of physical facts about the distribution and states of elementary particles in the universe? It seems to me that such non-trivial incompatibility would exist only if the theories implied incompatible things about chemical properties, which in turn would exist only if the conflict showed up at the level of observables or at the atomic or sub-atomic levels.[3] Similar considerations apply to Rorty's assumption that there could be two incompatible biological theories both compatible with the same facts about the distribution and states of elementary particles. Obviously more could be said about this, but fortunately there is no need to pursue these thoughts here. It is enough to note that Rorty is making a strong assumption, for which he offers no support, when he implies that there could be non-trivially incompatible pairs of chemical and biological theories all compatible with all the physical facts about elementary particles. It is an interesting, counter-intuitive assumption, by no means to be passed off as comparable with Quine's thesis that physics is underdetermined by the totality of *observables*. I think that is enough to show Quine is justified in claiming that the underdetermination of translation by the totality of physical facts is 'additional'.

6.3 Quine's reasons

Now for the argument in 'On the Reasons'. Strictly, what Quine argues for is not the general indeterminacy thesis but the following:

> T. Translation of physical theories is indeterminate at least to the extent that physical theories are underdetermined by all possible observations.

As he says, if you see physics as underdetermined only in its highest theoretical reaches, 'then by the argument at hand I can claim your concurrence in the indeterminacy of translation only of highly theoretical physics' (RIT, p. 181). But of course his view is that 'the empirical slack in physics extends to ordinary traits of ordinary bodies'; and given this by no means implausible premiss

[3] We might perhaps construct a pair of empirically equivalent rival chemical theories as follows. One of them is the result of conjoining with the accepted theory some such sentence as: 'And there are chemical demons which ensure that our laws hold'; the other is the result of conjoining the negation of that sentence. But presumably we should not want to maintain that such incompatibilities were anything but trivial.

his present argument, if sound, yields the indeterminacy thesis in its full generality. I shall try to show that his argument for the restricted thesis (T) is in fact unsound.

The background is that we are aiming at the radical translation of a radically foreign physicist's theory, and the whole argument is contained in the passage quoted below from 'On the Reasons for Indeterminacy of Translation', pp. 179 f., which for convenience I divide into four parts. (The conclusion, (5), is not part of the quotation.)

[1] The starting point is the equating of observation sentences of the two languages by an inductive equating of stimulus meanings. [2] In order afterward to construe the foreigner's theoretical sentences we have to project analytical hypotheses, [3] whose ultimate justification is substantially just that the implied observation sentences match up. [4] But now the same old empirical slack, the old indeterminacy between physical theories [sc. the underdetermination of physical theories], recurs in second intention. Insofar as the truth of a physical theory is underdetermined by observables, the translation of the foreigner's physical theory is underdetermined by translation of his observation sentences. If our physical theory can vary though all possible observations be fixed, then our translation of his physical theory can vary though our translations of all possible observation reports on his part be fixed. Our translation of his observation sentences no more fixes our translation of his physical theory than our own possible observations fix our own physical theory.

(5) Therefore (T) translation of physical theories is indeterminate to the extent that physical theories are underdetermined by all possible observations.

That is the entire argument. Outlining his main points, Quine contends that, where *A* and *B* are two empirically equivalent but incompatible physical theories, it might be possible for us to 'adopt *A* for ourselves and still remain free to translate the foreigner either as believing *A* or as believing *B*'. Nothing could possibly show that the foreigner did in fact believe one of the two theories rather than the other. Indeed, 'the question whether . . . the foreigner *really* believes *A* or believes rather *B* is a question whose very significance I would put in doubt' (RIT, pp. 180 f.).

This argument was originally offered as 'the . . . real ground' of the indeterminacy doctrine (RIT, p. 178). It is undoubtedly interesting, and an examination of it will be worth while even though Quine himself has since abandoned it—especially since his two reasons for abandoning it are, as I shall argue, unsound (sections 6.4 and 6.8).

6.4 A bad reason for rejecting Quine's reasons

Dummett has urged that if the translators regard the foreign theory as true, then it must be translated, if at all, into a theory they also regard as true (1974, p. 388).[4] And Quine himself has offered, as a reason for rejecting his argument in the last section, the apparently related principle that 'one of our goals in choosing our analytical hypotheses of translation should be maximum agreement regarding the truth of sentences, other things being equal'. He concludes that if our physics is A, we should ascribe A to the natives rather than B.[5]

But there are two things wrong with these suggestions. First, and chiefly, even if the proposed principle were accepted, it would not dispose of Quine's argument (the one set out in the last section). Second, in any case the indeterminacy thesis ought to be regarded as rendering the principle untenable. In other words, the principle threatens the indeterminacy thesis itself.

First, then, suppose our own theory is C, and that the foreigners' theory cannot be translated into C, but only into each of two different theories A and B, which we, the translators, neither accept nor reject. (There seems no reason to assume this sort of case could be ruled out a priori.) In this situation the principle before us could not be applied. For *ex hypothesi* we could not translate the foreigners' physics into C, which is the theory we actually accept; yet the existence of A and B would prevent our saying their physics could not be translated into English at all. In such a case, then, if Quine's argument is sound, it shows that translation of the foreigners' physics is indeterminate. So the principle does not dispose of the argument. (Nor is it relevant to say such cases could never arise in real life. If that were a relevant consideration it would rule out the indeterminacy thesis at a stroke. The practical difficulty of complete alternative schemes of trans-

---

[4] Actually he says 'it must be translated into a theory accepted as true by speakers of the translators' language'; but either this is to be understood as equivalent to my version, or it leaves room for a possibility he does not discuss, which is that some speakers of the translators' language regard it as false.

[5] In a letter to the present writer dated 13 September 1976. See also ESW, p. 322 and 'Comments on Newton-Smith' (1979b).

lation has never been supposed to affect the interest of the indeterminacy thesis.)

Even if acceptance of the principle were sufficient to demolish Quine's argument, the indeterminacy thesis itself, so long as it remains unrefuted, would give an excellent reason for rejecting the principle. For suppose we knew the foreigners' physics could be translated just as well by B as by A. According to the proposed principle, if we ourselves accepted physics A we should have to translate the foreigners' physics into A. But what justification can there be for this principle itself? For by composing the two translation manuals each sentence of A could be translated into a sentence of B and vice versa, so that there would be no rational justification for our preferring A to B, hence, it seems, no reason why we should decide to represent the foreigners as adhering to A rather than to B. True, it might be more convenient for practical purposes to represent the foreigners as sharing our physics, if we could do that. But we know that such considerations are irrelevant when the indeterminacy thesis is in question. And from the theoretical point of view the indeterminacy thesis seems to destroy any rationale the principle might have. The principle—whether it is to maximize agreement or to represent the foreigners, where possible, as sharing our theory—would obviously be justified if agreement were a matter of fact. But if the indeterminacy thesis is true agreement is *not* a matter of fact. If a foreigner's utterance of a given sentence S can be construed as agreement with my utterance of T according to one manual, but as disagreement according to another (which renders S by some sentence inequivalent to T) then there is no such thing as agreement *tout court*. The most we have is coincidence in dispositions to assent and, as we have seen, the lack of such coincidence has no theoretical interest here since the theory to which we assent is fully intertranslatable with one to which we might just as well assent.

It seems, then, that the principle, in spite of its endorsement by Quine himself, provides no good reason to reject his argument for the indeterminacy thesis unless we already assume the thesis is false. Still, there is another very good reason for rejecting the argument. To see what it is, let us first look again at steps (1)–(3) set out in the last section.

6.5 The argument must not assume that analytical hypotheses generate indeterminacy of translation

For Quine in the quoted passage the 'starting point' of the radical translation of the foreigner's physics is 'the equating of observation sentences'. Now in general the sentences of physical theory, regardless of the extent to which they are supposed to be underdetermined by observables, are not observation sentences.[6] So there will not be much—if any—equating of theoretical sentences in the early stages.

Now consider steps (2) and (3):

[2] In order afterward to construe the foreigner's theoretical sentences we have to project analytical hypotheses,

[3] whose ultimate justification is substantially just that the implied observation sentences match up.

Step (2) is uncontroversial. There seems no way to construct a useful translation manual at all without devising analytical hypotheses (2.3). But (3) needs a close look. The claim that the justification for a given scheme of analytical hypotheses is 'just that the implied observation sentences match up' is familiar to us. We know Quine is inclined to think analytical hypotheses are inevitably underdetermined by the matching up of observation sentences, and that this underdetermination extends far enough to result in indeterminacy of sentence translation. But is the present argument supposed to *depend* on this doctrine? If so, contrary to Quine's own declarations, the argument makes no essential use of the doctrine of the underdetermination of theory, and step (4) is redundant. For if it is an assumption of the present argument that the underdetermination of analytical hypotheses by the matching of observation sentences is alone sufficient to produce indeterminacy of sentence translation, then the full indeterminacy thesis— not just the restricted thesis (T)—follows from steps (1)-(3) alone. Clearly Quine does not intend the argument to depend on this assumption. He explicitly aims the argument at those who resist the arguments of *Word and Object* but accept the underdetermination of physics. (See the quotation near the beginning of 6.3.) So although the Quine of *Word and Object* seems to think he can get to the general indeterminacy thesis by means of steps (1)-(3)

---

[6] This is not to deny that, as Quine accepts, observation sentences may contain theoretical terms. (1979b, p. 67.)

alone, his present argument, if it works at all, must work without depending on the assumption that (1)–(3) entail T.

6.6 *The* non-sequitur

We can now see that the argument of 'On the Reasons' involves a *non sequitur*. First an example, then an explanation in general terms.

Fred regards physics as underdetermined by observables only at a very high level of theoreticity, say at the highest levels of particle physics. Protons, electrons, positrons he thinks are guaranteed by observables; but he doesn't think the same goes for quarks. He accepts a certain quark theory (viz. a certain set of *sentences*) but holds that an incompatible theory could be devised at that high level, yet still be compatible with all observables. Fred also assumes that Chinese physics is determinately translatable up to and including talk of protons, electrons, positrons. Of course Quine would say Fred was wrong. But we know the present argument is not intended either to establish that particular point or—this is crucial—to depend on an assumption to the effect that Fred is wrong and that Chinese physics is not determinately translatable up to the level at which he himself introduces quark theory. So I do not see how the description of Fred's beliefs so far could be thought to import any begged questions. Fred is just the sort of chap the argument of 'On the Reasons' is intended to convince. And the question is whether the argument can succeed in convincing Fred that his quark theory—that set of sentences— is subject to the indeterminacy of translation even though Fred believes translation of all physics below that level is determinate.

On Fred's own assumptions he can use Chinese physics text books to check his translations of what he counts as Chinese quark-sentences. This is because on his assumptions he can understand and translate *determinately* all those Chinese books which do not presuppose a knowledge of what he takes to be Chinese quark theory. So—still on his assumptions—he is as well-placed for learning what Chinese quark theory is as are Chinese students of physics who are setting out to learn that theory. However, when Fred translates Chinese expositions of what he takes to be their quark theory he finds (according to my story) that these expositions are indistinguishable from expositions of his own quark theory in his own language, English. Now Fred continues to insist that quark theory itself is underdetermined by observables; but he sees no reason there for concluding that translation of quark theory is indeterminate. On the contrary he maintains that there is a large class C of theoretical sentences of Chinese physics which (*a*) are not observation sentences, yet (*b*) are determinately translatable; and that his supposedly determinate translations of all members of C supply him with a sufficiently solid basis to ensure that his translations of Chinese high-level particle physics are determinate too. (C includes all the theoretical sentences that do *not* belong to high-level particle physics.)

Now of course Quine will dispute both of Fred's claims: he will insist both that the members of C are not determinately translatable and that even if they were, that would not guarantee the determinate translatability of the high-level non-C sentences. But the point is that neither of these contentions is supported by his present argument, still assuming, in accordance with the conclusion of the last section, that steps (1)-(3) must not be regarded as establishing them by themselves. These contentions come out of thin air. It is true that Fred has not managed to show either that the translation of the members of C is determinate, or that if it were, that would entail the determinacy of translation of the high-level non-C sentences. On the other hand it is also true that Quine's present argument does nothing to show that Fred is mistaken.

The *non sequitur* can be pinpointed as follows. After steps (1)-(3) Quine says:

[4a] Insofar as the truth of a physical theory is underdetermined by observables, the translation of the foreigner's physical theory is underdetermined *by translation of his observation sentences.* [My emphasis.]

(So far as I can see (4a) contains the gist of the points made by the four sentences at (4) in Quine's statement of the argument quoted in 6.3.) But (4a) is not the conclusion for which he is arguing. What he actually concludes is, in effect:

(5′) To the extent that the truth of a physical theory is underdetermined by observables, the translation of the foreigner's physical theory is underdetermined *by the totality of Quine-acceptable facts.*

(Note that (5′) is equivalent to T. I use it instead of T to dramatise the discrepancy between (4a) and T.)

To close the gap between (4a) and T it would be necessary to show that translations of observation sentences are the only facts on which the translation of underdetermined theories could possibly be based. Of course step (3) appears to imply just that; but we have seen that Quine cannot sensibly intend to appeal to it. Step (3) certainly prevents the non sequitur from becoming apparent; but once (3)'s inadmissibility is acknowledged the gap in the argument is plain. And as the story of Fred illustrates, there is at least a plausible case for thinking the gap cannot be filled. Why should the determinacy of translation of higher-level theoretical sentences not be guaranteed by behavioural dispositions relating to lower-level theoretical sentences? Quine's only reply to this sort of question seems to be to appeal to his other arguments for the indeterminacy thesis.

Or do these last remarks rest on an excessively strict interpretation of the phrase 'observation sentence' as it occurs in (4a)? Someone might suggest that, contrary to Quine's usual explanations, we are required to count as observation sentences whatever sentences of physics are thought to be determined by the totality of observables; so that all the members of Fred's class C of lower-level theoretical sentences ought to be counted, just for the purposes of the present argument, as honorary observation sentences. On this interpretation the transition from (4a) to (5') would be at any rate intelligible, though still problematic. Unfortunately this interpretation, though it brings (4a) closer to (5'), leaves (4a) itself without visible means of support. For if the 'observation sentences' to be matched up are taken to include all the members of C, (4a) becomes a bald assertion of something uncomfortably close to the indeterminacy thesis itself, and the argument is exposed as having no counter to Fred's claim that determinate translation of C would bring with it determinate translation of the high-level remainder of physics.

So there is a *non sequitur* no matter how you interpret the argument, provided (1)–(3) are not supposed to establish the indeterminacy thesis by themselves. If 'observation sentence' is given its usual Quinean sense (on which see 2.1, 3.9), (5') does not follow from (4a). And if the phrase is given the sense suggested in the last paragraph, (4a) is left without support. It looks as if the argument in 'On the Reasons' establishes no connection at all between the extent to which a theory is underdetermined by observables and the extent to which translation of theoretical sentences is underdetermined by the facts.

6.7 Evidence for theories and for the acceptance of theories

It seems clear that those observables which bear most directly on the admissibility of a given physical theory will not generally include those which bear on the question of whether or not a given group of people actually accept that theory. Observables of the first sort will tend to be confined to items corresponding to observation sentences such as 'This is melting', 'The reading is now 4.9 volts'; while among those of the second sort items corresponding to observation sentences like 'She uttered "Photons have no mass"' will predominate. Reflection on this point will help to show more clearly why the argument in 'On the Reasons' fails.

Recall the case of Fred. Suppose he discovers that one group of Chinese physicists seems to have a high-level physical theory which is still empirically adequate, but different from the one he originally translated into his (and our) quark theory; and that this rival theory is not translatable easily, if at all, into his quark theory. Now, there is no difficulty in distinguishing the two rival Chinese theories— theories-as-sets-of-sentences—simply on the basis of which sentences the different groups of Chinese physicists are disposed to assent to. And since one of these Chinese theories goes smoothly into Fred's quark theory while the other does not, Fred has a very strong reason for saying that the first Chinese theory is the same as his quark theory, and the other is a different theory. So here the observables seem to yield powerful evidence about just which theory the first lot of Chinese physicists actually use. Nor is there anything in the argument in 'On the Reasons' which would entitle us to reject this assumption. Of course Quine will say that Fred's theory might also have been intertranslatable with countless physical theories that were all different from the first Chinese theory. But that is beside the point. For that Quinean claim either depends on other arguments for the indeterminacy thesis than the one before us, or else it merely begs the question. The above development of the story of Fred makes a prima facie case for supposing that the thesis of the underdetermination of physical theory is quite compatible with the view that the totality of possible observations determines just which physical theory is held by a given group of people. Certainly the story falls far short of *establishing* the compatibility, but it does expose the failure of the argument in 'On the Reasons'.

6.8 Quine's suggestions about identity of theories

The question of what it is for theories to be the same has seemed
to raise a difficulty for Quine's argument. In his own words, 'If
two theories conform to the same totality of possible observations,
in what sense are they two?' (NNK, p. 80). Merely terminological
differences, as when 'neutron' and 'proton' are interchanged, must
not be allowed to constitute difference of theory, it seems, on pain
of making the underdetermination thesis trivial. Again, if the two
theories are alike except that one assumes an infinite space while
the other has a finite space in which bodies shrink in proportion
to their distance from the centre, 'we want to say that the difference
is rather terminological than real; and our reason is that we see
how to bring the two theories into agreement by translation: by
reconstruing the English of one of the theories.' (Loc. cit.). On
the other hand it will not do, he insists, to maintain that empirical
equivalence by itself is enough to render the difference purely
verbal: that would simply rule out the underdetermination thesis
by definition. His own proposal is to make theory identity depend
on something like translatability. He expresses it slightly differently
in two papers. In 'The Nature of Natural Knowledge' he suggests
that we might say we are faced with two theories 'where we no
longer see how to state rules of translation that would bring the
two empirically equivalent theories together' (NNK, pp. 80 f.). In
'On Empirically Equivalent Systems of the World' he confines
himself to the case of theories formulated within our own language,
thereby avoiding overt talk of translation. He also assumes the
theories are couched in a language with just truth functions, quantification, and a finite lexicon of predicates (ESW, p. 320). Where
a *theory formulation* is a sentence ('typically a conjunctive sentence
comprising the so-called axioms of the theory'—ESW, p. 318)
'two formulations express the same theory if they are empirically
equivalent and there is a reconstrual of predicates that transforms
the one theory into a logical equivalent of the other' (ESW, p.
320);[7] and theories are the equivalence classes of the equivalence
relations thus defined: 'The theory expressed by a given for-

[7] A 'reconstrual' of predicates is 'a mapping of our lexicon of predicates into our open
sentences', as, for example, of 'heavier than' into 'x is heavier than y', or of 'molecule' into
'x is an electron'. Two formulations are 'logically equivalent' if they imply the same 'observation conditionals'—material conditional sentences whose antecedents are conjunctions
of pegged observation sentences and whose consequents are pegged observation sentences.
(On pegged observation sentences see 6.1.)

mulation is the class of all the formulations that are empirically equivalent to that formulation and can be transformed into logical equivalents of it or vice versa by reconstrual of predicates.' (ESW, p. 321.)

Several authors have argued that if these proposals are accepted the argument in 'On the Reasons' must be abandoned.[8] For if, as envisaged there, we can translate the foreigner's physics equally well into A and into B, it seems we must also be able, by composing our two translation manuals, to translate any sentence of either into a sentence of the other, thereby 'bringing the theories into agreement by translation'. And on the first of Quine's present proposals for identity of theories this seems to mean that A and B are not after all different theories. On that proposal, if A and B really were different, we should not be able to translate the foreigner as holding whichever of the two we chose: if his theory could be translated into A it could not also be translated into B. So that proposal appears to demolish the argument in 'On the Reasons'. Nor does the second of the present proposals seem to avoid this consequence. For he does not require the reconstrual of predicates always to carry a predicate to a simple one-word predicate: it may be mapped to a many-word open sentence (providing this has the right number of free variables). So it seems that if the foreigner's theory can be translated equally well into our A or B, the composition of the two translation manuals will still always induce a reconstrual of predicates between A and B, in which case A and B will be, contrary to the assumption of Quine's argument, not different theories, but different formulations of the same theory. Again the argument in 'On the Reasons' seems to be wrecked.

Since Quine's proposals about identity of theories have much to commend them, and since we have seen that the argument in 'On the Reasons' is dubious on independent grounds, the last paragraph may seem to provide just one more reason to abandon that argument. However, it has been argued that Quine ought to abandon his proposals for identity of theories as well, on the grounds that they are at odds with his naturalistic view of language, and even conflict with the indeterminacy thesis itself.[9] Let us examine these claims.

[8] S. Blackburn, 1976, R. Kirk, 1977a and 1977b, Bechtel, 1980. In the private letter of 13 September 1976 Quine himself accepted—unnecessarily, if I am right—that his proposals on the identity of theories destroyed the argument in 'On the Reasons'.

[9] Bechtel 1980, p. 318 n. 5. See also the other items referred to in note 8 above.

His proposals have been thought to conflict with his linguistic naturalism because they seem to introduce a conception of sameness of meaning of just the kind he has hitherto rejected. By implying that trivially different theory formulations are really only formulations of 'the same theory' he appears to be gripped unawares by 'the idea of there being meanings somehow lying behind language use' (Bechtel, 1980, p. 318). His proposals also seem to threaten the indeterminacy thesis. For if intertranslatability is a criterion of identity of theories, the foreigners' theory will be the same as our own if we can translate their language into ours at all, even if we have two or more translation manuals. Moreover, two such manuals would induce a mapping of parts of our *own* theory to other parts. So it is hard to see how, if intertranslatability is a criterion for identity of whole theories, the existence of such a mapping should not be held to constitute an overwhelming reason for saying the correlated theory-*parts* were identical too. If this is correct, there could be no incompatibility between empirically adequate translation manuals because they would always map a formulation of one theory-part to a formulation of that same theory-part.

I shall not take space to discuss the merits of such attempts to involve Quine in inconsistency because I think he can disable them by a very simple move. We know it is basic to his position that the indeterminacy thesis does not require inequivalence between sentences to be a matter of fact. (See 3.6) Analogously, he can avoid seeming to commit himself to the view that identity of theories (when not just a matter of identity of sentences) is a matter of fact. (Cf. 1981b, p. 24.) My suggestion is that where A and B are intertranslatable systems of sentences, the Quinean position should be merely that it is *compatible with the facts to say* that A and B are not different theories, but different formulations of the same theory, rather than that these are different theories full-stop. In this way the unwelcome implication that identity of theories is a matter of fact is clearly disowned.

However, merely to exclude the identity of theories from the realm of fact would not be enough. It would leave the thesis of the underdetermination of our theory of nature unexplained. If identity of theories is not a matter of fact, how can we intelligibly speak of two different theories being compatible with all observables? Once again we can invoke an analogy with the indeterminacy thesis. What makes the indeterminacy thesis interesting is that according to it two empirically adequate translation manuals might translate a given French sentence, say, by English sentences that would ordinarily be regarded as inequivalent—even if the Quine-acceptable facts were also compatible with those sentences being said to mean the same. Similarly the underdetermination thesis is interesting if according to it two theory formulations that would ordinarily be taken to be formulations of different theories (*incompatible* theories according to 'On the Reasons') might yet be empirically equivalent—even if there existed a translation manual by which those formulations were intertranslatable. To the extent that translation between two theory formulations is obvious or straightforward it seems sensible to regard them as just different formulations of the same theory, as Quine has proposed; although no doubt there are cases where from some points of view or for some purposes we should still want to count them as different. To the extent that we find translation between the two theory formulations difficult, forced, or unnatural, it seems sensible to regard them as expressing different theories, even though from some points of view or for some purposes it might still be desirable to treat them as versions of the same theory.

To summarize, my suggestion for interpreting Quine's proposals about the identity of theories has two parts. First, his proposals are not to be seen as representing the identity of theories as a matter of fact. Second, he is not to be read as insisting that the intertranslatability of two theory formulations *compels* us to count them as versions of the same theory: whether we do so will depend partly on our interests, partly on how straightforward we find the translation manual.

Evidently this interpretation is thoroughly compatible with Quine's linguistic naturalism. Sameness of theories is put firmly in the same boat as sameness of meaning: a useful *façon de parler*, not a mirror of reality. This interpretation also blocks the line of argument which seemed to show that his proposals were at odds with the indeterminacy of translation. For that line of argument assumed—what my interpretation denies—that Quine requires intertranslatability, however deviously achieved, to *entail* identity of theory. Suppose it is conceded that identity of theory is not a matter of fact, and that where the translation manual is not straightforward we do well not to treat the case as one of theory identity.

Then immediately it becomes clear that if there is Quinean underdetermination of theories at all, there may be many instances of it where the result of composing the two acceptable translation manuals is not straightforward and does not correlate sentences that we should ordinarily regard as equivalent. And this holds even though the empirical adequacy of such a composite manual would permit us to say, if we perversely insisted, that the two sentences were nevertheless equivalent. (Similar considerations also show that Quine's proposals need not be construed as undermining the argument in 'On the Reasons'—but I have said why I think that argument fails.)

6.9 Conclusion

I have tried to show that the indeterminacy thesis is neither a special case of the underdetermination thesis nor in any way supported by it. 'Pressing from above' seems to be a complete failure. On the other hand some light has perhaps been shed on the interpretation of both the indeterminacy thesis and the underdetermination thesis, and Quine's proposals on the identity of theories have turned out to be compatible with his other views, contrary to what some have argued.

7

Syntax

In *Word and Object* Quine briskly remarks:

Obviously the grammatical theories can differ in word segmentations, in parts of speech, in constructions, and still have identical net outputs in the way of whole sentences and even of English sentence translations. But I am talking of difference in net output (p. 73. Cf. MR, p. 443).

He also says that phonematic analysis does not affect the philosophical point he wants to make (*WO*, pp. 28 f.); and he has asserted that there are 'no important illusions' about the process whereby we are made familiar with the sound of a word and able to reproduce it (OR, pp. 27 f.). Nor does he anywhere hint at serious difficulties over sentencehood. On the contrary he seems to take for granted—rightly, as I shall argue—that talk of sentences is not open to damaging theoretical objections comparable to those he urges against talk of meaning and sameness of meaning (*WO*, pp. 5–13 and *passim*; 1970a, ch. 2; MR, pp. 442 f.). So it looks as if he does not think that indeterminacies outside semantics might support the doctrine of the indeterminacy of translation.

However, people occasionally suggest that the doctrine can be given independent support from that quarter, and in this chapter I shall examine the suggestion. Indeed, some of Quine's other remarks may at first seem to support the idea (*WO*, p. 35, OR, p. 35, RIT, p. 182). In these passages he claims that once we have made our (underdetermined) decisions on what Gavagese expressions correspond to our pronouns, identity, plurals, and other individuative apparatus, we can settle by interrogation whether *gavagai* are rabbits or stages or parts. But these passages turn out to be beside the present point. There is no implication that those crucial decisions could be taken *independently* of semantic considerations; and in fact it is obvious that hypotheses about how the expressions in question might contribute to reference and communicational utility will have a heavy influence on the decisions. So Quine himself does not after all seem to be endorsing the suggestion we are to examine, that syntactic indeterminacies might independently help to establish the indeterminacy of sentence translation.

7.1 Quinean indeterminacy and syntax

No one doubts that the non-semantic parts of grammar are subject to indeterminacies of various kinds. For example, speakers of the same language disagree, on occasions, over the pronunciation of words, over whether an expression belongs to their language, over the acceptability of utterances. So the very data on which linguists work are to some extent conflicting: doing justice to some people's practices involves flouting others'. Again, there are wide areas of disagreement among linguists about goals, methods and theoretical frameworks. However, the indeterminacies associated with these disagreements are not grounds for accepting the existence of the non-trivial indeterminacy of sentence translation; nor are they even analogous to it.

Consider disagreements over pronunciation. People told they are pronouncing a certain word idiosyncratically quite often deny it. Some may be able to make discriminations others cannot (between light and dark 'l' for example); or they may disagree over the importance of a difference both acknowledge. Such disagreements obviously have no tendency to support the indeterminacy doctrine; nor do they generate anything analogous. They would do that only if competent linguists with full background knowledge could disagree non-trivially in such cases. But competent linguists, who could make all the relevant discriminations, could not disagree seriously over their importance. We can be confident of this because language learning depends on the possibility of learning and recognizing *norms* of pronunciation. Serious disputes over what the norms are obviously cannot arise. You say *tomahto*, I say *tomayto*. But that just means we speak dialects with slightly different norms, or else that the norms allow two pronunciations. The norms are there, fixed by communal practice; and such disagreements do not threaten their existence. (Such norms are discussed in *WO*, pp. 85–90.) From now on, therefore, I shall follow Quine and ignore problems of phonetics and phonology.

What about disagreements over the acceptability of utterances? Actual disagreements of this sort, assuming they are between mature members of the same linguistic community, only ever concern cases both parties would agree are marginal. It never happens that one party wants to rule out as inadmissible something the other party finds quite unproblematic. No sane English speaker, for example, challenges the acceptability of 'dog', 'speaking', or 'Where are the potatoes?' So there can be no question of something analogous to Quinean indeterminacy being implied by *actual* disagreements over acceptability. (Whether such disagreements are in principle possible will be discussed later.)

Finally, disagreements among linguists about goals, methods, and theoretical frameworks cannot be a source of anything like Quinean indeterminacy. Such disagreements among scientists are entirely compatible with there being objective matters of fact to be right or wrong about. The disagreements merely make it harder to tell whether or not the substantive views held by the different parties really conflict. For example, do schemes of phonological analysis based on distinctive features necessarily conflict with those based on phonemes, or is the difference just a matter of using different concepts? The answer will depend on the exact nature of the putatively rival theories, not solely on the fact that they take different approaches.

Grammars are universally recognized to be, to a considerable extent, instrumental: the terms and statements occurring in them often have systematic roles and are not necessarily intended either to have objective reference or to be uniquely correct. If for example one English grammar classifies 'more' under the heading 'ADV' and another does not, it does not follow that they are in significant conflict. Perhaps 'ADV' may have to be regarded as deriving its sense solely from its role in each particular grammar, and not as independently intelligible.[1]

Now if the non-semantic parts of grammars were *purely* instrumental, and moreover the classes of items to be generated or accepted by them were constrained by objective criteria, obviously there would be no room for significant indeterminacies outside translation. But of course things are not so simple. For one thing, Chomsky and many other linguists hold that grammars are constrained not only by the practical or aesthetic demands of economy, manageability and the like, but also by the requirement that they

---

[1] This is the 'formal' or 'tactical' conception of syntactic categories, as opposed to the 'notional' or 'cognitive'. See Lyons, 1968, p. 134, or Stockwell, 1977, who says: '. . . only the grammar as a whole defines each category by putting it to use' (p. 38).

somehow reflect psychological reality: ' . . . linguistic theory is . . . concerned with discovering a mental reality underlying actual behaviour' (Chomsky, 1965, p. 4). On this view grammar is part of psychology. For another thing, it is not altogether obvious that sentences—fundamental among the categories of items to be generated or accepted by grammars—are not subject to something like Quinean indeterminacy. I shall deal with these points in the next two sections.

7.2 Psychological reality

As we noticed earlier, Quine accepts as an implication of the indeterminacy doctrine the unsettling claim that it is not generally a matter of fact what beliefs, desires, intentions, and other propositional attitudes we have. Now the view that psychological reality constrains the internal structure of grammars as well as their outputs might have been taken to imply that it *is* a question of fact what propositional attitudes we have. So if it did have this implication, Quineans would maintain that it left room for the relevant sort of indeterminacy in some of the non-semantic parts of grammars. However, this sort of indeterminacy would clearly be an integral part of the indeterminacy of translation, not a distinct variety. There are no grounds for supposing it exists over and above whatever grounds there may be for accepting the indeterminacy of translation. So if the view under consideration were concerned only with the psychological reality of propositional attitudes we could now say goodbye to it.

In fact, though, the view actually held by Chomsky and his followers seems not to be based on assumptions about propositional attitudes. On the contrary it has to do with things of which we are normally unaware, in ourselves as well as in others: the internal structures and processes whereby our utterances are produced and understood:

Any interesting generative grammar will be dealing . . . with mental processes that are far beyond the level of actual or even potential consciousness. . . . A generative grammar attempts to characterize in the most neutral possible terms the knowledge of the language that provides the basis for actual use of language by a speaker-hearer. ('Aspects of the Theory of Syntax', pp. 8, 9.)

Chomsky's position is certainly objectionable to Quine. For example, Quine has complained of the obscurity of the idea that a person's behaviour could be guided by a system of rules of which that person was not consciously aware—that there are rules 'heeded inarticulately' (see MR *passim*). Again, the assumption that for a given language—even for idealized speaker-hearers— there is some distinguishable cognitive entity describable as 'knowledge of the language' conflicts with the inextricability thesis (chapter 4). Of course Quine is not going to deny that there *are* realities underlying people's linguistic capacities: he is committed to the realities of physical structure and state, and whatever facts about dispositions may be solidly based on these (see MR, p. 444, *RR*, pp. 8–15, MVD, and Appendix B). But he disagrees with Chomsky over the nature of these underlying realities. So for each area of conflict it seems possible to formulate an indeterminacy thesis, or range of theses: 'Two incompatible assignments of "internalized rules"/"knowledge of the language"/ . . . could both fit all behavioural dispositions/physical facts/ . . . '.

To the extent that such indeterminacy theses challenge only contentious theoretical claims, rather than widely held assumptions like the one about the objectivity of synonymy, they lack the interest of Quine's actual indeterminacy doctrine. Nor, again in contrast with the other case, is it clear how far these disputes are substantive.[2] But there is no need to develop these points here. It is enough for our purposes to notice that in any case such indeterminacy theses could not provide any independent support for the semantic indeterminacy. Suppose someone agrees with Quine's rejection of characteristically Chomskyan non-conscious mental processes, but insists, against Quine, that it is generally a matter of fact what propositional attitudes we have, and that propositional attitudes, if real, do determine sameness of meaning (as is widely agreed: see 1.3). Then the only way to attack this position would be by defending the indeterminacy thesis itself. For it would be necessary to show that *only* Chomskyan internalized rules, separable knowledge of language, etc., could underlie the possession of propositional attitudes not subject to Quinean indeterminacy. But any attempt to do that would require an attempt to show that facts about physical states and behavioural

---

[2] Chomsky's suggestion that there may be behavioural evidence favouring one rather than the other of two extensionally equivalent grammars, which he makes in replying to Quine (1975, pp. 179–82) implies that his position may be less sharply opposed to Quine's than at first appears.

dispositions—Quine-acceptable facts—are not by themselves enough to determine propositional attitudes. In other words (assuming the futility of trying to show that determinate propositional attitudes would *not* determine sentence translation) it would require an attempt to defend Quine's actual indeterminacy thesis. We can therefore thankfully leave these other possible theses on one side.

7.3 Sentences and languages

Let us agree that 'sentence' and 'language' are to some extent theoretical words. Different theorists, with different ideas about how to balance such factors as simplicity and intuitive acceptability, cannot be expected to agree exactly over what counts as a sentence of a given language. My earlier statement of what it is for a translation manual to fit the facts is sensitive to this point. I concluded that a translation manual is empirically adequate if a competent linguist, free from prejudices and practical constraints, is disposed to accept that the facts (or the totality of possible evidence) are consistent with its classifications of sentences as meaning the same. So two manuals which disagreed over sentencehood might still both be compatible in that sense.

A possible inference from the theoreticity of the terms 'sentence' and 'language' would be that whether a given utterance is a sentence of a given language is not a question of fact. But that would be misleading in view of two further considerations. One is that these words, like 'meaning', belong to our ordinary language, not just to the dialect of linguists. The other is that these words are rather closely linked to certain facts. Of course the fact that they belong to ordinary language does not automatically make them non-theoretical. But it does exert a certain constraint on linguists' use of them. Whatever linguists count as a sentence of the language spoken by a given community had better not be very remote from what might be spoken or written, or at least understood, by its members (unless it belongs to the region where theoretical simplicity predominates over other considerations: see below). And what they might speak, write or understand is going to be subject to constraints imposed by their verbal dispositions. Sentencehood and languagehood *are* indeterminate, certainly. But the question here is whether the indeterminacy is analogous to the sort Quine alleges for translation, and if so, whether it could possibly make a contribution to the indeterminacy of translation. I shall argue that the answer to both these questions is 'No'.

We can begin with an imaginary example. There is no a priori objection (though no doubt there are psychological objections) to the suggestion that there might be a tribe whose verbal dispositions were so conservative and consistent that we were able to devise for their language—Conformish—what has never yet been achieved for any natural language: a completely adequate generative grammar. For any deliberate utterance the Conformish produce or are disposed to produce (and they do *speak*: our grammar is not trivial) our grammar counts it as the utterance of a sentence of Conformish; and for any utterance that the Conformish are disposed never to produce, our grammar either counts it as a non-sentence of Conformish, or else its length and complexity put it beyond normally manageable limits. But remember: our grammar is empirically adequate. Imagine that Conformish is like a fragment of English, and that your favourite project for a generative grammar for English actually succeeds in generating, as its sentences, what the facts allow us to count as the sentences of Conformish. (Most if not all Conformish sentences will be English sentences too, but the converse will not hold.)

Now, are sentencehood and languagehood for Conformish subject to a non-trivial indeterminacy? So far as I can see the facts rule out any possibility of serious conflict between rival grammars here. Admittedly there is still room for conflict of sorts. For example, an eccentric grammar might refuse to apply the label 'sentence' to the standard forms of Conformish utterances; but since that eccentricity would conflict with the ordinary use of 'sentence' it could not seriously be described as a conflict over sentencehood. There might also be disagreement over sentencehood out in the regions where the length and complexity of expressions made them humanly unmanageable. But just because such items could never actually be used, to call them sentences at all is plainly no more than a matter of theoretical convenience.[3] If such disagreement showed up at the level of manageable utterances, Conformish behavioural dispositions would decide the issue unproblematically. The issue might also conceivably be decidable on the basis of Chomskyan or Quinean 'underlying realities'. Otherwise this sort

[3] As linguists recognize, of course. Cf. Bach, 1974, pp. 24-6. See also Stich, 1975, p. 804.

of seeming conflict would be no more serious than the first: a matter of achieving essentially the same results by different means. I conclude that for Conformish, at least, sentencehood and languagehood can be taken not to be subject to any significant indeterminacy.

But now, Conformish is by definition quite like English. So is there any special reason why sentencehood and languagehood for natural languages in general should be expected to be unlike Conformish in this respect, and subject to a non-trivial indeterminacy?[4] What differences might conceivably introduce such indeterminacy?

One apparently relevant consideration is that the class of grammatical or non-deviant sentences for a natural language will not generally coincide—as it seems to for the peculiar case of Conformish—with the class of *acceptable* utterance types. Acceptability is one thing, grammaticality is something else. (See Chomsky, 1965, pp. 11 f.; Lyons, 1968, pp. 152–5.) Indeed, by suitably preparing speakers of a given language it seems we could get them to accept, in the context provided by the preparation, virtually any string composed from words belonging to the language. So if our aim were to provide a grammar for English that would include as sentences *all* utterances acceptable in some context, the grammar could take the form 'Any finite sequence of English words is a sentence' (Putnam, 1961, p. 87). This one-sentence grammar would be significantly incompatible with a grammar of the sorts actually favoured by linguists.

But this is a trivial indeterminacy of sentencehood and languagehood. The one-sentence grammar has a different aim from the more conventional varieties. It aims to define all and only those utterances 'which speakers of English might conceivably use or hearers of English might conceivably understand'.[5] But the usual types of grammar aim to define a much more restricted class of expressions. The expressions which *they* count as grammatical will be so counted partly because of the explanatory power of the theory according to which they are grammatical. I assume, as is

---

[4] Perhaps I had better state explicitly that 'languagehood' here is to be understood in such a way that *x* and *y* may be the same language even if Quine is right and the language is susceptible of conflicting semantic interpretations. Similarly, *mutatis mutandis*, for sentencehood. The present issue is simply whether, even if there is semantic indeterminacy, other sorts of indeterminacy support the claim that it exists.

[5] Putnam, 1961, p. 86. As he convincingly argues, this programme 'would either be trivial or impossible of execution'.

widely accepted, that among the things to be explained are the fact that certain sorts of utterance are more intuitively acceptable than others to speakers of the language, the fact that the language can actually be acquired in a finite time, and the fact that differences in the syntactic structures of sentences are systematically relatable to differences in the uses to which they can be put. For such explanatory purposes the one-sentence grammar is useless. In effect, then, the one-sentence grammar is operating with an eccentric definition of 'sentence'; and its incompatibility with conventional grammars is only apparent, or, if construed as genuine, not significant from our point of view. The indeterminacy, if that is what it is, is trivial precisely because of the difference in what the two grammars are aiming at. (Cf. thesis VII in Appendix A.) So the fact that Conformish differs from actual languages in the perfect coincidence of grammatical with acceptable sentences seems not to matter.

The point that grammaticalness is to some extent dependent on a theory's explanatory power may appear to leave room for indeterminacy. Indeed it does (cf. Stich, 1972). But the question is whether such indeterminacy could be significant. It must not arise from the use of divergent definitions of 'sentence' or 'language', and it must not merely reflect divergent verdicts on borderline cases. Now we have already recalled that even native speakers, not to mention professional linguists, sometimes differ over the grammaticalness and acceptability of utterance types. It follows that empirically adequate grammars can conflict. However, there never seems to be any conflict over cases not universally admitted to belong to the border regions.[6] Is this agreement over the central area just a result of the sorts of factors that according to Quine prevent real-life linguists from producing examples of translational indeterminacy, or does it reflect something objective?

In fact the case of languagehood and sentencehood contrasts strikingly with that of translation. If someone said they had devised a permissible German-English translation manual which rendered, say, 'Das Photon hat keine Masse' not, as usual, by 'Photons have no mass', but by 'Electrons have negative charge', we should be sceptical, but we (post Quine) could not sensibly reject their scheme without either knowing more about it, or else having an

---

[6] 'Without any precise definition of sentences for a given language, it is quite possible to manipulate the notion of sentence in a reliable way': Gross, 1972, p. 2.

argument against Quinean indeterminacy more compelling than any that have appeared so far. However, if someone claimed to have a translation manual according to which 'Das Photon hat keine Masse' was not even a German sentence, we should feel able to reject that part of the scheme out of hand, without needing to know any more about it. For 'Das Photon hat keine Masse' must be counted as a German sentence by any grammar that does not either misuse the word 'sentence' or conflict with the facts. The same goes for countless other examples, including, it is safe to say, the overwhelming majority of expressions occurring between full-stops in the overwhelming majority of German books in prose.

How can we be so positive? The answer is clear in the light of two considerations: the reasons for trying to produce a grammar in the first place; and the Quine-acceptability of behavioural dispositions. For, as noted earlier, one reason for attempting to discover a grammar for a language is to explain why certain utterances are in fact acceptable to speakers of that language. Moreover, that certain utterances *are* acceptable is discoverable by reference to the facts, such as the facts about the utterance types they are disposed actually to employ, and to assent to or dissent from. It is a matter of fact that the members of a certain population are labelled, say, 'German speakers';[7] and the linguist provisionally classifies as acceptable at least those utterance types which members of that population actually use. Conceivably the demands of scientific theorizing will make it desirable to exclude some of those acceptable utterances from the category of grammatical sentence. But plainly the nature of the project itself guarantees that the great majority of utterance types which are both acceptable to all mature German speakers, and constructed with due attention, will have to be counted as grammatical German sentences. (These remarks seem entirely consistent with Quine's: MR, pp. 445 f.)

While the devising of non-standard schemes of *translation* calls for, and might conceivably be justified by reference to, elaborate compensatory adjustments to the translation of countless sentences,

---

[7] You may correctly point out that I do not even claim to have established the determinacy of reference (chapter 5). Strictly speaking, therefore, I am not entitled to say it is a matter of fact that we label such and such people 'German speakers'. However, all that matters for the purpose of the present argument is that no one—certainly not Quine—would wish to use the (conceivably) disputable factuality of our labelling them German speakers as a basis for an argument for indeterminacy. That they are German speakers is something we are all ready to treat as a fact.

the points just mentioned ensure that there is no conceivable sort of compensatory adjustment as a result of which sentences acceptable to German speakers and constructed with due attention could permissibly be counted as deviant or non-grammatical. The nature of the project for devising a grammar guarantees that there will be no significant indeterminacy of languagehood or sentencehood.

Two concluding points, which hold even if the above reasoning is rejected. First, since it is an empirical question whether there is an actual population as linguistically tame as the Conformish, any indeterminacy of sentencehood there may be in actual languages must be a consequence of contingent facts about languages, not a necessary concomitant of any conceivable language. (Notice that such indeterminacy would be independent of syntactic complexity: Conformish itself can be imagined to be as complex syntactically as you like.) And being an empirical matter of fact, such indeterminacy would pose no deep philosophical problems of the sort that would be posed by Quinean indeterminacy of translation, the arguments for which are supposed to apply to natural languages in general. Second, even if disagreement over borderline cases were held to constitute a significant indeterminacy of languagehood or sentencehood, that would still have no tendency to support the indeterminacy thesis. Disagreement over sentencehood and languagehood is obviously compatible with agreement over how to translate any given *utterance type*, sentence or not.

7.4 Is there an 'argument from parsing'?

M.C. Bradley has urged that in *Word and Object* Quine presents an 'argument from parsing' which is 'potent enough *by itself* to yield the indeterminacy' (1976, p. 28). He is not concerned to defend the indeterminacy thesis, only to establish that the argument he claims to discern is distinct from the argument from the alleged underdetermination of analytical hypotheses—in spite of the fact, which he concedes, that Quine himself does not treat it as distinct. Let us examine these striking claims.

Bradley summarizes the argument from parsing thus:

[1] The parsing of the alien tongue is underdetermined by the behavioural totality viz. by the totality of behavioural dispositions etc.. But [2] translation involves parsing, so [3] translation is underdetermined by the

behavioural totality. ('Quine's Arguments for the Indeterminacy Thesis', p. 27, my numbering.)

We need consider only whether this is an argument for Quinean (i.e. significant-conflict-involving) *semantic* indeterminacy of *sentence* translation. If it is not, as will soon become clear, we need not go on to consider whether it is good for anything else.

In fact the argument is obviously unsound when regarded as an argument for the semantic indeterminacy of sentence translation. Step (3), so understood, just does not follow from (1) and (2) because different parsings below sentence level might always be compensated for so as to leave the translation of whole sentences unaffected. That is the lesson of Quine's Japanese example. Nor does Bradley offer any reasons for supposing that Quine has an argument to bridge this gap. Bradley points to Quine's insistence that the notion of a term, and with it the notions of articles and pronouns, singular and plural, copula, and identity predicate, are 'provincial to our culture' (*WO*, p. 53. See 2.3) This thought may indeed help to soften resistance to the indeterminacy thesis. But we have seen that neither it nor whatever else goes into 'pressing from below' amounts to a solid argument (chapter 5). I conclude, as Quine himself seems to imply in the passage quoted at the beginning of this chapter, that there is no argument from parsing anything like potent enough to yield the indeterminacy of sentence translation.

Another suggestion of Bradley's had better be mentioned here. In connection with the stream of spoken noise encountered by Quine's jungle linguist, he remarks: 'Even that it is intelligent discourse is presumably underdetermined by the behavioural totality; that it breaks thus and so into *sentences* must be underdetermined if intrasentential parsing is' (op. cit., p. 35). Clearly the first part of this sentence must be supposed to apply to all language users, not just to Quine's remote tribe. But why should Quine be assumed to be committed to such a view? Certainly it is not part of the indeterminacy doctrine that the totality of behavioural dispositions of English speakers, Japanese speakers, and everyone else is compatible with their utterances not being intelligent discourse; nor has he offered any argument to that effect (nor has Bradley). True, dualists and other anti-behaviourists might be disposed to accept that view; but that is beside the point—especially when we bear in mind that in Quine's best statements of the indeterminacy doctrine it is not just the behavioural totality, but the totality of physically statable facts, which must be taken into account (3.1). So the first part of the quoted sentence seems to be doing Quine an injustice. In the second part it is assumed that any indeterminacy of intrasentential parsing must result in indeterminacy of sentencehood. We have seen that Quine appears to reject this assumption. In any case, if the assumption is true, then the fact that sentencehood is *not* subject to any significant indeterminacy (see the last section) shows that in the relevant sense parsing is determinate after all. Either way, then, we have been given no reasons to revise our earlier conclusions.

7.5 *Conclusions*

The possibility of significant indeterminacies in areas of language outside that covered by semantics has not been ruled out altogether. It has been ruled out, I think, for phonetics and phonology, and for languagehood and sentencehood. But it has not been completely ruled out for the rest of syntax. However, the point of investigating the possibility of non-trivial indeterminacies outside semantics was to discover whether they might yield any independent support for the semantic indeterminacy doctrine. I claim that the above discussions have shown there could be no such independent support.

In five chapters—2, 4-6, and 7—I have set out and examined the rather confusing network of general considerations adduced by Quine and others in defence of the indeterminacy doctrine. The result is that none of the arguments for the indeterminacy thesis appears sound. However, even if the Quinean arguments are no good, it does not follow that the thesis is false. Perhaps a good argument for it may yet be found. Perhaps, too, the failure of attacks on it (to be discussed in chapter 9) may be regarded, à la Popper, as lending it support. And of course the position would be dramatically transformed if an actual example of Quinean indeterminacy of translation could be discovered or devised.

8

Alleged Instances

Quine has been wary of claiming to have found actual instances of the indeterminacy of translation. But others (more Quinean?) have offered to fill the gap. In the light of our earlier discussions some of these alleged instances can easily be seen to be impostors. Others require more extended consideration. I suspect that a quick glance at some of them—especially the mathematical ones—has helped to make the indeterminacy thesis appear less radical, and more worthy of acceptance, than it is.

In the first section I shall briefly consider some cases which are rather obviously not instances of the right sort of indeterminacy. (I don't mean that those who originally suggested them couldn't see the obvious. It is only in the light of our rather extended discussions that these cases can now easily be seen not to fit.)

8.1 Four clear non-instances

(a) Hartry Field has proposed as an example of Quinean indeterminacy of translation the fact that 'we can translate certain outdated physical theories into current theory in a variety of ways'. In particular he says we can translate Newtonian 'mass' either into 'relativistic mass' or into 'rest mass', as these expressions occur in relativity theory (1974, p. 209, and 1973). Depending on which translation we choose, certain tenets of Newton's theory acquire different truth values under their different interpretations in relativity theory. Field claims that there is no fact of the matter as to which of these translations is 'the correct one'. Now, he is surely right to imply that *if* these are both admissible translations of Newton's 'mass', neither is uniquely correct. But evidently neither is better than a rough translation of Newton's term (as of course Field is well aware). It is not as if relativity theory simply *included* Newton's, in which case straight homophonic renderings would be available. Relativity theory replaces Newton's and is strikingly different by any standard. So, since it has emerged that the indeterminacy thesis cannot sensibly be supposed to be instantiated by conflicting rough translations, this alleged example must be rejected. (It is clearly akin to the Aristotelian example mentioned in chapter 1.)

It is worth adding that what has just been said does not settle the question whether Newton was *referring* to rest mass or relativistic mass (or whether Aristotle was referring to the zygote or the embryo). As we noted at 1.1(*c*), the question of reference is generally distinct from the question of translation. We might well want to say Newton was referring to both rest mass and relativistic mass, but in a way we now regard as inappropriate; and similarly that Aristotle used 'kyēma' to refer both to the zygote and to the embryo, but that the theory in which his concept was embedded was inadequate.

(*b*) Next, let us return briefly to a formal case: that of divergent set-theoretical explications of the natural numbers, discussed at 5.4. Both the Zermelo and the von Neumann schemes match the ordinary natural number system in most of their structure; but each has additional features with implications for the structure of the numbers themselves. (These additional features are of course irrelevant for arithmetic.) So far as I know, no one has maintained in print that this case actually instantiates the indeterminacy of translation. However, Harman has seen it as analogous:

Quine's thesis of the indeterminacy of radical translation claims that translation from one natural language into another resembles translation of number theory into set theory in that various equally good alternative but non-equivalent general schemes of translation are always possible, and one may speak of the 'correct' translation of a single sentence only relative to some envisioned general scheme of translation. ('An Introduction to "Translation and Meaning"', (1969), p. 14.)

Harman concedes that there is a big difference between the number theory/set theory example and translation between natural languages (op. cit., p. 17). But he seems to think the chief difficulty is that in any example one might offer 'the language in question must be quite structured in the way that number theory and set theory are and natural languages as a whole are not', and he points out that, in contrast with number theory and set theory, we cannot even give a complete syntactical account of, for example, English. If I am right, though, this is not a difficulty at all. No one has offered a plausible a priori reason why a complete syntactical account of English should be impossible, or why there could not have been a tribe of near-English speakers, like the Conformish of 7.3, whose syntax was completely specifiable. The fundamental objection to the number theory/set theory example is the one stressed by Quine: 'the sentences about numbers that take on opposite truth values under different explications are sentences that have no clear truth values before explication' (1968b, p. 296. See 5.4).

(c) The next suggestion is attributable to Kripke. We take both the translated theory and the translating theory to be the same, and to be set theory without the axiom of choice. The proposed rival to the homophonic manual follows the latter in translating every sentence by itself with just two exceptions: the axiom of choice is translated by its denial and vice versa.[1]

Harman comments that this is not a good example of Quinean indeterminacy because the second scheme of translation is 'less simple or more *ad hoc*' than the homophonic one. But this objection seems to be off target. If being less simple or more *ad hoc* than the homophonic is a sufficient reason to reject a proposed rival to it, then rivals to homophonic translation are hardly conceivable. What could be as simple as the homophonic manual? There seems no need to include relative simplicity or *ad hoc*-ness among the constraints on Quinean translation (cf. 3.3 and 3.6). In fact the suggestion is open to a far more damaging objection. But before explaining it I had better note that Harman discusses the suggestion in the context of Quine's remark that the two translations 'might even be patently contrary in truth value, provided there is no stimulation that would encourage assent to either' (*WO*, pp. 73 f. Cf. 3.8). Since Kripke's example has both translated and translating theories lacking the axiom of choice (which of course has been proved independent of the rest of set theory) the two rival translations of the axiom of choice can be known to be contrary in truth value even though their truth values are left unfixed.

Now, if a rival to homophonic translation is to be a translation manual in the relevant sense, the rival manual must license the statement that the sentences it translates *mean* the same (3.6). And for this to be possible the sentences must be meaningful—not just the bare formulas of an uninterpreted calculus. So we are bound

---

[1] Attributed to Kripke by Harman, 1969, pp. 25 f.

to assume that in the present case the sentences of that single theory which is both translated and translating theory—set theory without the axiom of choice—have been somehow made meaningful, perhaps by informal explanations. In particular such explanations (or interpretations or whatever) must have made meaningful both a sentence that can be said to formulate the axiom of choice and the negation of that sentence. Otherwise neither could be offered as a translation of the other. But once this point is acknowledged, the present suggestion can be seen to be either false, question-begging, or irrelevant.

The suggestion is false if the explanations, interpretations, behavioural dispositions, or whatever it may that renders the theoretical sentences meaningful, result in there being Quine-acceptable facts which actually determine relations of sameness of meaning among those sentences, since in that case the axiom of choice cannot, compatibly with the facts, be said to mean the same as its negation: the rival to homophonic translation would not be permissible. On the other hand the suggestion is obviously question-begging if it assumes that the definitions etc. do *not* result in facts which determine relations of sameness of meaning among the sentences in question. Finally, the suggestion is irrelevant if it is not concerned about whether the *totality* of facts, rather than some subset of those facts, determines synonymy relations among the sentences of the theory. (Perhaps Kripke made the suggestion—mistaken but understandable in view of some of Quine's remarks—on the assumption that dispositions to assent to or dissent from the sentences of the theory were to be the sole relevant constraints on translation.)

(*d*) It is occasionally suggested that non-projectible predicates like Goodman's 'grue' might provide illustrations of Quinean indeterminacy. Following Goodman, we suppose 'grue' applies to all things examined before *t* just in case they are green, but to other things just in case they are blue (Goodman, 1955/65, pp. 73 f.). Now, provided *t* is some time in the future, linguists who encountered a tribe using this predicate might well be inclined to translate it by 'green'. If their manual fitted the facts, therefore, we should have an instance of Quinean indeterminacy. For 'grue' can certainly also be said not to mean the same as 'green'.

However, it should be obvious that such a translation manual would not fit *all* the facts. Only up to time *t* (whenever that might be) would 'grue' and 'green' appear to be roughly equivalent. From then on there would be a striking difference, objectively detectable: the presence of something blue would prompt assent to 'Grue?' So the stimulus meanings of 'Green' and 'Grue' are different, and we no longer have an obvious illustration of the indeterminacy thesis (see 3.9). (A given baby could not learn 'grue' the way it could learn 'green', so that at best 'green' would be only a rough translation of 'grue'.)

8.2 *The transposed spectrum etc.*

Colour words may at first seem to admit a more pertinent possibility than 'grue'. Discussing his ideas about relativizing to a background theory, Quine remarks that his point 'is reflected better in the riddle about seeing things upside down, or in complementary colours; for it is that things can be inscrutably switched even while carrying their properties with them' (OR, p. 50). This remark clearly need not commit him to accepting the genuineness of the alleged possibilities. But it does show that he has made some connection between it and the indeterminacy doctrine; and occasionally the connection is made explicit.[2] However, even if transposed qualia etc. are possible, the possibility does not illustrate the indeterminacy doctrine.

Assume for the sake of argument that it is indeed logically possible that in some sense the way you see red things is the way I see green things, and so on systematically through the spectrum, respecting complementarity, while the Quine-acceptable facts fail to show the difference. There are two distinct ways in which this might be thought to vindicate the indeterminacy thesis.

One suggestion would be that it entails that a rival to homophonic translation which interchanged 'red' and 'green', 'blue' and 'orange', etc., would be permissible. To refute this suggestion it is enough to point out that 'Red', 'Green', etc. are one word observation sentences. Most English speakers confronted by ripe tomatoes, for instance, are disposed to assent to 'Red' and dissent from 'Green'. So, since permissible manuals must respect these dispositions, no manual that interchanged those two words would be permissible.[3]

The other suggestion would not be quite so crudely mis-

---

[2] Cf. Harman's remark in the discussion reported in *Synthese* 27 (1974), p. 489.
[3] Quine makes this reply to the remark of Harman's referred to in the last note.

conceived, although it would go against well known Wittgensteinian considerations. The idea would be that, first, I might have
two special words, say 'ra' and 'ga', for referring to the 'private'
experiences I have when I see red and green things respectively;
and correspondingly you might have special words, say 'ru' and
'gu'. Then it would be said that the facts would be compatible
with two different manuals. One manual would render your 'ru'
by my 'ra' and your 'gu' by my 'ga', the other would interchange
'ra' and 'ga'. But now, is it a question of fact which private colour
experiences you and I have? If so, then the facts will determine
that at most one of the proposed schemes of translation is correct.
My 'ga' will correctly render your 'gu' if and only if the two
private experiences are objectively alike. And this will be an objective matter to be right or wrong about, hence there will be no
indeterminacy. (One might of course see this proposal as an objection to Quine's ideas about the facts; but then it could hardly
be supposed to illustrate the indeterminacy thesis.) If on the other
hand it is not a matter of fact which private experiences you and I
have, the whole story is a red (green?) herring. For in that case
'ra' (said by me) will mean something like 'what typically happens
when I see something red', and will not be translatable by any of
your special words (on the ground that my special words apply
only to my experiences, yours to yours) or else, if it is held to be
translatable (on the grounds that it is indexical, like 'I') it will be
translatable only by your 'ru' and not by your 'gu'. Again, no
indeterminacy. So, whether or not the content of private experiences is a matter of fact, the present suggestion cannot serve
to illustrate the indeterminacy thesis.

This suggestion only needed to be properly looked at to be
quickly scotched. But I suspect that, left unexamined, such suggestions have helped to make acceptance of the indeterminacy thesis
easier than it ought to have been. Now for some rather more
impressive suggestions.

8.3 Massey's three alleged rivals to homophonic translation

Gerald Massey has constructed what he calls a 'full-blown rival to
the homophonic manual for a rather rich language', one which
'supports not only the indeterminacy thesis but the added weight
of the inscrutability of reference as well' (1978, pp. 44 f., 49). In

fact he has constructed three: the *dualizing* manual *d*, the *contradictory* manual *c*, and the *Cretan* manual *e*.

His non-homophonic manual *d* exploits the logical principle of duality. It applies to *L*, a first-order language with identity and modality but without singular terms. *d* is a general recursive function from expressions of *L* to expressions of L, defined as follows. For every general term *X*, *d*(*X*) is the complement term of *X*. Thus while the homophonic *L-L* manual *h* (which is of course just the identity function) has it that 'dog', say, is true of all and only dogs, *d* has it that 'dog' is true of all and only non-dogs; and so on. Thus the *d*-reference of a general term is the complement of its *h*-reference. Connectives and operators are translated by their respective duals: negation by negation, disjunction by conjunction, conjunction by disjunction, the existential (universal) quantifier by the universal (existential) quantifier, possibility by necessity, necessity by possibility. Finally, wherever there is assent (dissent) according to the *h*-linguist, there is dissent (assent) according to the *d*-linguist, and 'the *d*-linguist inverts assertion and denial just as he inverts assent and dissent' (op. cit., p. 51).

To illustrate the way *d* works, suppose the *h*-linguist wishes to inquire whether all dogs are carnivores. This linguist asks '(x) $(\sim Dx \lor Cx)$?' and, as expected, gets the native's sign of assent 'Yes'. But the *d*-linguist takes the native to have thereby *dissented* from '$(\exists x)(\sim \text{compl}(D)x \ \& \ compl(C)x)$', also as expected. Similarly, if the *h*-linguist asks '$\Box(x)(\sim Dx \lor Cx)$?' and gets the response 'No', the *d*-linguist takes the same performance to constitute assent to '$\Diamond (\exists x)(\sim \text{compl}(D)x \ \& \ compl(C)x)$'. And so on.

In view of the nature of duality, Massey concludes that no matter what the linguists ask and no matter how the natives respond, both the *h*-linguist and the *d*-linguist will be equally convinced, on equally good grounds, that their respective manuals correctly translate *L*, in spite of the fact that the *d*-translation of a sentence will be true or false just in case its *h*-translation is respectively false or true.

If Massey is right this is a striking vindication of the indeterminacy thesis. The latter, as understood here, requires only *some* significant conflict over sentence translation. Massey's *d*, however, translates *every* sentence by a sentence which is not just counted as significantly different from its homophonic translation, but actually differs from it in truth value. And as if that were not enough, the dualizing manual *d*—if Massey is right in thinking it to be permissible—also vindicates the doctrine of the inscrutability of reference. For since *d* translates every general term by its complement term, *d* nowhere agrees with *h* about reference: for every general term, its *d*-reference is the complement of its *h*-reference. As Massey comments, 'more referentially divergent manuals are scarcely conceivable' (op. cit., p. 50). These consequences are so remarkable that it is worth investigating Massey's claims in some detail. In the next two sections I shall argue that none of his manuals is a permissible rival to the homophonic one.[4]

8.4 Empirical inadequacy of the dualizing and contradictory manuals

Evidently *d* would be ruled out immediately if the translatability of truth functional connectives and the preservation of stimulus analyticity and stimulus contradictoriness could be regarded as absolute constraints on translation, as Quine is sometimes taken to have implied by his remarks in *Word and Object* about conditions $(1')$–(3) (see 2.4). But Massey points out that they cannot be so regarded because they depend on analytical hypotheses about assent and dissent, as indeed Quine has emphasized (e.g. in 1968b, p. 312). Quine 'is prepared to pass over whatever traces of underlying indeterminacy there may be in the signs of assent and dissent themselves' (op. cit., p. 317). But Massey wants to show that the indeterminacy over assent and dissent is not to be sneezed at. It is a mistake, he thinks, to treat analytical hypotheses about assent and dissent 'as if they were genuine hypotheses, as if there were something for them to be right or wrong about'. And he maintains that *d* is permissible in spite of the fact that it 'violates all three constraints viz. conditions $(1')$–(3) everywhere' (op. cit., p. 49).

You may nevertheless suspect that Massey's *d*-linguist must bump up against *some* objective constraints when engaged in the resolutely perverse inversion of assent and dissent, assertion and denial. Further investigation confirms this suspicion, not only for the case of the dualizing manual *d*, but also for that of the 'contradictory' manual *c*, where each sentence is translated by the result of prefixing the negation sign to it, and where assent/dissent and assertion/denial are inverted just as they are in *d*.

That *c* and *d* cannot be empirically adequate becomes clear when

---

[4] This section borrows substantially from pp. 409 f. of my earlier work (1982a). However, the objections in the following sections are new and take account of Massey's reply.

we reflect that both the *d*-linguist and the *c*-linguist agree with the homophonic linguist (and with one another) over which *beliefs* an *L* speaker's utterance expresses on any occasion. For the *d*-linguist takes *L* speakers always to be denying the dual, and the *c*-linguist takes them always to be denying the contradictory, of whichever proposition the *h*-linguist takes them to be asserting. This is not to imply that all or any of them (or I myself) are necessarily committed to the objective soundness of such notions as proposition and belief. The point is that the differences between their manuals are consistent with the *d*-and *c*-linguists following the *h*-linguist in their use of those notions—assenting to the same set of sentences in which 'belief' or its cognates occur. Given that all three manuals must be consistent with this agreement, any conflicts about what the natives were doing with their utterance could be resolved by discovering what, according to these manuals, the natives *thought* they were doing. For example, suppose *h* interprets the *L*-expressions '*Ux*' and '*Ax*' to mean, respectively, '*x* is an utterance in L' and '*x* has the force of assertion'. And suppose all *L* speakers are disposed to respond with 'Yes' to the queried sentence

$$(1)\ (x)(\sim Ux \lor Ax).$$

(It seems reasonable to expect *L* speakers to have this disposition, since an equivalent one is surely possessed by natural language speakers. (*L* has only declarative sentences, remember.) The possibility that they do not will be considered shortly.) On these suppositions Massey's position requires there to be agreement among *h*-, *d*-, and *c*-linguists that *L* speakers *believe* that utterance in *L* has the force of assertion, even though *d* renders (1) by its dual and *c* renders it by its contradictory. For the *d*-linguist takes *L* speakers to be disposed to dissent from the proposition that there is something which is both not a non-utterance and a non-assertion; and the *c*-linguist takes them to be disposed to dissent from the proposition that it is not the case that utterance in *L* has the force of assertion. But this is overwhelming evidence against the claim of *d* and *c* to the effect that among *L* speakers utterance has the force of *denial*, evidence which the *d*-and *c*-linguists cannot consistently reject. If you concede not only that *L* speakers' behaviour is *consistent* with their utterances having the force of assertion (as of course is assumed when *h* is assumed to be permissible), but also that all *L* speakers *believe* their utterances have the force of assertion, there seems to be nothing you can consistently appeal to which might block the conclusion that their utterances *do* have the force of assertion.

It would not help Massey to suggest that *L* speakers might be disposed to respond to (1) with 'No'. That would only make *h* empirically inadequate in its turn, contrary to the original assumption (for then the *h*-linguist would have to withdraw the claim that utterance has the force of assertion), and again rule out the sort of conflict Massey says there could be between permissible translation manuals. Nor would it help to suggest that *L* speakers might disagree as to whether utterance implied assertion, since then they would simply fall into two empirically distinguishable groups, and the pair *h* and *d* would not jointly fit the facts about either group, when Massey requires them to fit all the facts about everyone. Nor, finally, would it help to say that *L* speakers might have no views on the matter, since that could only imply a degree of doubt as to whether *h* was permissible after all—whether '*Ux*' and '*Ax*' should be understood by *h* in the ways indicated above. But the behavioural dispositions of *L* speakers have to be consistent with *h* for the whole discussion to have a point, so we must assume those dispositions are consistent with the *h*-linguist taking (1) to express the view of any reasonably intelligent and articulate *L* speaker. (You could hardly support the indeterminacy thesis by having it depend on the contingent obtuseness of the population concerned.)

I conclude, then, that *d* and *c* are not permissible rivals to *h*.

8.5 Empirical inadequacy of the Cretan manual

However, Massey has a third putative rival to the homophonic manual, which he brings on stage in order to meet the objection that the *d*-linguist and the *h*-linguist, in spite of their conflict over the translation of *sentences*, agree over their translation of *statements*, when these are regarded as expressions of belief.[5] This is the 'Cretan' manual *e* (for Epimenides).

Over the translation of terms, connectives and operators, *e* follows *d*. But it follows *h* over assent and dissent, assertion and denial. The *e*-linguist squares the natives' apparent defiance of all good sense (as it seems to be on this system) by taking them to be

---

[5] This is not of course the same objection as the one given in the last section.

asserting falsehoods on all and only the occasions when the *h*-linguist takes them to be asserting truths, and taking them to be speaking truthfully only on those rare occasions when the *h*-linguist takes them to be lying. Massey briefly rebuts the suggestion that it is a 'sociological fact' that people by and large try to tell the truth. He does not consider a more serious challenge: that it is incoherent to assume that the speakers of a language could be untruthful normally and in the long run. However, I shall not pursue this familiar (though tricky) point. Instead I shall argue that the Cretan manual *e* conflicts with the empirical facts.

It is certainly conceivable that a community might exist for a long time while its members spoke untruthfully as often as, on normal assumptions, people actually speak truthfully. And certainly a consistent policy of making false assertions, not only to strangers but to one another and to their children, would frustrate linguists attempting radical translation. But Massey seems to assume that these facts are enough to show that the Cretan manual is empirically adequate, when it should be clear in the light of our earlier discussions that they do nothing of the sort. For, as we know, the issue raised by the indeterminacy thesis is not whether two conflicting translation manuals could both fit some of the facts—of course they could—but whether conflicting manuals could fit *all* the facts.

According to Massey both the homophonic manual *h* and the Cretan manual *e* are permissible—both fit all the facts. But according to the *h*-linguist *L* speakers are normally truthful. And people who are normally truthful know that this is what they are. They also know they are not systematic dualizing liars. Even if this loose talk of being 'truthful' and 'knowing' what one is doing is ruled out, we can at least be sure that all *L* speakers will be disposed to assent to such sentences as:

(2) $\sim(x)(\sim Sx \lor Lx)$.

For this sentence is interpreted by the *h*-linguist to mean, in effect, that it is not the case that all speakers of *L* are systematic dualizing liars; and of course the *h*-linguist takes this to be true. Observe that Massey is bound to accept that *L* speakers are disposed to assent to sentences such as (2) simply by his (inescapable) assumption that *h* is empirically adequate. (And after all, we are all disposed to assent to such sentences when they relate to English.)

But now consider how the *e*-linguist interprets such sentences as (2). By definition this linguist translates (2) by its dual, viz. by

(3) $\sim(\exists x)(\sim(complS)x \ \& \ complLx)$,

and understands this to mean in effect that every L speaker *is* a systematic dualizing liar. However, also by definition, the *e*-linguist takes L speakers to be, in Massey's words, 'asserting falsehoods whenever the *h*-linguist takes them to be asserting truths' (op. cit., p. 52). So, since the *h*-linguist takes them to be asserting a truth when they assert (2), the *e*-linguist must take them to be thereby asserting a falsehood. Thus the *e*-linguist takes them to be asserting in effect that every L speaker is a systematic dualizing liar, but also—by Massey's own definition—takes this to be a falsehood. That is, the *e*-linguist takes it to be false that every L speaker is a systematic dualizing liar. Yet at the same time this linguist's whole case rests on the claim that that is precisely what they are. So the fact that L speakers are disposed to assent to sentences like (2) reveals that the *e*-linguist's manual is not empirically adequate. The attempt to accommodate that fact immediately exposes a fundamental inconsistency in the *e*-linguist's position.

In any case the suggestion that there need be no relevant differences at all between a tribe X using L for normal truth telling and a tribe Y following a policy of systematic dualizing mendacity falls foul of considerations that even Quineans could hardly challenge. Admittedly Quine is committed to rejecting the idea that it is generally a matter of fact what beliefs we hold. But that does not commit him to maintaining that there would be *no* relevant objective differences between X and Y. Surely there would be a considerable difference in the structure of their behavioural dispositions. (For example, unlike normal truth tellers, systematic dualizing liars would presumably be disposed always to dissent covertly, or when no one else was present, from sentences to which they overtly assented.) But since I think the earlier argument is conclusive I shall not pursue this line.

Massey's three ingenious and entertaining examples, though more thought-provoking and persuasive than the others so far discussed, have all turned out to be mistaken. But there are one or two other superficially attractive candidates to be considered.

8.6 Duality in projective geometry

A case which at first glance looks promising was mentioned by
Frege to illustrate a point about the objectivity of reference (1884/
1959, pp. 35 f.). It exploits the principle of duality in projective
geometry, according to which any figure which is not defined by
means of some measurement corresponds to a dual figure, and any
theorem to a dual theorem, so that a proof of the one theorem,
when the appropriate transformations are applied, is a proof of its
dual. In particular, under the rule planes are substituted for points
and points for planes, while lines remain lines. (Example of a pair
of duals: (1) Three points not in a line determine a plane; (2)
Three planes not passing through a line determine a point.) Frege
imagines two rational beings who can perceive only the properties
and relations of projective geometry, and says that even if the
private experiences which one of them associated with a point were
like those the other associated with a plane, and vice versa, it
would be impossible, in view of the duality, to tell the difference.
However, let us forget Frege's dubious notions about private experiences and adapt his example to our needs.

Anna speaks German and Bill speaks English. It seems that
Bill has two ways of translating Anna's projective geometrical
utterances. He can use the normal method of rendering 'Punkt' by
'point', 'Ebene' by 'plane', and so on; or he can render her 'Punkt'
by 'plane', her 'Ebene' by 'point', and so on—thereby translating
each of Anna's utterances by the geometrical dual of its normal
translation. Since the two rival translations will generally not be
synonymous, this may look like a rather neat illustration of the
indeterminacy thesis. Closer inspection shows that it is not; but
the case illustrates some useful points.

Notice first that if (*i*) Anna and Bill have normal sensory capacities, and (*ii*) their use of the vocabulary of projective geometry
is normally embedded in the rest of their respective theories, then
the facts will rule out the proposed rival to the normal translation
manual. At any rate, we could not assume that the rival manual
was permissible without begging the question. Take the proposed
rendering of Anna's 'Punkt' by 'plane'. Each of these words can
be used in its own language as a one word observation sentence,
and as such the words have very different stimulus meanings. Nor
is it a coincidence that the same words serve both as observation
sentences and as terms in the abstract theoretical reaches of

geometry. 'Plane' as an observation sentence and 'plane' as a projective geometrical term are linked by stretches of intervening theory and verbal practice. The properties of points and planes are explicitly distinguished in the rest of geometry, where relevant asymmetries between points and planes abound. These links from observation sentences to asymmetrical theories, and thence to projective geometry, constitute a strong prima facie case for thinking that the glaring difference in stimulus meanings between the one word observation sentences 'Punkt' and 'Plane' block translation of the projective geometrical term 'Punkt' by 'plane'. But even if we supposed Anna and Bill to lack normal sensory capacities, asymmetries in the theories embedding projective geometry would still seem to rule out the proposed translations. I am not saying some defence of the odd translations would be impossible in that case. But none has been offered, and these considerations are enough to destroy this example's claims to intuitive acceptability on assumptions (*i*) and (*ii*). So if duality is to have a chance of providing a convincing or even merely persuasive example of the indeterminacy thesis rather than a question-begging application of it, we must assume Anna and Bill's projective geometry is uninterpreted.

If Anna and Bill's projective geometry is to be regarded as uninterpreted there would seem to be no obstacles to rendering her 'Punkt' by his 'plane', etc. So is this what we have been looking for? The answer may not be immediately obvious. On the one hand, if their projective geometry is uninterpreted, the only difference between a sentence and its dual is that 'point' and 'plane' are interchanged. Nothing that matters to the uninterpreted theory would have been altered if in the original presentation those words had been switched round throughout. This may well incline us to say these two words mean the same—in which case, of course, we do not have a case of indeterminacy of translation, which requires rival translations that do *not* mean the same. On the other hand, even within the uninterpreted theory, a pair of dual sentences must be distinguished from one another. The two classes of 'points' and 'planes' must be counted as distinct—even though the properties of members of the one have not so far, within the theory, been distinguished from one those of the other. And this may lead us to conclude that 'point' and 'plane' do not mean the same after all, in which case perhaps they do illustrate the indeterminacy of translation. So the two considerations seem to take us in opposite directions. However, they are not really at odds.

To start with we must not assume that the uninterpreted theory determines two actual sets, one with members denoted by the word 'point', the other with members denoted by the word 'plane'. If the theory did determine two actual sets, there would be an objective matter to be right or wrong about. 'Point' ('plane') could permissibly be translated only by a word which denoted whatever 'point' ('plane') denoted, hence not by any word denoting the members of the other set (for the theory requires the two sets to be disjoint). So there would be no room for genuinely rival translations. It may now be suggested that we could forget these considerations if 'point', 'plane', and the rest may be taken to mark the possession of different properties. But we must not assume that either, and for substantially the same reason. If the theory entails that 'point' marks the possession of different properties from those marked by 'plane', then neither 'point' nor 'Punkt' can permissibly be translated by 'plane', and again we have no candidate for indeterminate translation.

Here it is useful to notice three features of *predicate letters*.

(*i*) Predicate letters work as if they assigned things to definite sets, or assigned definite properties to things, though they do not. ('$(\exists x)(Fx)$' looks as if it assigned something to a set of F's, or assigned a property F-ness to something, when there is no such set or property.)

(*ii*) Any given predicate letter will serve as well as any other, when any relations that may have been set up with other expressions in a given context are ignored. ('$(x)(Gx)$' taken alone will do as well as '$(x)(Fx)$' taken alone.)

(*iii*) Even when the differences between different predicate letters have to be respected in view of relations set up for some particular purpose (e.g. in a particular chain of argument) a different selection of letters would have done exactly the same job.

These features of predicate letters ensure that where one or both of a pair are used in sentences for certain purposes within a given context, exactly the same purposes would have been served in that context by using instead the sentences resulting from interchanging them. So one cannot sensibly claim that the letters have 'different meanings'.

Of course 'point' and 'plane' are not predicate letters. (As normally used they can be regarded as partially interpreted predicates.) But when we regard projective geometry as an uninterpreted theory, they do resemble predicate letters in three ways corresponding to (*i*)–(*iii*) above. First, neither word denotes the members of any definite set, nor does it assign a definite set of properties. Second, if we take any sentence in which just one of these two words occurs, and consider it without regard to any wider context, the sentence conveys neither more nor less than would have been conveyed by the result of substituting the other word throughout. Third, if we take in isolation a whole set or sequence of sentences incorporating both 'point' and 'plane', the result of interchanging these words throughout would have done the same job as the original set or sequence.

So, as with predicate letters, one cannot sensibly claim that 'point' and 'plane' have different meanings in uninterpreted projective geometry. True, within a given context one cannot arbitrarily substitute one for the other because the theory requires these words to work *as if* they applied to disjoint sets, or assigned different properties. But because neither is associated with any particular set or properties, substitution throughout a given isolated context results in an equivalent or synonymous sequence of sentences. It follows that the two allegedly rival schemes of translation from Anna's German to Bill's English are not in genuine conflict, and for that reason do not illustrate the indeterminacy of translation.

The compatibility of the alleged rival schemes can be brought out by noting that *within the uninterpreted theory* 'x is a point' means very much the same as 'x is a member of *one* of the two supposed sets', which in turn means very much the same as 'x is a plane'. Similarly, 'x is a point and y is a plane' means much the same as 'x is a member of one of the two sets, and y is a member of the other'—which in turn means much the same as 'x is a plane and y is a point'.

The moral is that in struggling to devise a clear illustration of the indeterminacy thesis you can find yourself introducing so many special assumptions that what was originally a clear case of incompatible translations (if not a clear case of two empirically adequate translations) is reduced to a case of disguised synonymy. The present case only looked promising because of our familiarity with the meanings of 'point' and 'plane' in geometry as a whole. But, as we saw early on, those connections with the rest of geometry ensure that the two words are not genuinely intertranslatable (or at any rate cannot be assumed to be so without begging the question). It is only by cutting projective geometry off from its roots in the rest of geometry and treating it as an uninterpreted theory that we make the words appear intertranslatable. But it turns out that by doing so we prevent them from being conflicting translations.

One other case can usefully be mentioned here. Michael Levin has argued that the idea of 'forcing' employed by Cohen in his famous independence proofs for set theory can be used to provide an example of the indeterminacy of translation. Indeed he calls it 'a shining example of translational indeterminacy', though I think it can be shown to be no such thing. I shall not attempt here to show in detail what has gone wrong with Levin's argument, but I do want to emphasize one or two points.[6]

Levin assumes that the only constraint on the translation of versions of set theory is that theorems must be matched with theorems, and logical relations between the sentences of one theory must be matched by parallel relations among their translational images in the other theory (p. 27). He does not explain why further possible constraints can safely be ignored; and this gap in his reasoning seems to weaken his case substantially. But that is a relatively minor objection. The main trouble with his argument, I think, is that he commits the error (noted at 1.1(e)) of applying a double standard for synonymy. When judging whether the sentences offered as translations of a given sentence by two 'rival' translation manuals are synonymous he applies his own (entirely reasonable) intuitions (p. 29). But when judging whether the two sentences themselves are admissible as translations of the given sentence he applies only the weak constraint mentioned above. It is not surprising that this double standard yields an apparent case of indeterminacy. But as soon as one attempts to correct the error, the case collapses. If the relaxed constraint on synonymy is applied to the two translating sentences they come out as synonymous too, so there is no indeterminacy for that reason. If instead our ordinary intuitions of synonymy are applied, the two sentences no longer

[6] See Levin, 1979. For criticism, see Kirk, 1983.

qualify as translations of the given sentence, so again there is no indeterminacy.

It is important to note such points because the alleged mathematical and set theoretical instances of the indeterminacy tend to be presented in a way which suggests that disputing them is as futile as setting out to prove, say, that π is rational. They seem to lend the indeterminacy thesis the authority of the established mathematical theorems they exploit. Not that I have any quarrel with some of the incidental points Levin makes. He is surely right to say it is an error to assume 'that forcing *really is* a weakened form of entailment rather than simply being *construable as* a weakened form of entailment' (p. 30). But I find it significant that in spite of the fact that he gives an acceptable statement of the indeterminacy thesis at the start of his paper, at the end he asserts: 'Proponents of the generalized indeterminacy thesis can take this as typical of the debunking that can always be found for the illusion that one interpretation, *primus inter pares*, is correct' (p.31). What he describes as an illusion certainly is one. But as we have seen, to oppose the indeterminacy thesis is not necessarily to be gripped by that illusion. There is no need to resort to meta-mathematics for counter-examples to the illusion. They can easily be found wherever two languages differ noticeably in conceptual scheme (as what languages do not?). (Cf. 1.1(*b*) and 1.1(*c*).) But to illustrate the indeterminacy thesis is not so easy.

8.7 Conclusion

The inadequacy of the cases discussed in this chapter obviously does not guarantee that no genuine instance of the indeterminacy of translation could be found. But perhaps this study of the various ways in which they fail will help to forestall further premature announcements.

That concludes part II, in which I have examined the arguments for the indeterminacy thesis. Now for the arguments against it.

Part III

The Case Against Quine's Doctrine

Whistling in the dark is not the method of true
philosophy

QUINE

9

Unsuccessful Attacks

In this chapter I shall examine a number of objections to the indeterminacy thesis. I believe they include all the published ones that have not been considered, either directly or by implication, in the course of the discussion so far (especially in chapter 1). I think it will be clear that not one of these objections succeeds, although more than one seems to provide a promising basis for an attack on the thesis.

9.1 The triangle argument

I begin with two excessively crude arguments, each of which must have been entertained at least for a moment by all Quine's readers. Bad though they are, it will be useful to note where they go wrong. The first is the 'triangle' argument.

According to Quine, rival translation manuals could render a sentence X of one language by sentences Y and Z of another which one or both manuals counted as inequivalent. But—so goes the triangle argument—the very facts which make Y and Z both permissible translations of X cannot fail to make them permissible translations of each other, in which case they will not be inequivalent, and at least one of the manuals will not be permissible after all.

There are two things wrong with this little argument. First, it assumes that if it is permissible to say Y and Z mean the same, then it cannot also be permissible to say they do *not* mean the same. But of course that assumption simply begs the question. The point of the indeterminacy thesis is precisely that two permissible manuals can be in conflict over sameness of meaning. Second, the argument ignores the role of 'compensatory adjustments' in Quine's conception of rival translation schemes. His conception requires the facts to make it permissible to say X means the same as Y, and also to make it permissible to say X means the same as Z. But that does not mean his conception also requires the facts to make it permissible to say X *both* means the same as Y *and* means the same as *Z*. His thought is that by construing the facts in one way you can take *X* and *Y* as synonymous; and by construing them a different way—making appropriate compensatory adjustments—you can take *X* and *Z* as synonymous. But it does not follow (or rather it does not follow without reasoning which the triangle argument fails to supply) that there is also a way of construing the facts by which you can take *Y* and *Z* as synonymous. (It is not as if 'means the same as' were an extensional context.)

9.2 *The argument from truth conditions*

The second crude argument rests on the notion of truth conditions. The claim is simply that differences in the meanings of sentences will be reflected in differences in the truth conditions for those sentences, which differences will be objectively discoverable; and that therefore if two translation manuals conflict, it can only be because at least one of them has failed to take proper account of the truth conditions of crucial sentences.

The Quinean can reply as follows. Obviously the truth conditions for the sentences of one language, L_1, must be assumed to be, if characterizable at all, characterizable in some language or other. So, for the particular case of L_1, let them be characterizable in L_2, and let *T* be a theory in L_2 assigning truth conditions to the sentences of L_1. Now, either (*i*) *T* gives as truth conditions no more than such physical or dispositional facts as are acceptable as facts to Quine, or else (*ii*) it goes beyond these. If (*i*) *T* is assumed to state the truth conditions wholly in Quine-acceptable terms, then the indeterminacy thesis entails that *T* leaves the meanings of sentences in L_1 underdetermined in the relevant way, so that an empirically adequate rival to *T* could be devised. Thus on the first assumption the argument merely begs the question. If, however, (*ii*) *T* goes beyond the Quine-acceptable facts, then the indeterminacy thesis entails that there is a rival to homophonic translation in L_2 which maps *T* onto a different theory in which, for some sentence of L_1, the truth conditions for that sentence are not equivalent to those assigned to it by *T*. So again the argument from truth conditions begs the question.

9.3 *The argument from structure*

The following argument improves substantially on the triangle argument by offering some justification for the contention that the two sentences at the base of the triangle mean the same. If the structure of our language, and its relations with non-linguistic reality—structure and relations both being realized in our verbal dispositions—are such that two translations of a given foreign sentence are both equally good, how can it be permissible to count those sentences as inequivalent, as the indeterminacy thesis requires? How can those internal and external relations of our language which make Y one good translation of X, and Z another, be such as to permit a translator to say that nevertheless Y and Z do not mean the same?

Such thoughts are a natural response to the indeterminacy thesis, and have long been a potent influence against it. Bennett offers a straightforward version of this approach:

The 'reverberations across the fabric' [of that system of interconnected sentences which constitutes our language and theory: cf. TDE, pp. 42 ff., *WO* ch. 1, SO, pp. 16 f.] have their own detectable pattern; and the two translations of S cannot both be secure unless $E1$ and $E2$ both reverberate in precisely similar ways. For example, if any experiences would render problematic the acceptance of $E1$ but not that of $E2$, then there could be behavioural evidence favouring the translation of S by one of them rather than by the other. Or if $E1$ were relevant to some theoretical issue, while $E2$ did not have an exactly analogous relevance to an exactly analogous theoretical issue, then again there could be a basis for preferring one translation. In short, every single fact about $E1$ must be mirrored by a fact about $E2$. By any reasonable standard, therefore, the two sentences are synonymous, and so the indeterminacy of translation thesis is false. (*Linguistic Behaviour*, 1976, p. 262.)[1]

This reasoning may well strike non-Quineans as cogent, but by itself it will not do. Take the claim that every fact about $E1$ must be mirrored by a fact about $E2$. In some sense of 'fact' and some sense of 'mirrored' exponents of the indeterminacy thesis must certainly concede this claim. Specifically they must concede that the facts about each of these two sentences are symmetrical to the extent that they bear on translatability. The trouble is that the indeterminacy thesis is precisely to the effect that $E1$ and $E2$ could be counted as inequivalent in spite of this symmetry. So if 'facts' in the symmetry claim is to be understood to mean Quine-

---

[1] For variants of this argument see Dummett, 1974a, p. 372 (on which see 9.5), Boorse, 1975, Papineau, 1979, pp. 189 f. I should argue that Davidson's remarks (1974a, p. 322 and 1977, p. 139) also constitute a version of the structure argument against the indeterminacy thesis rather than ways of spelling out how that thesis might be true: see Kirk, 1985.

acceptable facts, the word 'therefore' in the last sentence quoted signals that the question is being begged: there is no argument, just an assertion. Yet obviously it would not help if 'facts' were understood to include truth conditions or other items regarded as problematic by Quine (e.g. 'facts' about propositional attitudes: this version of the argument was rejected in 1.3 and 1.4). For it would again be question-begging to assume that the sort of symmetry Bennett envisages would be preserved when such language was used. 'Facts' of these sorts are what Quine holds to be underdetermined by the objective facts. Of course it is plausible to assume that the degree of symmetry that must exist even in the Quine-acceptable facts will ensure that E_1 and E_2 must be counted as meaning the same. But if plausibility were an admissible consideration we should all be doing something else now. Quineans might be willing to concede that the symmetry will make it permissible to say E_1 and E_2 mean the same, since that would be compatible with saying it would nevertheless also be permissible to say they do not mean the same. But nothing in the argument from structure compels them to concede that it would be impermissible to deny that E_1 and E_2 mean the same.

These defects mean that the argument from structure fails. However, I believe the ideas behind it are essentially correct, and I think my arguments in chapters 10 and 11 provide it with the solid grounding it needs.

9.4 The argument from constraints

It is a familiar idea that we shall have determinacy of translation if only we can manage to discover or invent enough respectable constraints on translation. In this section I shall discuss only one version of this approach; but I think my conclusions will apply quite generally. The approach I shall examine is that of David Lewis in his paper 'Radical Translation' (to which the page numbers refer). Lewis does not offer this explicitly as an argument against the indeterminacy doctrine; but it is often regarded as such, and it is obviously pertinent. The problem Lewis addresses is that of getting from the totality of those truths about a person which could be stated in terms of physics and chemistry, to 'what he believes, what he desires, what he means, and anything else about him that can be explained in terms of these things' (p. 331). Where P is 'the whole truth [past, present and future] about Karl as a physical system', A^o is a specification of his system of beliefs, desires, and other attitudes in terms of our language, A^k a specification of them in Karl's language, and M a specification, in our language, of the meanings of expressions of his language, Lewis's problem is: Given P, solve for A^o, A^k, and M.

Lewis explains that he is not really asking how *we* could determine A^o, A^k, and M, but 'how do *the facts* determine these facts? By what constraints, and to what extent, does the totality of physical facts about Karl determine what he believes, desires, and means?' (pp. 333 f.). He presupposes 'a sort of minimal materialism': 'that P determines all the rest to the extent that anything does—that where determination by P leaves off, there indeterminacy begins' (p. 334). (Davidson comments that his own view is not that the psychological and semantic facts supervene on P alone (1974c, p. 345). Presumably he would take into account facts about other people and the rest of the world.) Lewis's constraints are 'the fundamental principles of our general theory of persons, [which] tell us how beliefs and desires and meanings are normally related to one another, to behavioural output, and to sensory input' (p. 334). As well as doing this, the theory makes an empirical claim about human beings, to the effect that for (almost) any human being there will actually be a system of beliefs, desires and meanings which conforms to the principles. Moreover, the relevant concepts of belief, desire, and meaning are 'common property': the theory 'must amount to no more than a mass of platitudes of common sense' (p. 335).

Now Lewis offers six principles as constraints on radical interpretation:

(1) (Charity.) This is to the effect that Karl should be represented as sharing our own beliefs and desires, or perhaps as having the beliefs and desires we should have had in his place, allowing for explicable error.

(2) (Rationalization.) Karl should be represented as a rational agent: 'the beliefs and desires ascribed to him by A^o should be such as to provide good reasons for his behaviour, as given in physical terms by P' (p. 337).

(3) (Truthfulness.) Karl should be represented as conforming to what Lewis calls a 'convention of truthfulness' in Karl's language. This involves a certain pattern of relations between

Karl's attitudes and his meanings, including, for example, that he will have (*i*) a desire not to utter 'It's snowing' unless it is snowing' (*ii*) a belief that those who share his language share this desire; (*iii*) a belief that it is snowing when he hears 'It's snowing' uttered; (*iv*) a belief that his compatriots respond similarly to utterances of 'It's snowing'; (*v*) a belief that they expect him to have these beliefs and desires (*i*)–(*iv*); etc.

(4) (Generativity.) '[The theory of meaning] should assign truth conditions to the sentences of Karl's language in a way that is at least finitely specifiable, and preferably also reasonably uniform and simple' (p. 399).

(5) (Manifestation.) 'Karl's beliefs, as expressed in his own language, should normally be manifest in his dispositions to speech behaviour' (p. 399).

(6) (Triangle Principle.) 'Karl's beliefs and desires should be the same whether expressed in his language or in ours' (p. 399).

In his paper Lewis is chiefly concerned to discuss *methods* by which solutions to the radical interpretation problem might be found—the 'unreal' problem of advancing from omniscience about P to omniscience about A^o, A^k, and M (see his pp. 334, 339 f.); whereas we are more concerned with the question whether there could be more than one empirically adequate solution. Does his discussion go any way towards answering our question?

He considers a related question in his concluding paragraph:

Could indeterminacy of beliefs, desires, and truth conditions . . . arise because two different solutions both fit all the constraints perfectly? This sort of indeterminacy has not been shown by convincing examples, and neither could it be shown—to me—by proof. *Credo*: If ever you prove to me that all the constraints we have yet found could permit two perfect solutions, differing otherwise than in the auxiliary apparatus of M, then you will have proved that we have not yet found all the constraints (p. 343).

But of course this is not an argument. As Davidson indicates in his reply, one of the points at issue is whether there are constraints sufficient to eliminate Quinean indeterminacy (1974c, p. 347). And the fact that Lewis presents his opinion as an article of faith makes plain his inability to provide an argument for it. (A conversational implicature, I take it.) Still, the six principles are worth pondering; and it will be highly relevant to consider the implications of Lewis's creed.

Lewis's Principle of Charity, to the extent that it does not beg the question against Quine, seems to be implicit in the Rationalization Principle. For if we could represent Karl as a rational agent *without* also representing him as having the beliefs and desires we should have had in his place, then it would be unacceptable, in the present context, to invoke the Principle of Charity purely for the purpose of reducing the number of possible solutions to the radical interpretation problem. The Principle of Charity is best seen either as a way of making explicit what is implicit in the Rationalization Principle, or as a merely heuristic device for finding candidate solutions. As to the Rationalization Principle itself, I have already argued that it cannot be rejected even by Quineans (3.5).

Lewis's Principle of Truthfulness might perhaps be challenged. (We have already discussed one challenge: 8.5). But it is at least plausible as an attempt to spell out part of the content of our ordinary notions of belief, desire, and meaning. To reject it would not be a convincing way of strengthening the Quinean position.

Something like the Principle of Generativity seems to be required for reasons discussed at 3.4. Again, Quineans would not strengthen their case by rejecting it.

Lewis himself points out that the Manifestation Principle is redundant, given Truthfulness, Rationalization, and the Triangle Principle (p. 342).

So what about the Triangle Principle? At first glance it might appear to beg the question against the indeterminacy thesis because it may seem to presuppose the impossibility of rivals to homophonic translation of *our* language. The principle requires Karl's beliefs and desires to be the same 'whether expressed in his language or in ours'; but the domestic version of the indeterminacy thesis has it that, given one interpretation in our language of Karl's language, hence of his beliefs and desires, there is a rival to these particular home language interpretations. In that case, according to Quine, it makes no sense to say Karl's beliefs are the same regardless of which language they are expressed in: the content of his beliefs is not a matter of fact at all (cf. 1.3 and 1.4). But this objection is premature. As I understand Lewis's Triangle Principle, it is meant to ensure only that for any *one* proposed interpretation, with its own versions of A^o, A^k, and M, the renderings of Karl's attitudes which it provides by means of A^o (in our own language) are consistent with those it provides by means of A^k (in Karl's language) and M (the theory of meaning for Karl's language, in our language). And this requirement, like those of Rationalization and Truthfulness, appears to do very much what Lewis claims, viz. it helps to spell out what our ordinary concepts of belief, desire and meaning involve—and after all it is these concepts that the indeterminacy thesis must attack.

So we are left with four principles: Rationalization, Truthfulness, Generativity, and the Triangle Principle, none of which could sensibly be challenged. The question remains whether these principles, together with any acceptable additions, are sufficient to ensure that there can be only one perfect solution to the radical interpretation problem. Lewis evidently does not see how this could be shown, nor do I. Why should he nevertheless believe what he does?

So far as I can see, you will believe such constraints determine a unique solution only if you are already an objectivist about the content of beliefs, desires, and other attitudes. For suppose that, like Quine, you hold that in general it is not a matter of fact what people believe, desire or mean. Then even if you accept the four principles noted in the last paragraph, you will not thereby show yourself to be committed to the view that these constraints are guaranteed to yield only a *single* interpretation of people's attitudes, given the totality of purely physical facts about people, or indeed about the whole world—the 'whole truth about nature'. For of course it is not generally true that a given data base and a set of constraints applying to it will yield a unique solution. On the contrary, it is not even generally true that adding more constraints automatically cuts down the number of possible solutions.[2]

Clearly, then, Lewis assumes that some factor associated with his constraints ensures that they, supplemented if necessary, will force a unique solution. He must assume that somehow or other the constraints are going to work systematically in this direction.

---

[2] Suppose for example we have a collection of lengths of wool, a yellow piece six inches long, two green ones five inches long, and some others all less than five inches. Then if we have to find which pieces satisfy the single constraint 'Maximize the length of x', there is a unique solution: the yellow piece. But if there is a second constraint 'x must not be yellow', and we want both constraints to be satisfied, there are two solutions: the green pieces.

Now I do not see how this factor could be the mere fact that—assuming it is true—the constraints do justice to the concepts of commonsense psychology. For why should our commonsense psychological concepts be supposed to have the required tendency to a unique solution—unless we assume they normally mirror objective psychological facts? If, however, we do assume that our commonsense psychological explanations, with their apparent references to the contents of our beliefs and desires, are not defined solely by a set of constraints, but report matters of fact, then of course a set of constraints which does justice to the concepts used in those explanations will tend to force a unique solution to the radical interpretation problem. If Lewis's credo is offered on this assumption, it is entirely understandable. Otherwise I, for one, do not understand it. In any case, with or without that assumption, it is no substitute for argument.

9.5 Dummett's objections

A version of the argument from structure appears in Dummett's discussion 'The Significance of Quine's Indeterminacy Thesis' (1974a). As one would expect, Dummett's examination of the indeterminacy thesis and related issues contains a number of thought-provoking suggestions. Unfortunately it suffers from two serious defects. First, he considers only versions of the thesis according to which the rival translation manuals must actually differ in truth value. (See 3.8 on why Quine is not committed to this.) Second, he assumes that on Quine's account there is, for any given language, a set of dispositions possession of which is necessary and sufficient for 'an ability to speak the language in a standard manner' (p. 372; cf. pp. 365 ff., 376–80). (See Appendix B for the reasons why Quine is not committed to this either.) The influence of these defects makes Dummett's discussion less cogent than it might have been. His reasoning leads him to conclude that the indeterminacy thesis must be understood as envisaging

the following . . . possibility: that two speakers of a language, each of whom conforms to all the linguistic dispositions the possession of which characterizes mastery of the language, and who have had exactly the same experiences, may yet disagree about the truth-value of a sentence of the language, even when both agree that its truth-value has been conclusively established, and even when this disagreement is not resoluble by appeal to linguistic practices common to all speakers of the language. (p. 373.)

But this conclusion is objectionable not only because of the un-justified assumption that Quinean indeterminacy requires dif-ference in truth value, but because Quineans will not feel bound to accept that the truth value of sentences whose translation is subject to the indeterminacy *can* be established conclusively, or even that there is such a thing as 'the best possible evidence' for them. On their view such sentences will be standing sentences with a high degree of theoreticity—verdicts on them will be subject to revision—and holistic considerations will ensure that the set of possible revisions is large and indeterminate.

Even waiving these objections, Quineans are unlikely to be convinced by Dummett's attempt to disprove the possibility to which he alleges they are committed. For he asserts that if there were a disagreement of the kind envisaged, and if the two people concerned, *a* and *b*, were to explore the sources of their dis-agreement, they would be able to discover that each was convinced by reasoning considered by the other to be 'fallacious' (p. 374): they would disagree over 'the validity of a form of inference' (p. 375). Such a disagreement would be reducible to a 'difference about meaning' (p. 376). Quineans can reply that these claims seem to presuppose that *a* and *b* not only start off with the same history of experiences and are endowed with the same intelligence—both acceptable assumptions—but that there was some time at which they shared (as we should say) exactly the same *beliefs*. For what people regard as having been conclusively established, like what they regard as evidence, must depend partly on what beliefs they have. If *a* and *b* start off with different beliefs, then even if they have the same history of experiences, their disagreement over the truth value of a sentence whose truth value they both regard as having been conclusively established need by no means arise from fallacious reasoning or a difference over meaning. It could be the result of those differences in their initial beliefs. Nor could this objection to Dummett's argument be overcome by adding identity of initial beliefs to the other assumptions. For there is no reason why Quineans should be bound to maintain that two people who started off with the same beliefs and had the same experiences might disagree over the truth value of a sentence whose truth value they agreed had been conclusively established—even if the content of beliefs were a matter of fact.

However, Dummett does later consider the Quinean reply that

it is only theoretical sentences that will be subject to the indeterminacy, and that for such sentences there can be no universally
agreed means of regarding them as conclusively established (p.
379). Unfortunately his arguments against the indeterminacy thesis
so interpreted appear no more persuasive than those noticed above.

According to Quine in his brief comment on Dummett's paper,
the latter has overlooked a certain possibility:

Are there two such sentences [translations of a given foreign sentence]
about which the speakers would disagree as to the truth-value? No; the
point is that the two translations of a native theoretical sentence may
have unknown truth-values, known only to be unlike. ('Reply to Michael
Dummett', p. 399.)

(The continuum hypothesis and its contradictory come close to
illustrating what he seems to have in mind, but see 8.1(*c*).) Replying
to this, Dummett seems to assume that the alleged possibility is the
only one on which Quine would now wish to insist. He says he
envisaged just this possibility in his paper, and rebutted it. He
does not claim to be able to show that such an indeterminacy of
translation cannot occur; but he does claim that 'the underdetermination of theory is the sole positive reason Quine has given for
believing that indeterminacy of translation actually occurs, and
that it is not a cogent reason'. Moreover he claims that the sort of
case envisaged in Quine's comment is the only kind of indeterminacy of translation which could obtain. (1974b, p. 416).

I concede immediately that the underdetermination of theory is
not a cogent reason for indeterminacy of translation (chapter 6).
But Quineans can and should resist Dummett's other claims here.
First, even if Quine did suppose that the sort of case he described
was the only one in which there could be indeterminacy of translation, he gives no reasons for this view. Nor does Dummett, as
we have seen. As to Dummett's rebuttal of the possibility alleged
by Quine, this amounts to the claim that where there is enough
symmetry of theoretical structure to permit two apparently different exact translations, there will be nothing to choose between
them; while if the translations really do differ in meaning, they will
not both be exact:

such meaning as [the theoretical terms occurring in the two sentences]
possess must derive either from their being taken as essentially belonging
to a particular theory or from their vague evocations of other theories in
which they are used: and either feature is likely to provide a ground for

choosing one translation rather than the other ('Reply to W. V. Quine', pp. 415 f. See also his main paper, 'The Significance of Quine's Indeterminacy Thesis', p. 392).

But we have already noted this argument from structure, and that it falls short of being a cogent refutation.

For these reasons I do not think Dummett's discussion makes a noticeable dent in the indeterminacy doctrine.

9.6 The argument from Quine's philosophy of science

Some people have argued that the indeterminacy thesis is inconsistent with Quine's own philosophy of science. Since there is much to be said in favour of the latter, the argument, if valid, would be powerful.

Quine's philosophy of science encourages us to take as true whatever 'theory of nature' fits the data best, and best conforms to our vague guiding principles of simplicity and conservatism (*WO*, pp. 20–5; 1968b, p. 303; *RR*, pp. 137 ff.). Indeed, it is his answer to the charge of relativism that 'within our own total evolving doctrine, we can judge truth as earnestly and absolutely as can be' (*WO*, p. 25). So it seems that on his view *the facts* are whatever are provided for by our total evolving theory of nature. And the objection goes that it is hard to see how these principles can leave room for the indeterminacy. Take those pairs of natural languages between which we already have working schemes of translation (idealizing as far as necessary). Quinean principles would not only favour these tried and tested schemes over any ingenious alternatives we might conceivably cook up. Those principles, it seems, would require us to regard such schemes as yielding *the facts* about sameness and difference of meaning between sentences of the languages in question, thereby ruling out the indeterminacy. Similarly in the case of radical translation, illustrated by English and Gavagese, Quinean principles appear to favour a scheme by which 'gavagai' is rendered by 'rabbit' rather than by any of the suggested alternatives, since such a scheme is likely to be both simpler in itself and easier to fit into our antecedent theory of nature, especially in view of what Quine calls 'the primacy of bodies' (FM, p. 181; cf. TPT, p. 9). Finally, in the domestic case, any rival to the homophonic scheme will by definition be less simple and harder to accommodate to the rest of our theory of nature, so it seems that again, by Quinean principles, we should have to regard the homophonic scheme as yielding *the facts* about what our compatriots mean.

Quine seems to have anticipated this objection in a rather dark passage:

May we conclude that translational synonymy at its worst is no worse off than truth in physics? To be thus reassured is to misjudge the parallel. In being able to speak of the truth of a sentence only within a more inclusive theory, one is not much hampered; for one is always working within some comfortably inclusive theory, however tentative. . . . In short, the parameters of truth stay conveniently fixed most of the time. Not so the analytical hypotheses that constitute the parameter of translation. (*Word and Object*, pp. 75 f.)

He elaborates this reply in a passage discussed earlier. He insists that the indeterminacy is not just a special case of the general thesis that most theories, if not all, are underdetermined by their data: the indeterminacy of translation is 'additional' (see 6.2). We saw that this point, properly understood, shows that his thesis is not a boring truism. But does it also meet the present objection, which is that by his own standards the thesis is actually false? Chomsky's reactions have already been noted. Gardner regards the physicalism to which Quine commits himself as mistaken.[3] And Rorty concludes that Quine is faced with a dilemma: 'he should either give up the notion of "objective matter of fact" all along the line, or reinstate it in linguistics' (1972, p. 459. Cf. 1980, pp. 202 ff.) Yet although Quine seems not to have managed to get across just why these attacks fail, I think they can be shown to fail.

What needs to be emphasized above all is that the guiding principles of simplicity and conservatism ('familiarity of principle' or 'relative empiricism': *WO*, p. 20; *RR*, pp. 138 f.) are supposed to be applied not just to sub-theories but to our *total* evolving doctrine (*WO*, p. 25; cf. *RR*, p. 137). Applying these principles to his own total system Quine concludes that:

(*a*) the best 'theory of nature' for today is that provided by today's physics, even though this theory, or bundle of theories, has its difficulties and gaps and is subject to revision. (The central point is made at *WO*, pp. 234 f., 264 f., FM, p.

---

[3] Gardner, 1973, pp. 389 f. However, I think Gardner's interpretation of Quine's physicalism is itself incorrect. Contrary to what he assumes, that physicalism need not include a commitment to the translatability of non-physical statements into the language of physics. See 1.10, and FM, p. 187 for Quine's actual view.

187. The incompleteness of physics is noted at FM, pp. 192 f.)

(*b*) Therefore, since our theory of nature says, in its own terms, what is the case in the world, there are no facts, no realities, other than those constituted or underlain by facts statable in terms of physics. This does not of course mean that all true statements are *translatable* into the language of physics (1.9-1.10).

(*c*) Therefore, if some psychological or semantic interpretation is not strictly implied by the physically statable facts, its sentences do not in general state facts at all—even if that interpretation is best when the principles of simplicity and conservatism are applied within the area of inquiry concerned.

(*d*) Theories of translation are not strictly implied by the physically statable facts. (The indeterminacy thesis.)

(*e*) Therefore questions about synonymy relations are not (or not generally) questions of fact.

Some comments are called for. The objection is, after all, that there is something arbitrary, indeed contrary to Quine's own principles, in refusing to accept as matters of fact whatever is not underlain by physically statable facts. Why should facts statable in terms of physics make statements true in a way nothing else can? Rorty asks: 'What more does it take [sc. on Quinean principles] for there to be a "fact of the matter" than a rational procedure for reaching agreement about what to assert?' (1972, p. 453); and goes on to claim, with some justice, that 'there just *are* rational procedures for preferring the "rabbit" manual to the "rabbit-stage" manual' (op. cit., p. 457). If Rorty's points are soundly based on Quinean principles, then the fact (if it is one) that the 'rabbit' manual is not strictly implied by the physically statable facts in the required sense ought not to debar its synonymy statements from the realm of factuality. However, Rorty seems to have mistaken Quine's position.

If you are a Quinean, what you take to be real—what statements you take to state matters of fact—is a decision that is to be guided by the principles of simplicity and conservatism. So suppose you decide that fact-stating sentences at any rate include many sentences couched in terms of today's physics. There can be no doubt that this decision conforms to your Quinean principles. But now there is a question as to what other kinds of sentences you ought to regard as stating facts, as conveying part of the truth about reality. Suppose, then, you boldly follow the approach indicated by Rorty, and take it to be a matter of fact that 'gavagai' means the same as 'rabbit'. Then you face the problem of relating this fact to the physically statable facts. If this fact, like those of chemistry and microbiology, turns out to be strictly implied by the physically statable facts, then of course all is well. It is just a complex physical fact: the realities involved are purely physical. But if this fact about sameness of meaning is *not* strictly implied by the physically statable facts, you are committed to a rather complicated view of reality. On the one hand you have the facts statable in terms of physics. On the other you have semantic facts, facts about propositional attitudes, etc., somehow floating free of the physical facts. Is such a commitment compatible with the principles of simplicity and conservatism? Evidently Quine thinks not. And while one might legitimately dispute this conclusion, I do not see how it could be held actually to conflict with his principles. To me it seems to be entirely in accordance with them. So I think Rorty was mistaken in assuming that on Quinean principles the existence of rational procedures for reaching agreement about what to assert in a given area of inquiry is alone sufficient to ensure that what is asserted is an objective matter of fact. It is also necessary to bring the results of such agreements into line with your overall theory of nature. When you do this, you may well find that the demands which simplicity and conservatism impose on your total theory require you to refuse to allow the assertions you make in that field of inquiry to be counted as stating facts—no matter how practically useful they may be.[4]

9.7 *The argument from optimism about semantics*
Katz asserts that Chomsky's conception of grammars as ideal-izations of speakers' knowledge of language 'makes linguistic theorizing like theorizing in the advanced sciences', so that 'notions of any sort' can be introduced by linguistics, provided they can be precisely stated and justified in terms of their value in explanations. He points to his own use of Chomsky's approach to syntactic theory as a model for a semantic theory (1.3), and declares that

---

[4] For another line of reply to the present attack on Quine, see Hookway, 1978, pp. 31 f.

Given the possibility of a semantic theory, Quine's thesis of the indeterminacy of translation has nothing to support it. Evidence about the semantic properties and relations of expressions in languages can be used to confirm the existence of synonymy or translation relations, even in the case of radical translation. . . . Since there are no a priori reasons to think that . . . the evidence cannot be made clear enough to compensate for inductive underdetermination, there is as much a fact of the matter about identity of sense as about anything else in science ('Semantic and Conceptual Change', pp. 338 f.).

Evidently Katz assumes that Quine's inextricability thesis is mistaken. (In fact, in the article from which I have quoted, he turns his claims against that doctrine too, a manoeuvre that Quineans can reject as question-begging.) But I will ignore that point. The main thing to notice is that even if semantic theory can be made as clear and scientific as Katz assumes, he offers no argument for his further assumption that the sort of evidence he alludes to will be relevant to deciding whether there is Quinean indeterminacy— when in *Word and Object* Quine explained why such evidence is *not* relevant. To repeat: there is Quinean indeterminacy of translation if the totality of facts about behavioural dispositions, and indeed the totality of facts statable in physical terms, is compatible with translation manuals which are in significant conflict. Katz, in effect, merely points out that the totality of Quine-acceptable facts may well be compatible with *one* Katzian translation manual. He does nothing to show that a rival to it could not possibly be devised. In justification he would no doubt maintain that the existence of a soundly based scientific theory is the best possible reason for taking its posits as matters of fact. But we saw in the last section why this point, though defensible, does not provide the means for demolishing Quine's position. Optimism about semantics leaves the indeterminacy thesis unscathed.

9.8 The argument from holism

Another feature of Quine's doctrine with which the indeterminacy thesis has been held to conflict is, ironically, his holism (chapter 4). He maintains that there is a 'structure of interconnected sentences' which forms 'a single connected fabric including all sciences, and indeed everything we ever say about the world' (*WO*, pp. 12 f.). At the same time he insists that a sentence is 'meaningless except relative to its own theory; meaningless intertheoretically' (*WO*, p. 24). And the objection is that, on this holistic account of meaningfulness, translation between different theories or different languages will be not indeterminate, but impossible. If a given sentence's meaningfulness depends on its place in its own theory, and if that theory is linked with others in a single structure, then only a sentence standing in exactly the same relations to exactly the same theories will be capable of serving as an exact translation of it. So between genuinely different languages there will be no indeterminacy of translation because no exact translation will be possible at all; while within a single language no sentence other than itself will adequately translate a given sentence. It seems, then, that Quine's holistic conception of meaningfulness destroys both the interlinguistic and the intralinguistic versions of the indeterminacy thesis.[5]

These considerations appear powerful, but they overlook two important facts. First, to say a sentence is 'meaningless except relative to its own theory' is not to say it is a matter of fact *which* meaning a sentence has. To be meaningful—usable in communication—cannot be assumed to be the same as to have some determinate meaning (4.10). Quine's remark actually commits him to no more than that the question of how to translate a given sentence cannot sensibly be raised unless the sentence is understood to belong to a theory; and obviously this relatively uncontentious claim leaves him free to maintain that there is scope for divergent translations. Second, in *Word and Object* Quine acknowledges that occasionally his holism has been 'excessive' (*WO*, p. 13n.), and follows his remarks about the single connected fabric with the qualification that 'some middle-sized scrap of theory usually will embody all the connections that are likely to affect our adjudication of the truth value of a given sentence' (*WO*, p. 13. Cf. ESW, pp. 314 f.). This qualification alone would be enough to disarm the present attack. For if the adjudication of a sentence's truth value does not require us to go beyond the limits of some middle-sized scrap of theory, neither can the adjudication of its claims to translate some foreign sentence; so there is no obstacle to substantially different languages having several theories in common, hence admitting a fair amount of exact translation.

The above two points in effect reduce the argument from Quinean holism to the old argument from structure discussed in 9.3.

---

[5] See Dummett, 1973, p. 414, 1974a, p. 385, Boorse, 1975, Papineau, 1979, p. 187.

It is not altogether without force; but without supplementation it seems to be question-begging.

9.9 Conclusion

The hitherto known objections to the indeterminacy thesis seem just as inconclusive as the arguments for it. Still, our investigations have cleared the ground and helped to improve our appreciation both of the character of the indeterminacy thesis and of the conditions to be satisfied by any adequate defence or attack. In the next two chapters I shall draw on this understanding to construct what I believe to be a refutation of the doctrine.

10

General and Domestic Theses Related

The English speaking linguist in *Word and Object* may be confronted by a jungle language markedly unlike English in both syntax and conceptual scheme. Yet Quine's thesis that translation between English and the jungle language is indeterminate is supposed to be 'just a different way' of putting a similar point about the domestic case. The case of radical translation between syntactically and conceptually divergent languages is intended to make his claims about domestic indeterminacy clearer and more vivid (*WO*, p. 27; cf. OR, pp. 46 f.; *RR*, p. 83).

In spite of these explicit indications to the contrary, there has been a tendency to see the indeterminacy thesis as essentially concerned with translation between languages that differ widely in both syntax and conceptual scheme. This tendency is encouraged by the 'Gavagai' discussion and the Japanese classifier example (2.3, 5.2) and also by some of Quine's other remarks here and there (e.g. SO, p. 6, 1969a, p. 103). Quite possibly, too, some readers have regarded his insistence on the equivalence of the intralinguistic and interlinguistic theses as just mistaken, and have found the doctrine plausible only when applied to translation between widely differing languages. So far as I know there have been no published attempts to justify the assumption that it could hold only in such cases. Anyway I think that assumption is wrong, and Quine is right here, as will follow immediately from the main conclusion of this chapter. I shall argue that if there is indeterminacy of translation at all, there must be indeterminacy in the domestic case too. I have to argue for this, rather than simply accepting its assumption by Quine, because in the next chapter I shall argue that there cannot be Quinean indeterminacy in the domestic case.

10.1 Is the domestic thesis just a special case of the general thesis?

It may seem that no elaborate argument is needed to show that intralinguistic indeterminacy is entailed by interlinguistic indeterminacy, since the former can be viewed as just a special case of the latter. However, this suggestion is not as straightforward as may appear. A translation manual represents sentences of two languages as meaning the same; but a Quinean reinterpretation for a single language does not represent each sentence of that language as meaning the same *in that language* as the sentence onto which it is mapped. On the contrary, it requires these sentences, in some cases, to be counted as *not* meaning the same. And whereas our ordinary notion of sameness of meaning seems to be both reflexive and symmetric, we must not assume that a Quinean reinterpretation which maps X onto Y will map either X onto X or Y onto Y. For if it did either of these things for each pair of sentences X and Y, it would not be, as the domestic thesis requires, incompatible with the homophonic scheme. (To reinterpret X by both X and Y, or X by Y and Y by X, is obviously consistent with interpreting X by X, as the homophonic scheme does.)

Still, a Quinean reinterpretation for what would ordinarily be counted as a single language *can* be regarded as a translation manual if we think of each of its speakers as having their own idiolect. Users of such a reinterpretation will then be construed as saying that their victims' sentences X^1, X^2, . . . mean the same, respectively, as the users' own sentences Y^1, Y^2, . . . , but do not in general mean the same as the users' own X^1, X^2, . . . , where 'means the same' denotes, as usual, a relation that is both reflexive and symmetric. (For further discussion see 11.1.)

Given the above interpretation of the domestic thesis, it does appear to be just a special case of the general thesis. And if it is, then to show there is no Quinean indeterminacy of translation in the domestic case will be to show that the general thesis is false. However, it is easy to imagine someone objecting that the domestic case is an exceptional limit case, and that what holds for translation between different languages need not necessarily hold when translated and translating langages are (or can permissibly be counted as) one and the same. To meet this objection it will be necessary to show that if there is Quinean indeterminacy of translation at all, it holds for the domestic case too.

10.2 Main argument

First an argument I shall not press. Suppose the general indeterminacy thesis were true, and we had two incompatible but empirically adequate manuals for, say, French and English. Each of these manuals would include a partial function from English sentences to French sentences (or to sets of purportedly synonymous sentences), and another partial function going in the reverse direction (1.14). So it seems we could compose these functions to produce a Quinean reinterpretation for English. We use the English-to-French function from one manual, and the French-to-English function from the other. The permissibility of the first pair of manuals would seem to guarantee that of the resultant Quinean reinterpretation. However, this argument may be vulnerable to an attack on the lines of an objection to the 'triangle' argument discussed in 9.1. For it is one thing to assume that the facts make each of the two translation manuals permissible, and something else to infer that the facts also permit both manuals to be used together. I do not say such an objection could be sustained, but I do not see how it could be quickly shown to be mistaken. It raises a prima facie difficulty with the argument from composition. So I shall leave that argument, and devote the rest of the chapter to another.

Assume for the sake of argument that the domestic version of the indeterminacy thesis is false. That is, assume that any possible scheme of reinterpretation for a given language will be either consistent with the homophonic scheme, or else impermissible. We shall see that on this assumption translation between any pair of languages will be determinate.

Suppose the inhabitants of Nottingham for some reason decide to forsake their native language and culture and adopt instead those of a community culturally and linguistically rather remote from their own, though not so remote as to preclude exact translation of many sentences. Chinese will be a good example. Suppose too they decide to carry through this project not by a mass migration to China, but by following some translation manual.[1]

Now, if Quine is right about interlinguistic translation there will be at least two ways in which the people of Nottingham could succeed in the linguistic part of their project. They could follow the generally accepted scheme for translating between Chinese and English or they could follow some Quinean rival. Let us begin, then, by supposing they decide to follow the usual scheme. (We

---

[1] The possibility that no exact translation between the two languages is possible will be dealt with below (10.5).

pretend that, as presupposed by the indeterminacy thesis, there really are two permissible manuals of translation between these languages, each manual being finitely specifiable in English: 3.3.) To make things relatively easy for themselves, the people of Nottingham agree to switch over to Chinese by way of a series of minor changes, announcing in advance the changes to be made at each stage. Let the first changes be just these: (1) Chinese 'wo' will be used instead of English 'I' and 'me'; (2) 'ni' will be used instead of 'you' (singular); (3) 'xuesheng' will be used instead of 'a (the) student'; (4) 'shi' will be used instead of the copula 'is' or 'are'; (5) 'bu' will be used instead of 'not'.

Once this little packet of changes has been put into effect the sentences 'wo shi xuesheng', 'ni bu shi xuesheng', etc., as now used by the people of Nottingham in their hybrid transitional language, will be translatable into normal English by 'I am a student', 'You are not a student', etc. More to the point, given our initial assumption of determinacy in the domestic case, the announcement of these linguistic changes will not itself be subject to the indeterminacy, from which it follows that the above English translations will not be subject to the indeterminacy either. For they were reached by following a set of rules determinately interpretable in English, applied to English sentences also determinately interpretable in English.

No translation of the Nottinghamians' new sentences which conflicted with the ones given above would be permissible. Suppose for example that some rival manual were to offer 'I am a rabbit' as its English version of 'wo shi xuesheng'. The assumption of determinacy in the domestic case entails that in Nottingham English *before* the adoption of (1)–(5), that particular English sentence was, objectively, not equivalent to 'I am a student'. (For since it is certainly permissible to say these two sentences do not mean the same, it would be permissible to say they *did* mean the same only if there were indeterminacy in the domestic case, contrary to our assumption.) So 'I am a rabbit' could be a permissible rendering of that Chinese sentence only if (1)–(5) had introduced some semantically relevant change in the Quine-acceptable facts— a change affecting not just the words used by the people of Nottingham, but the permissible interpretations of sentences incorporating those words. But clearly (1)–(5) cannot possibly affect interpretations: they can have no more bearing on what the sentences can be said to mean than a rule enjoining a simple change of pronunciation would have had—switching round 'l' and 'r' sounds, for example. The effect is merely that in whatever circumstances the Nottinghamians would have been disposed to use a sentence beginning 'I am . . . ' before the adoption of (1)-(5), they are now disposed to use 'wo shi . . . ', and similarly for the other changes. ('Circumstances' here should be taken to mean the totality of relevant Quine-acceptable facts.) So, since (1)-(5) cannot have introduced any semantically relevant changes, the facts about the hybrid transitional Nottingham language, just like the facts about English, given our assumption of domestic determinacy, rule out 'I am a rabbit' as an English translation of 'wo shi xuesheng'. Similarly for any other English sentence now permissibly said not to mean the same as 'I am a student'. Therefore the translation of that Chinese-like Nottingham sentence by 'I am a student' is determinate, given our assumption.

After the first lot of linguistic changes, then, English and the hybrid Nottingham language are still determinately inter-translatable, given determinacy in the domestic case. By similar reasoning English and each successive one of the whole series of transitional languages will remain determinately translatable after each lot of further changes, including the last member of the series which completes the programme. Determinacy of translation at each stage of the changeover is guaranteed by determinacy at each of the preceding stages. So eventually, leaving aside some points to be dealt with in the following sections, the people of Nottingham will end up not only speaking, but being disposed to speak, like Chinese (or at any rate like speakers of the standard Peking dialect). Yet by the above argument translation between their language and English will be determinate if domestic interpretation is.

May we conclude that translation between Chinese and English is determinate if there is no Quinean indeterminacy in the domestic case? Two or three points must be considered first. One arises from the reasonable supposition that any Chinese-English translation manual will leave some sentences of each language without exact translations in the other.

10.3 Failures of translatability

Untranslatable English sentences will of course be no problem for the people of Nottingham, who will simply arrange to cease using them. However, untranslatable Chinese sentences, or rather Chinese sentences left untranslated by that particular (normal) translation manual they have chosen to follow, are a different matter. It may be suggested that a different yet still permissible manual might have left a different set of Chinese sentences untranslated; which might appear to leave room for pockets of indeterminacy.

Suppose, then, that N is the manual actually used by the people of Nottingham, and that it renders X by Chinese Y, while some rival manual, P, renders X by Chinese Z. Suppose too that N cannot consistently translate Z into English, which of course entails that N counts Y and Z as not equivalent in Chinese. Then, regardless of whether or not P agrees with N in counting Y and Z as non-synonymous, there will be a Quinean indeterminacy: either because they produce what both agree are incompatible renderings of X, or because they conflict over the synonymy of Y and Z. However, indeterminacy of this sort cannot occur, given our initial assumption.

Notice first that the argument of the last section shows that for *any* English sentence and any Chinese sentence which the Nottingham manual N counts as a translation of it, and which therefore belongs to the Nottingham repertoire at the end of their programme of N-based changes, the translation of that Nottingham Chinese sentence by that English sentence is determinate (given determinacy in the domestic case). Leave aside for the moment the question whether Nottingham Chinese is really part of Chinese. The point is that by the earlier argument no permissible manual for translating between that particular Chinese-like language and English can conflict with N. It follows immediately that P, which does conflict with N because it renders English X by Chinese Z, when N renders X by Y and does not count Y and Z as synonymous in Chinese, is either not permissible or not in genuine conflict with N. But given the assumption that there is no domestic indeterminacy, the only way P could be permissible yet not in conflict with N would be if Nottingham Chinese were not really part of Chinese. Let us consider this possibility.

If N leaves some Chinese sentences untranslated, the Nottingham folk will not have seen their project through if, having got as far as N will take them, they do nothing to acquire the capacity to use those sentences. So let us suppose they somehow acquire that capacity—perhaps by taking lessons from native Chinese speakers. Observe that their acquisition of the remainder of Chinese cannot fail to be compatible with the Chinese-like dispositions they have already acquired. In particular, their use of the Chinese sentence Z, which we assumed to have been declared untranslatable by their chosen manual N, will be compatible with their present dispositions. For *ex hypothesi* N, being a permissible English-Chinese translation manual, conforms to *all* the Quine-acceptable facts about the English and the Chinese, including the totality of Chinese and English behavioural dispositions, not forgetting those relating to Chinese sentences left untranslated by N. It follows that no behavioural incongruities can result from grafting the remainder of Chinese on to the Chinese-like stock which the Nottingham folk have cultivated. When this part of the operation is completed, therefore, the people of Nottingham will be permissibly counted as speaking Chinese, just as they intended. Nottingham Chinese is Chinese. Finally, then, it follows from the conclusion of the last paragraph that P must be impermissible if domestic interpretation is determinate. No indeterminacy can result from the fact that the chosen translation manual leaves some Chinese sentences without English translations.

That ties up one of the loose ends left by the argument of the last section. A second loose end appears when we recall that the Nottingham folk opted for the standard English-Chinese manual N rather than for some Quine-inspired rival. What if they had used a Quinean manual Q instead of N?

10.4 Is there an alternative?

At first sight there may seem no reason why the argument of 10.2 and 10.3 should not have been applied to the case where the Nottinghamians, instead of following the standard manual N, had opted for its Quinean rival Q. Then, it seems, a parallel argument would have shown there could be no rival to Q; in which case the argument is somehow misconceived. But it is the objection that has gone wrong.

The objection overlooks the fact that what I have been calling the standard scheme for translating between English and Chinese, which we have imagined to be encapsulated in a translation manual N, is *known* to be permissible—tried and tested, vouched for by competent linguists and bilinguals. So the argument rests on a firm basis which the parallel argument would lack; for no Quinean rival to N is known to be permissible. Given the knowledge that N is permissible, then, the argument shows, first, that if there is no domestic indeterminacy there could be no permissible rival to N, and second, that it is indeed Chinese that the people of Nottingham would be speaking when they had completed their project. So the argument shows that, assuming determinacy in the domestic case, if the Nottingham folk had adopted Q they would *not* have ended up speaking Chinese. So the objection is misconceived.

That completes the main argument of this chapter. Quine's assumption that if there is indeterminacy of translation at all, there is indeterminacy in the domestic case, is vindicated. But before moving on to deal with the domestic case, I want to make it clear that the arguments are unaffected by the extent to which exact translation may be prevented by differences of conceptual scheme, and then to consider the relevance of Wittgenstein's conception of possible differences in 'form of life'.

10.5 Conceptual differences and translatability

The main argument assumes that some exact translation between different languages is possible. However, there is a spectrum of different opinions on the degree of translatability that can be expected. One extreme view is that 'for any sentence of one natural language, there is at least one sentence in every other natural language that expresses the same proposition' (Katz, 1972, p. 20).[2] The other extreme view is that exact translation between different languages is impossible: 'Traduttore, traditore': conceptual differences are held to preclude exact translation altogether.[3] Of course there are intermediate positions. But fortunately we need not enter this controversy. Neither of the two extreme possibilities affects the arguments of this chapter adversely, while the argument is expressly tailored to suit any intermediate position.

If *no* exact sentence translation between different languages is possible—foreigners are utterly inscrutable—then since the

---

[2] Grayling goes further: 'The criterion of languagehood is: translatability into our own language' (1982, p. 272). See also Davidson, 1974.

[3] 'For instance, the cultural and physical contexts of Chukchee utterances are, with a few exceptions, incomparable with the contexts within which English is spoken. Chukchee weapons, food, manners, standards of any sort, landscape, fauna, and flora are mostly unfamiliar to English-speaking cultures. Thus, practically no common frame of reference, no basis for a segmental, one-by-one comparison exists between these two languages. Translation here can be only a very rough approximation of what has been said and intended originally'. Lenneberg, 1953.

indeterminacy thesis must be supposed to be about exact translation, it can hold, at best, only in the domestic case. So this
extreme view renders the argument of 10.2 redundant: the only
possible Quinean indeterminacy would be domestic. The other
extreme view—foreigners are utterly transparent—would let the
argument of 10.2 go through unproblematically, and 10.3, which
deals with the residue of supposedly untranslatable sentences,
would be redundant. So neither of these extreme views about the
scope of translation requires modifications to the argument of the
chapter.

10.6 Translatability and form of life

It may be suggested that differences in Wittgensteinian form of
life would be natural breeding grounds for indeterminacy of translation. This must have been far from Quine's thoughts (though see
1.11); but the suggestion ought not to be dismissed out of hand.

Consider Wittgenstein's odd adder. This individual, though at
first appearing to have learnt how to follow the instruction to add
n to a given whole number, is eventually unmasked as finding it
natural to apply the rules in a way that strikes the rest of us as
bizarrely wrong.[4] Our training in the use of a rule cannot determine
our future applications of that rule. We respond to our training as
we do, and generally agree in what we count as what the rule is,
what it applies to, what it is to follow the rule or go on in the same
way, not because the training or the rules determine our behaviour,
but as a combined effect of training and facts about our 'natural
history'—facts which could conceivably have been otherwise.

Now, if there were two linguistic communities which differed in
their relevant innate tendencies and predispositions in the way
Wittgenstein imagined, the differences would obviously present
severe difficulties for translation and interpretation. The question
we have to consider is whether such differences could generate a
variety of Quinean indeterminacy of translation. They could do so
only if they did not altogether *prevent* translation, of course; and
it is natural, and I believe correct, to think that this is just what
they would do. But we need to be sure this is correct.

The main point to notice is that if there were differences of the
sort in question between a given pair of languages, no one could
have command of both languages at the same time. This may not

---

[4] See *Philosophical Investigations*, secs. 143, 185-9.

be immediately obvious. But suppose it were possible for one person to have simultaneous mastery of both. In that case someone whose natural predispositions and tendencies allowed them to speak one of the languages in a way acceptable to native speakers could also possess natural predispositions and tendencies which enabled them to speak the other equally acceptably. But this would be possible only if the same set of natural dispositions enabled someone to speak both. And that is impossible. For the point about forms of life is that given *our* predispositions, we agree on what is acceptable, while anyone with a different set of predispositions would not agree with us. Having both sets would involve having incompatible predispositions.

But does the impossibility of simultaneous mastery of both languages rule out the possibility of a translation manual between them? Of course there might be areas of language where the two communities' predispositions and tendencies overlapped, in which case sentences confined to those areas could be translated. But that is beside the point. The question is whether *differences* in form of life might generate Quinean indeterminacy; so we can ignore linguistic areas where agreement reigns. Given that presupposition, we can see there could not be a translation manual for the two languages. A translation manual must be finitely specifiable: it cannot be supposed to consist of a bare infinite pairing of sentences (3.4). But such a specification must be in some language or other; and the trouble is that no single language could do justice to two languages grounded in different forms of life. For since no one person could master both languages simultaneously, no one language could provide the means to specify translations over a potential infinity of possible cases. We could not, for example, correlate one of the foreigners' phrases with 'add 2', or with any other English phrase, precisely because, *ex hypothesi*, the foreigners do not project the uses of their expressions as we do ours. No translation manual would be possible, therefore; hence no Quinean indeterminacy could be generated by different forms of life.

The conclusion of this chapter is that if there is Quinean indeterminacy of translation at all, there is indeterminacy in the domestic case. So—for the purpose of the next chapter—if there is no Quinean indeterminacy in the domestic case, there is none at all.

Domestic Determinacy

It is time to look hard at what now seems to be the heart of the indeterminacy doctrine: the domestic indeterminacy thesis. I shall argue that it is false. First we need to take note of one of its implications.

11.1 What domestic indeterminacy would involve

The domestic version of Quine's thesis becomes reasonably clear when we notice that if there is a permissible rival to a standard manual for, say, English, then there is indeterminacy of translation between English and each of a range of close 'twins' of English, such as the Martian language to be described shortly. (A 'standard' manual for English is one which (a) includes the homophonic manual; (b) licenses only such statements of synonymy between non-identical sentences as would be acceptable to most mature English speakers.) Suppose for example that the Martians speak a language exactly like English except that each of their morphemes is the reverse of the English morpheme by which it is most naturally translatable. It fits the Quine-acceptable evidence—it is permissible—to translate their 'tibbar' by our 'rabbit', their 'elucelom' by 'molecule', and so on. Let the morpheme-to-morpheme correlation under which Martian and English are thus translatable be **m**, let **M** be the translation manual which uses **m**, and let **q** be a function which takes English sentences to English sentences for a perverse Quinean rival, **Q**, to the homophonic manual **H**. Then by applying first **m** to the sentences of Martian and then **q** to the result we get a composite function **q(m)** from Martian sentences to English ones. Similarly, by applying first the inverse of **q** and then the inverse of **m** we get a composite function from English sentences to Martian ones. Obviously, these two functions will serve as the basis for a perverse Martian-English translation manual **R**, which rivals the humdrum morpheme-to-morpheme manual **M** just as **Q** rivals the homophonic English manual **H**. Now, Martian is defined so that all the relevant facts about it—about behavioural dispositions, brain states, and whatever else Quine will accept as facts—are exactly like the relevant facts about English, except that each Martian morpheme is the reverse of its m-correlate. And the point I want to make now is that if **Q** is a permissible rival to **H** for translation or interpretation within English, then **R** is a permissible rival to **M** for translation between Martian and English.[1] (If this strikes you as obvious, skip the rest of this section.)

We know that the interest of Quine's thesis depends on its bearing on our ordinary unreconstructed notions of sameness of meaning, translation, 'use', etc. Now the interlinguistic version of the thesis, as I have explained it, bears on these notions in a fairly clear and straightforward way. It claims that if considerations of practicality and plausibility are ignored, then that totality of facts which permits us to say that the speakers of a foreign language use their sentence X as we use our sentence Y (or mean by X what we mean by Y) will in some cases also permit it to be said that they use X as we use Z, and not as we use Y. (See 3.13.) However, Quine describes this interlinguistic thesis as just a way of putting the same point as is put by the intralinguistic thesis (see 10.1). Whatever else this characterization may imply, it must surely imply that there is no essential difference between the sort of conditions that must be met by the statement that other English speakers mean by S what I mean by T, and the sort of conditions that must be met by the statement that all Martian speakers—including myself, if I speak Martian—mean by their sentence S' what English speakers mean by T. To explain. When testing the Martian-English manual **R**, we have to consider whether the behaviour, dispositions, and other relevant facts about Martian speakers and English speakers are compatible with our saying that Martian speakers use S' as English speakers use T. If, but only if, the totality of Quine-acceptable facts is compatible with that and other statements licensed by **R**, then **R** is permissible. And the present point is that the intralinguistic thesis will have a relevant bearing on our ordinary notions of meaning etc. only if rivals to homophonic translation such as **Q** have to pass an essentially similar test. This

---

[1] The case of Martian and English is not so science-fictional as it might seem. There are mutually unintelligible dialects of Chinese which share the same syntax, and we noticed earlier that much the same holds for Japanese and Korean. Here is another example: 'In central India speakers switch from the Indo-Aryan Marathi to the Dravidian Kannada by a simple process of morph for morph substitution. In effect they control one grammar with two lexica.'—J. Gumperz, in Kelly (ed.), 1969, p. 246.

means that the intralinguistic thesis requires us to treat other English speakers who use (what are objectively) English sentences just as if they were foreigners using non-English sentences. Evidently this task would have been easier if they had spoken English with a distinctive accent; and it would have been superfluous if they had mangled their morphemes more drastically (as we can imagine the Martians have actually done). The point is that such differences in the sentences involved cannot affect the nature of the task itself. If this is correct, other English speakers may permissibly be said to use X as we use Y only if Martian speakers may permissibly be said to use the m-correlate of X as English speakers use Y. In other words, if Q is permissible (fits the facts), so is R. Notice that this point holds no matter what complicated assumptions about the translation of English sentences may have been required in order to accommodate Q to the facts: if Q is permissible, corresponding adjustments will automatically ensure that R is permissible too.

There will be domestic indeterminacy of translation for English, then, only if there is indeterminacy of translation between English and Martian, when this latter sort of indeterminacy has exactly the same form as what is claimed to hold for interlinguistic cases generally. I shall argue that this sort of indeterminacy cannot exist.

11.2 Strategy

The argument exploits the fact that a child can be regarded as acquiring a language by a succession of short steps, for example, acquisition of particular recognizable words or one-word sentences, 'Bird', 'Dog'; acquisition of a given construction, the 'Where?' construction as in 'Where dog?'; acquisition of a given preposition or cluster of prepositions: 'To water', 'Down stairs'. I need to show two things. First, that if we take a point early in a child's acquisition of, say, English, and exactly the same point in a child's acquisition of the Martian language imagined in the last section, then we see that there can be no Quinean indeterminacy of translation between these two languages at this early stage. Second, I have to show that if there is no indeterminacy in translating between an initially acquired fragment of English and the exactly corresponding initially acquired fragment of Martian, then there is none at the immediately following step either. It will then follow, as in mathematical induction, that there is no indeterminacy

of translation at all between Martian and English. Since there can
be no reason to suppose that what holds for English does not hold
for other natural languages, I take this conclusion, together with
that of the last section, to be enough to show that Quine's domestic
thesis is quite generally false.

In the next section I shall explain and defend the assumption
that a child can be regarded as acquiring a language by a succession
of steps of the sort this argument presupposes. (Bear in mind that
much of what seems obvious to opponents of the indeterminacy
thesis is likely to be contested by its defenders.) Then I shall try
to show that there can be no indeterminacy at a very early stage in
the child's acquisition of English; and finally that if there is no
indeterminacy between an arbitrary initial fragment of English and
the corresponding fragment of Martian, there is none at the next
step, whatever that might be.

11.3 Steps in language acquisition

The main idea is a modification of the simple thought that we
acquire our natural languages by a series of short steps or stages.
Parents often describe these steps as the acquisition of 'words';
and developmental psychologists are ready to count the number of
words in different syntactic categories that children of different
ages typically have. Of course it is too simple to think of the
acquisition of a language as just the acquisition of one word after
another. For one thing, new syntax is acquired as well as words.
For another, words sometimes come in clusters. There is a time
when one cannot be said to have grasped any member of a certain
cluster; there is a later time when one can be said to have grasped
every member of the cluster; but there is no intervening point at
which one can be said to have grasped just one or two members
but not the rest. (The first cluster of colour words is an example.)

For the purposes of the present argument I shall nevertheless
make two simplifications. First, I shall ignore the acquisition of
syntax, since we have seen that syntax cannot be supposed to make
an independent contribution to Quinean indeterminacy of sentence
translation (chapter 7). Second, I shall pretend that every step in
the acquisition of English beyond the basic stage to be described
in the following section is a matter of acquiring an atomic *predicate*,
or a cluster of atomic predicates none of which can be acquired
independently of the rest. Once the application of the argument to

predicates has been grasped, I think its extension to other types of expression (e.g. proper names) will be seen to be unproblematic. Any serious objections to my argument are likely to be objections to its whole conception, I expect, not to the details.

I assume, then, that for the purpose of this argument any given natural language can be regarded as capable of being acquired by means of a succession of minimally short steps, each step beyond a certain elementary basis consisting of the acquisition of one further atomic predicate or predicate cluster. The steps are minimal in the sense that the increment constituted by a given step cannot be regarded as consisting in its turn of the successive acquisition of semantically relevant increments. But some comments are needed.

First, the assumption does not imply that there is an objectively unique sequence of such steps. All it requires is that, for at least one case of acquiring the language in question, the facts allow an analysis into minimally short steps—not necessarily a unique analysis. For, second, neither this assumption nor the argument as a whole requires the language to be capable of acquisition *only* via a sequence of short steps. (There might be language pills: you take a Chinese language pill today, say, and tomorrow you speak Chinese as well as anyone who has acquired it by traditional methods.) All the argument requires is that it be *possible* for a person to acquire a given natural language by such steps. Next, the assumption does not imply—what is obviously false—that for any given language there is only one possible order in which its components can be acquired. It is not assumed that, e.g. 'Cat' must be acquired before 'Dog', or 'category' before 'endogenous'. The argument will be conducted in terms of an arbitrarily chosen learner of English and a parallel learner of Martian. It does not presuppose any particular ordering of the steps by which the learner acquires English. Finally, the assumption does not beg the question against Quine's holism by presupposing that once a given predicate has been acquired in the relevant sense, the person's use of that predicate is somehow fixed once for all. The assumption requires only that we can sensibly speak of a child as knowing or having acquired a certain fragment of English at a given time, and as enlarging that grasp of English by noticeable stages. It *is* assumed that the question whether the child counts as having acquired a given predicate is decidable; and certainly that assumption involves some idealization. But it is not further assumed that there is no scope for improving on one's grasp of a given predicate.

I shall deal later with other possible worries about the assumption.

11.4 A determinately translatable base

In this section I shall try to show that there is a stage fairly early on in the child's acquisition of English where there can be no indeterminacy of translation between it and the language spoken by a child who has reached an exactly corresponding stage in the acquisition of Martian. Three considerations are decisive: the translating language matches the translated language point for point (11.1); the use of words (or their childish approximations) is subject to public checking; observation sentences have to be translated by stimulus synonymous observation sentences if such translations are available (as of course they are in this case)(3.9).

Emma is starting to speak English; Marcia is starting to speak Martian (viz. the Martian language imagined in section 11.1). There is a one-to-one correlation between the sound patterns they respectively produce so that all the dispositions and other linguistically relevant facts about Emma are transformed into the linguistically relevant facts about Marcia by simply substituting Marcia's sound-patterns for Emma's under the correlation, and using the morpheme-for-morpheme correlation m for making any necessary substitutions in the verbal contributions of mature English speakers. To illustrate these points we can suppose the correlation includes the following:

Emma	Marcia
Bird	Drib
Cat	Tac
Big	Gib
Where?	Erehw?

Then any Quine-acceptable characterization of the circumstances in which Emma is disposed to utter 'Bird' is also a characterization of the circumstances in which Marcia is disposed to utter 'Drib'; whatever holds for the circumstances in which Emma is disposed to utter 'Where cat?', and for the circumstances in which she is disposed not to utter it, holds also, *mutatis mutandis*, for the circumstances in which Marcia is disposed to utter, and, respectively, not to utter, 'Erehw tac?'; and so on.

Now it would obviously be question-begging to move without further argument from this statement of the (Quine-acceptable) facts to the conclusion that translation between Emma's fragment of English and Marcia's fragment of Martian is determinate. However, I do not think much further argument is needed for the special case of Emma and Marcia. The reason is that, even if we suppose they each have an active vocabulary of the order of 200 basic expressions—such as two year old children can have—their utterances are too simple, and too closely keyed to publicly checkable circumstances, to leave room for the sorts of compensating adjustments that would be required for the construction, within these rather limited language fragments, of permissible rivals to the ultra-simple morph-for-morph manual that gives such perfect results here.

I expect Quineans would concede this point without argument. Many of the expressions in question could serve as one-word observation sentences ('Ball', 'Bed', 'Bird', 'Boat', etc.); and the matching up of stimulus meanings will guarantee that there is no room for conflicting versions. For Emma and Marcia's dispositions match exactly, and we are concerned only with translation between Emma and Marcia's languages, not between one of them and some adult language. However, I had better give some argument for a similar conclusion for their other utterances. First let me say a little more about what those utterances are.

Emma has about 150 nouns ('ant', 'apple', 'ball', 'bed', . . .) all of which can be used as one-word observation sentences, but which also combine in simple constructions with expressions of other categories to make indefinitely many other sentences. There are half a dozen adjectives: 'big', 'dirty', 'nice', ... Three or four prepositions: 'in', 'to', 'down', some also serving as adverbs. A handful of proper names. Four or five number words. Ten or so verbs, some of them, e.g. 'Look', 'Read', also serving as imperatives. A demonstrative pronoun 'this'. The interrogative adverb 'Where?' The sentence and noun phrase conjunction 'and'. The negative 'not', which can be prefixed to most other expressions. And there are some other devices for forming sentences: simple concatenation, as in 'Dog big', 'Nice: go down seaside'; an expression 'Ere-e-is' (from 'There it is') followed by a noun phrase and translatable as 'There's . . . '; an expression 'S' (for 'It's'), as in 'S hot' ('It's hot'); and 'Adopti' (from 'I've dropped it'), followed by a noun phrase, as in 'Adopti book'.[2]

It does not take much study of this (modified) fragment of English to see that most, though certainly not all, of its declarative sentences are highly observational, and that its non-declarative sentences are also intimately linked to publicly checkable types of circumstance. We have already noted that Emma's one-word observation sentences ('Dog', 'Duck', 'Cow', etc.) will be determinately translatable into Marcia's parallel Martian. Clearly the same will be true for most of her composite declarative sentences too. Consider a few samples: (1) 'Boat wet', (2) 'Ere-e-is, bird', (3) 'Adopti book', (4) 'S hot'. As actually used, all these sentences deal with the here and now in ways which preclude their being admissibly rendered by any of Marcia's sentences other than their respective correlates under the morpheme-to-morpheme correlation m. The stimulus meanings of Emma's (1)—(4) are (a) richly informative, and (b) exactly match those of Marcia's counterparts under m, while no other sentences share the same stimulus meanings. As Quine says in connection with colour words, ' "Red" is a good translation to the extent that it resembles the native sentence umbra for umbra and penumbra for penumbra' (*WO*, p. 41). In the cases in question, umbras and penumbras coincide precisely when Emma's sentences are matched with their counterparts under m in Marcia's language, but not when they are matched with sentences of Marcia's language that we should not ordinarily count as equivalent to those counterparts. Nor, of course, is there any question of Marcia's having some phrase parallel to 'undetached bunny part' to set against Emma's 'bunny'.

The only possible exceptions to this conclusion (for Emma's declarative sentences) are those sentences which contain 'gone', 'nice', 'and' or 'not'. Emma's 'Bunny gone' is certainly often used when a rabbit disappears from sight, in which use it is highly observational, and determinately translated by Marcia's 'Ynnub nog'. It is also highly observational when produced on sight of an empty rabbit hutch. However, such a sentence can be produced quite out of the blue, when it might naturally be taken to express the child's recollection that some particular rabbit(s) has (have) been absent for some time. The question is whether this reflective

---

[2] This specification is consistent with what is reported by linguists and psychologists, except that 'and' and 'not' might not always be present so early.

use of the sentence—as a standing sentence—offers any scope for it to be translated in a way that would be rejected by a translator using the morpheme-to-morpheme manual.

In fact it does not. Consider the child's (second-order) dispositions to *lose* the disposition to utter 'Bunny gone' in this reflective way. She is disposed to lose it in just those circumstances in which she is disposed to utter (or assent to) 'Bunny'. (Some obvious qualifications are needed here to take care of rabbit-pictures, models, etc.) By our assumptions this second-order disposition of Emma's is matched by an exactly corresponding disposition of Marcia's. And since no sentence that we should not ordinarily count as equivalent is similarly linked up with exactly this second-order disposition, it follows that none of Marcia's sentences could serve as a rival to 'Ynnub nog' as a rendering of Emma's 'Bunny gone'—even though the latter is not purely or straightforwardly observational.

Since 'nice' is strongly evaluative, those of Emma's sentences which include the word will not generally be straightforwardly observational either. However, just because the word makes that sort of evaluative contribution to sentences, Marcia's language offers no scope for devising perverse non-standard renderings of sentences containing it.

As for Emma's use of 'not' and 'and', these can be dealt with on the lines proposed by Quine himself in *Word and Object* pp. 57–61 (see 2.2). His points apply to the present case in a specially clear-cut fashion, since Marcia's vocabulary affords no serious alternatives to the straightforward scheme of taking 'ton' to do the work of Emma's 'not', and 'dna' to do the work of 'and'.

So much for declarative sentences. The non-declarative sentences can be dealt with even more straightforwardly. We have just imperatives ('Look', 'Read', 'Push', etc.) and interrogatives introduced by 'Where?'. Clearly the relevant first-and second-order dispositions will leave no room for indeterminacy in translating any of these sentences between Emma's English and Marcia's Martian.

I conclude that translation generally between these two languages is not subject to Quinean indeterminacy.[3] This conclusion

---

[3] David Cooper (1975) argues that there is what he calls indeterminacy of translation for a child's fragment of English. However, I am not contradicting the thesis he actually maintains, which is that the indeterminacy holds between the child's English and *adult*

is entirely consistent with what Quine himself has said. His view seems to be that the scope for indeterminacy increases with the level of *theoreticity* of the sentences involved. (More on this below. See also 1.8.) However, in the following sections I shall argue that if translation between English and Martian is determinate at any given stage, it will be so after the next step has been taken, whatever that step may be.

11.5 Carrying determinacy upwards (I): a special class of cases

To bring out the main idea of this part of the argument I start with cases where the parallel acquisition of English and Martian has reached a rather more advanced stage than the one discussed in the last section. These are cases where the English speaker understands expressions of the following forms: 'We say "——" when . . .' (or 'in these circumstances'), and 'The new predicate applies to ——'. The argument is given in steps A1–A6 below.

> A1. Let E_n and M_n be any pair of parallel initially acquired stages of English and Martian respectively reached by Emma and Marcia, such that E_n includes expressions of the forms just mentioned; and assume that all translation of whole sentences between E_n and M_n is determinate under a translation manual T (i.e. T is uniquely permissible)
>
> A2. Let the next step in Emma's acquisition of English, the step which takes her from E_n to E_{n+1}, be acquisition of the atomic predicate P (or of the inseparable cluster of predicates $P_1, \ldots, P_k$). Note that it follows immediately from the definition of 'step' in section 11.3 that any E_n speaker will be capable of being *somehow* brought to grasp how these new predicates are used.
>
> A3. Now since E_{n+1} is by definition a relatively slight extension of E_n itself, there can be no a priori reason why Emma should not hit on precisely that extension all by herself, without outside help. It is after all the sort of thing people have done before.
>
> A4. Moreover, thanks to the idioms she is assumed to possess

English. According to me this illustrates not Quinean indeterminacy of translation but common or garden indeterminacy of sense: thesis XI. Incidentally, the example of Emma's English and Marcia's Martian illustrates some of the differences between the translator's task and that of the Davidsonian meaning theorist. Notably, as translators we need not use these childish languages, nor even translate them into our own—even if that were possible.

(see A1 above) she could *explain* her use of $P_1, \ldots P_k$ to other E_n speakers entirely by means of E_n, supplemented, where necessary, by practical demonstrations. At any rate, given what we noted at A2, we can legitimately assume that this is possible. The crucial point here is that she would not have to use the new predicates in her explanations because she could always replace any sentence in which they occurred by a sentence in which they were merely mentioned.

A couple of examples will help to illustrate the main points in the argument so far. Suppose that for some reason E_n included no colour words, and no general word 'colour'. I expect it will be granted that it is theoretically possible that Emma should arrive independently at a modest vocabulary of colour terms, say 'black', 'white', 'red', 'green'. (We can assume for simplicity's sake that 'red' covers every hue that mature English speakers would include in the region from maroon to orange, while 'green' covers the rest—leaving out black and white.) Such a colour vocabulary is a straightforward example of 'inseparable' predicates in the relevant sense. So let us suppose the acquisition of these predicates is the step which takes a speaker of E_n to E_{n+1}. Now it is easy to imagine ways in which Emma could teach these predicates to other E_n users without herself actually having to use any of them. She could do so by such expedients as saying: 'I'm going to teach you some new words: "black", "white", "red", "green". I use "red" for all these things [pointing] and for anything like them; but not for any of these things [pointing]. To these I apply "green". . . . Does "red" apply to this? . . . This? . . . ' And so on.

Another example. Emma is ignorant of modern science, but has nevertheless been theorizing about the composition of things, and has hit upon a version of Democritus' atomic theory. What extends E_n to E_{n+1} is the new predicate 'atom'. To convey a grasp of this new predicate, Emma simply states the theory in E_n, perhaps as follows: 'Sticks and stones and all other solid objects are made up of tiny subvisible things of different shapes and sizes. Change and decay, and the different properties of things, are explained by the way these tiny things can be combined and disconnected. In very dense objects the shapes of these tiny things enable them to lock together very tightly. In liquids they are smoother. The little things have always existed and cannot be destroyed.' Given the sort of grasp of the theory that can be conveyed in such terms—presumably a perfect grasp—the transition from E_n to E_{n+1} is made by means of the bald announcement: 'The word for these tiny things is "atom"'. So much for step A4.

A5. Now for the crucial step. By A1 all Emma's explanations in E_n of the new predicates that extend E_n to E_{n+1} are determinately translatable into Martian M_n. So if nevertheless the step from E_n to E_{n+1}, and the exactly parallel step from M_n to M_{n+1}, were to introduce some indeterminacy of translation between E_{n+1} and M_{n+1}, then that indeterminacy would be introduced by the simple transition from mentioning the new predicates to using them—or even, as in the 'atom' example, by learning the linguistic form of the new word, the mere pattern of sounds or marks.

A6. However, such information must be counted as semantically irrelevant: it cannot affect the permissibility or impermissibility of a translation manual. To assume otherwise would be to endorse some kind of magical view of meaning. And this means that if the standard translation manual T_n for E_n and M_n is uniquely permissible, so is its successor, T_{n+1}, for E_{n+1} and M_{n+1}.

This point is particularly obvious in the 'atom' case. By A1, the atomic theory itself (minus the *word* 'atom') is determinately translatable: any manual for Emma's English and Marcia's Martian must be compatible with the standard manual T_n's renderings of the sentences of that theory, and also with T_n's rendering of the decisive sentence 'The word for these tiny things is "atom"'. Suppose, then, that some non-standard manual Q_{n+1} for E_{n+1} and M_{n+1} were to reject T_n's rendering of one of the new sentences. Q_{n+1} would have to accept T_{n+1}'s rendering of every sentence of the theory which contained a phrase like 'these tiny things' instead of 'atoms', and it would have to accept T_{n+1}'s rendering of 'The word for these tiny things is "atom"'; but it would have to reject T_{n+1}'s rendering of just such a sentence where 'atom' was substituted for 'these tiny things'. For example, if Q_{n+1} rejected T_{n+1}'s rendering of (1) 'Atoms are indestructible', it would still have to accept T_{n+1}'s rendering of both (2) 'These tiny things are indestructible' and (3) 'The word for these tiny things is "atom"'. Here it is particularly clear that the mere introduction of 'atom' as a substitute for 'these tiny things' cannot possibly have made room for an indeterminacy that had hitherto been excluded. If T_n is uniquely permissible in this case, so too is T_{n+1}. (And remember, the resources of the translating language exactly match those of the translated language. The only additional resource that M_{n+1} has over M_n is 'mota', the Martian counterpart of 'atom'.)

11.6 Carrying determinacy upwards (II): generalizing

We can hardly assume that at every stage after the basic one discussed in section 11.3 speakers of E_n will have at their command expressions like ' "——— " applies to . . . ', or 'The new word for the things I have been describing is "——— " '. However, if the argument of the last section is sound, determinacy of translation at any early stage in the acquisition of English and Martian will automatically extend to the next stage.

The reason is simple. There can be no essential difference between the kinds of addition to the language that we have just been discussing—'atom' and colour words—and the kinds of addition that are possible when the languages include semantic expressions of the sorts in question. For obviously there is no reason why colour words or 'atom' should not have been introduced *before* the languages included that simple semantic vocabulary. Nor could the determinacy or indeterminacy of translation of sentences including colour words or 'atom' depend on whether or not those words happened to have been introduced with the aid of semantic words. For the question whether translation between a given pair of languages is subject to the indeterminacy is to be settled by the actual character of those languages at whatever stage they may have arrived, regardless of the route by which that stage was reached. Two people can both count as speakers of English (or of some early fragment of English) even if one has learnt 'atom' via the semantic vocabulary and the other has not. (Cf. *WO*, p. 27.) Really the sort of semantic vocabulary that was exploited in the argument of the last section is just a convenient means for achieving results that could be achieved—though perhaps less conveniently—by sticking to the material mode. If follows that we can generalize the conclusion of the last section and conclude now that if translation between parallel initially acquired fragments of English and Martian is determinate at any stage, it is determinate at the next stage too.

There is one sort of difference between later and earlier stages in the acquisition of a language which has seemed relevant to the question of indeterminacy. That is the degree of theoreticity of the terms or sentences involved. Quine's idea seems to have been that the scope for indeterminacy increases as the level of theoreticity goes up, and what is said is less and less directly linked to the here and now. (See *WO*, pp. 76 f., EN, p. 89, RIT, *RR*, pp. 35 ff., ESW, p. 314. On levels of theoreticity, see 1970b.) The argument of the last section, if sound, provides a further reason for supposing that that was a mistake. It shows that there is no necessary connection between the extent to which a speaker's *theory* is underdetermined by the evidence for it, and the extent to which *translation* of that theory is subject to the indeterminacy. (See also chapter 6.)

That completes the argument.

11.7 Objections and replies

It would be tedious to try to anticipate all possible objections. I will deal with the six which look the most threatening.

Objection 1: 'You seem to have forgotten Kripke's sceptic, who will challenge even the first stage of your argument—even the claim that Marcia's "Ynnub nog" is translatable only by Emma's "Bunny gone".'

Reply 1: My reply is implicit in what I said in the earlier discussion of Kripke's sceptic and the indeterminacy thesis. I think the appeal to the sceptic in this discussion is either beside the point or question-begging.

Kripke's sceptic is introduced as an exploiter of the gulf between finite historical data—for example, actual utterances in context or occurrences of thoughts—and the potential infinities of interpretations consistent with those data. 'The sceptic argues that when I answered "125" to the problem "68 + 57", my answer was an unjustified leap in the dark; my past mental history is equally compatible with the hypothesis that I meant quus, and therefore should have said "5"' (Kripke, 1982, p. 15). Indisputably that particular gulf exists; but since it has nothing to do with the indeterminacy thesis (1.1) the sceptic in that guise is no threat to my argument. Translation manuals have to take account not only of actual historical events, but of the totality of behavioural dispositions.

Now of course Kripke applies the sceptic's ideas to dispositions too. But it is noteworthy that when he does so, all the weight of his argument is on the points (noted in 1.11) that my dispositions will not justify my present response (e.g. to the query about '68 + 57'), nor tell me what I ought to do in each new instance, nor supply an analysis of what it is to mean, for example, addition by 'plus'. And, as I remarked in the earlier discussion, it seems quite possible to agree with Kripke over these points without also conceding that the totality of dispositions leaves room for significant conflict over sentence translation. No doubt my merely being disposed to produce what is in fact the sum when I am asked to apply the operation indicated by ' + ' to two numbers does not justify the claim that I mean addition by ' + ', nor does it supply an analysis of my meaning addition by ' + '. But that is beside the point if the question is whether the totality of people's behavioural dispositions permits rivals to a standard translation manual. So far as I can see, Kripke's arguments are not intended to support an affirmative response to this question, nor do they do so. (I argued in 1.11 that his claim that dispositions are finite gives no support to the indeterminacy doctrine.)

It matters that we have to take account of the *totality* of dispositions. A person's dispositions form a complex system which includes dispositions to acquire and lose lower-order dispositions, and to correct or revise the productions of other dispositions (see Appendix B). And of course, when considering the permissibility of translation manuals the system must be taken into account holistically (3.7). These points provided reinforcement when I argued in section 11.4 that no permissible manual for Emma and Marcia's initial languages could conflict with the standard manual's rendering of 'Ynnub nog' by 'Bunny gone'. A further illustration may help. Suppose it were suggested that, gruesomely, Marcia's 'Ynnub nog' could be translated by 'Bunny gone' only in Nottingham (or only on Tuesdays, or only until midnight tonight) and otherwise by 'Duck gone'. Since by definition the two children's dispositions at all levels are relevantly in agreement, and neither of them is disposed to treat the sentences in question differently at different places (days, times) the Quine-acceptable facts rule out the perverse translation (cf. 8.1).

I conclude that gesturing towards Kripke's sceptic does not amount to an objection to my argument.

Objection 2: 'In defending your claim that there is no indeterminacy of translation between Emma's initial segment of English and Marcia's corresponding segment of Martian (section 11.4) you argue that no sentence translations which rivalled the standard ones would fit the Quine-acceptable facts, and you have just been backing up that contention. But you have overlooked the possibility that a non-standard manual's conflict with the standard manual might consist solely in its declaring some of Marcia's sentences *untranslatable* into Emma's English. Marcia's meanings might be represented in such a way that for certain sentences of her language there was just no equivalent in Emma's language—though it might be claimed that Emma could later acquire the verbal resources to construct suitable equivalents.'

Reply 2: That sort of conflict could exist only if there were also conflict over the translation of sentences actually belonging to Emma and Marcia's languages. Suppose the non-standard translator went the whole hog and maintained that no sentence of either language was translatable into the other. The implication would be that these children's use of words differed to such an extent that each lacked any means of doing with her sentences what the other could do with hers. But that claim conflicts with the Quine-acceptable facts: it would be quickly refuted by producing the standard manual. So if some translation manual has that implication, it is not permissible for that reason. Any permissible non-standard manual, therefore, would have to allow that at least some of Marcia's sentences were translatable by Emma's. However, and for a similar reason, no permissible non-standard manual could agree with the standard manual in all its actual translations, while confining its eccentricity to the bald claim that each of the sentences it did not translate was untranslatable into the other language. For of course these untranslated sentences would also be translatable consistently with the rest of the standard manual. It follows that any permissible non-standard manual would have to conflict with the standard one in its actual translations of sentences. But the present objection does not touch my argument that the facts would rule out the possibility of such conflict.

Objection 3: 'You've ignored the possibility that if Quine is right there will be many different ways of speaking both English and Martian—as many as there are permissible Quinean permutations of the set of sentences of each language. So even if you've shown that some Quinean rivals to a standard translation manual will not be permissible, you haven't shown that all permissible rivals are ruled out.'

Reply 3: This is just a mistake. All the argument requires is that Emma and Marcia be permissibly counted as speaking their respective languages at the stage in question. In one sense it is a platitude that there will be indefinitely many different ways of speaking each language. For there are indefinitely many different patterns of propositional attitudes that might be possessed by people who all spoke the same language; and each pattern would show up in different complex systems of verbal dispositions. But the argument is unaffected by the existence of this variety of ways of speaking a language because all the argument requires is that the people to whom a translation manual applies speak their language in *some* (unspecified) way. No constraints are imposed on the manner of speaking it.

A thought lurking behind this objection had better be made explicit. It is that if Quine is right there are what might be called 'straight' and 'devious' ways of speaking any language. The 'straight' way of speaking L corresponds to the homophonic manual for L: for each sentence X of L, you utter X if and only if you (or perhaps a 'standard' speaker of L) are (or would normally be?) disposed to utter X. But for each permissible Quinean permutation q for L there is (according to this way of thinking) a devious way of speaking L. Where $q(X) = Y$, speaking L deviously consists in uttering Y when a straight speaker of L would have uttered X. However, once this thought has been brought into the open it can be seen to be misconceived. For could it be a question of Quine-acceptable fact whether a particular person spoke L straight or deviously? If it were, then for straight speakers of L to apply q to devious speakers of L would be objectively justifiable in a way that it would not be justifiable for them to apply q to one another. But of course that is not Quine's idea at all. His point is that we could apply q indifferently to *any* other speaker of our language. The presence of any relevant differences in the facts would triv-ialize his thesis. So the alleged distinction between straight and devious ways of speaking L cannot be supposed to be a matter of fact. At best it will be a matter of interpretation (as Davidson has pointed out, 1979, p. 17). And that reinforces the points made in the last paragraph. For if there is no factual difference between straight and devious *L* speaking, the argument cannot depend on how the language in question is spoken.

Objection 4: 'Your argument works as far as it goes. But really it's just a long-winded restatement of a point made by Putnam, that *from within* the language there's no problem about what the words refer to or mean. As he says,

A sign that is actually employed in a particular way by a particular community of users can correspond to particular objects *within the conceptual scheme of those users.* 'Objects' do not exist independently of conceptual schemes. *We* cut up the world into objects when we introduce one or another scheme of description. Since the objects *and* the signs are alike *internal* to the scheme of description, it is possible to say what matches what. (*Reason, Truth and History*, p.52.)

But you have completely failed to show that there's no room for indeterminacy when the linguists doing the translating are not *themselves* within our conceptual scheme. Nothing in your argument proves that linguists from Alpha Centauri would have to accept the standard manual for English and Martian.'

Reply 4: First, I think Putnam in the passage you quote allows internalists an entirely unearned benefit. How could they reply to the following challenge from a Quinean sceptic? 'It's only a *theory* of yours that "rabbit" refers to rabbits. All your behavioural dispositions, and indeed all the physical truths you accept, are compatible with your word "rabbit" referring to something quite different. So it's not a matter of fact that your word refers to rabbits. You're not much better placed to say what it refers to than your extreme metaphysical realist opponents.' They might reply that what they understand by reference is summed up in statements like ' "Rabbit" refers to rabbits'. Putnam again: 'For me there is little to say about what reference is within a conceptual system other than these tautologies' (loc. cit.). But this reply leaves it obscure what constitutes being in the same conceptual system. Do the French share our conceptual system? If so, is it supposed to be a tautology that their word 'lapin' refers to rabbits? If not, how could we have become so confused that we nevertheless continue to insist that their word *does* refer to rabbits? There seems to be substantially more to be said about reference than Putnam's tautologies, so I don't think my argument is just an elaboration of the points he makes.

But let's look at the objection itself. What about these Alpha

Centauran linguists? Here as on earlier occasions they are no help to exponents of the indeterminacy thesis: to attack that thesis is not to endorse what Putnam calls metaphysical realism. Recall that a translation manual is permissible if and only if it is acceptable to a competent linguist who can speak both languages but deliberately disregards considerations of simplicity and practical convenience (3.3, 3.6). So if the Alpha Centaurans cannot speak English and Martian they are irrelevant. But if they can, these exotic creatures might just as well be ordinarily eccentric human linguists, with odd ideas about simplicity and manageability. Since my argument makes no assumptions whatever about the simplicity or manageability of translation manuals, the objection fails.

—'But they might have peculiar ideas about the meaning of "means the same"!' In that case what could justify describing their ideas as ideas about sameness of meaning? What sense does it make to suggest there might be a different concept of *that*? Only, presumably, some analogy that we could accept as such. But mere analogy isn't enough, for reasons I emphasized in chapter 3. It's got to be our untutored notion of sameness of meaning, otherwise we're no longer talking about the indeterminacy thesis (3.3, 3.6). Still the objection fails.

Objection 5: 'You have used the assumption that if translation between E_n and M_{n+1} is determinate, then when these languages are extended to E_{n+1} and M_{n+1}, translation of the 'old' sentences, the sentences that are also sentences of E_n and M_{n+1}, will remain determinate. (See step A5 in 11.5.) But you have not justified this assumption. Admittedly it is plausible. But it overlooks the possibility that in spite of the fact that the *sentences* of E_n are all retained in E_{n+1}, the addition of whatever new predicates are required for E_{n+1} has an effect on the permissibility of synonymy statements about those 'old' sentences when they are regarded as belonging to E_{n+1}. In other words you have begged the question against Quine on a central issue: holism. On the holistic approach, adding new predicates to a language is not at all like, say, putting more books on the shelf alongside the ones already there, while leaving these untouched. It's more like fixing an additional strut to a bridge or adding another herb to a stew: the relationships and functions of other components of the system are going to be modified. If Quine's holism is correct, your argument is at best incomplete.'

Reply 5: This objection has already been met, though implicitly. There are two decisive considerations. First, the 'steps' which the argument exploits are minimal ones (as explained in section 11.3). At each step the learner's grasp of the language is extended by an increment whose acquisition cannot itself be regarded as the successive acquisition of smaller, semantically relevant increments. Second, Emma and Marcia acquire their respective languages by exactly parallel steps, so that any realignments of the predicates of E_n which may be occasioned by Emma's acquiring the new predicates which take her to E_{n+1} are matched by exactly corresponding realignments of the predicates of M_n, caused by Marcia's acquisition of M_{n+1}. Obviously this parallelism ensures that the standard manual T_{n+1} for E_{n+1} and M_{n+1} is an *extension* of T_n, the manual for E_n and M_n. It also ensures that the present objection fails.

Suppose Q is a rival to T_{n+1}: a manual for E_{n+1} and M_{n+1} which rejects at least one of T_{n+1}'s translations or statements of equivalence; and assume, as in the argument, that T_n is uniquely permissible. In order for the present objection to apply, the conflict between Q and T_{n+1} must not be confined to their renderings of 'new' sentences—ones which do not belong to either E_n or M_n. For the objection is that the transition from E_n (M_n) to E_{n+1} (M_{n+1}) involves changes in what may permissibly be said about the 'old' sentences. Without loss of generality, then, we can suppose that Q rejects T_{n+1}'s rendering of an 'old' sentence S of E_{n+1}. Now because T_n is assumed to be uniquely permissible,

(*i*) Q must be consistent with whatever T_n says about sameness of meaning among the sentences of E_n and M_n: it must treat as statements of fact whatever synonymy statements are licensed by T_n.

(*ii*) But since Q rejects T_{n+1}'s rendering of the 'old' sentence S *qua* sentence of E_{n+1}, Q must license the statement that S does not mean the same in E_n as it does in E_{n+1}.

(*iii*) Yet, since T_{n+1} is an extension of T_n, the same facts also permit it to be said that S in E_n does mean the same as S in E_{n+1}.

However, the character of the difference between E_n and E_{n+1} (M_n and M_{n+1}) ensures that (*i*) and (*iii*) rule out (*ii*). For I have already shown that, in view of the minimal increment represented by the new predicates, adequate explanations of those new predicates could be provided in the original language E_n, supplemented where necessary by practical demonstrations, statements of theories, etc. If that is correct, the transition to actual *use* of those predicates cannot make a semantically relevant difference: it cannot affect the permissibility of translation manuals. In particular it cannot make it permissible to say that S before the transition does not mean the same as S after the transition. So the objection fails.

Objection 6: 'You haven't allowed for the possibility that a succession of very slight variations in what schemes of translation were permissible at each stage in the acquisition of English and Martian might eventually allow room, for some n, for a permissible rival to T_{n+1}. Your argument forces a choice in favour of the standard manual at each stage. And indeed, if the variations in permissibility at any given stage are only slight, as is plausible, each choice seems inevitable. But someone could concede that those choices were forced while still insisting on the possibility of a rival to the standard manual for the complete languages English and Martian. The possibility would be silently accruing, so to speak, from those successive increments of looseness of fit that your argument ignores.'

Reply 6: The picture of an unnoticed build-up of looseness of fit may be seductive, but it's misconceived. True, if it was a mistake to assume that English can be acquired by a succession of small 'steps' my argument fails for that reason. The reader must judge if that assumption is justified (11.3). But given that assumption, the objection would work only if we could do exactly the same sort of thing for a *non*-standard rival to T as my argument does for T. For clearly, if a rival to T is permissible at all, there must be exactly the same possibility of building up this rival manual by successive increments as there is for the case of T itself. I believe my argument rules out this possibility because at each stage T_n supplies *exact* versions in M_n for the sentences of E_n, while no exact rival versions are permissible. Rough versions will also be available, of course. But T_n will be compatible with the statement that they *are* rough versions; so there will be no scope for building up from them to an outright permissible rival to T_n.[4]

---

[4] Another objection may be nagging the reader. Haven't I somehow begged the question by assuming that it even makes sense to speak of sentences meaning the same independently of some implicitly or explicitly specified translation manual? Recall Harman's words: 'one

11.8 Conclusion

I have argued that there is no Quinean indeterminacy of translation
in the domestic case. Since we saw in the last chapter that if that
is so, there is no Quinean indeterminacy at all, it follows that the
indeterminacy thesis is false. (And by the argument in section 5.9 it
also follows that reference is not subject to Quinean indeterminacy
either.)

Of course the argument does not yield an actual recipe for
constructing a uniquely correct translation manual for a given pair
of different languages, except for artificial cases like Martian and
English.[5] It only guarantees that if we have managed—by whatever
means—to devise a translation manual which fits all the possible
evidence, no manual inconsistent with it will also fit all the possible
evidence, assuming, as throughout, that both manuals are aiming
at 'literal' or 'cognitive' synonymy. Still, that is worth knowing. It
means that in the exact translation of sentences, at least, there is
something to be right or wrong about. So if my arguments are
sound, at least one common assumption about meaning and translation is vindicated. Clearly my arguments mesh in well with the
argument from structure discussed earlier. In effect they provide
the argument from structure with the solid foundations we saw it
lacked.

There are other common assumptions about meaning and translation which have not been vindicated, however, and other Quinean doctrines which remain untouched by my arguments—or so I
shall now try to show.

may speak of the "correct" translation of a single sentence only relative to some envisioned
general scheme of translation' (1969, p. 14). But this objection was anticipated and disposed
of in 3.12.

  [5] I am sceptical of the suggestion that such a recipe could be found, nor do I see why
we should think we need one. After all, we no longer look for such recipes for constructing
scientific theories. Cf. McGinn, 1977, pp. 534 f.

Part IV

Implications

12

Quineanism without Indeterminacy

In this chapter I consider the implications for Quine's other views of the falsity of the indeterminacy doctrine. If the arguments earlier in this book are sound, rejection of the indeterminacy doctrine is compatible with all the other central Quinean doctrines except for the strong indeterminacy of reference and its team-mate, onto-logical relativity.

12.1 Jettisoning the indeterminacy doctrine

In chapters 2 and 4 I argued that rejection of the indeterminacy was compatible with Quinean holism. In chapter 4 I argued that the thesis of the inextricability of semantic and factual knowledge did not entail, or even provide support for, the indeterminacy of translation, so that giving up the indeterminacy doctrine need not involve giving up the centrally important Quinean doctrine of inextricability. In chapter 5 we saw that, as Quine himself points out, weak indeterminacy of reference, as exemplified by the Jap-anese classifier case, is also entirely consistent with determinacy of sentence translation. True, strong indeterminacy of reference and ontological relativity do seem to entail indeterminacy of sentence translation; but these doctrines are so intimately linked with indeterminacy of sentence translation that it seems best to regard them as applications or extensions of the latter rather than as distinct doctrines.

In chapter 6 I argued that the thesis of the underdetermination of our theory of nature does not entail or even provide support for the indeterminacy thesis. Finally, since the whole discussion has been conducted in terms of the Quine-acceptable evidence or facts, it seems clear that determinacy of translation is compatible with Quinean naturalism and physicalism.

However, although naturalism, physicalism, inextricability, and the underdetermination of our theory of nature—those central pillars of Quineanism—are left undisturbed by the collapse of the indeterminacy thesis, you may think that giving up the indeter-

minacy doctrine must involve giving up the most distinctive component of Quine's contribution to the philosophy of language, his
semantic nihilism. You may also suspect that to accept determinacy
of translation must involve acceptance of a doctrine of analyticity,
which he has discredited on independent grounds. But are these
anxieties justified? First let us consider his rejection of the analytic-
synthetic distinction.[1]

12.2 *Quine's rejection of the analytic–synthetic distinction*

On occasions Quine has made it appear that he rejects the analytic-
synthetic distinction solely because of doubts about meaning and
synonymy. For example, in 'Two Dogmas' he dismisses the proposal to define analytically true sentences as those that could be
reduced to truths of logic by substitution of synonyms for synonyms on the ground that the notion of synonymy could not be
adequately clarified. So if, as may seem reasonable,[2] determinacy
of sentence translation brings with it determinacy of synonymy in
general, you might think we could override his objections to such
definitions of analyticity. (Given synonymy of whole sentences we
can define synonymy of other expressions, by saying, for example,
a word is synonymous with a word or phrase if substitution of
the one for the other in a sentence always yields a synonymous
sentence.)

However, he has always had other objections to analyticity,
arising from his holistic conception of language and meaningfulness. These considerations seem to tell against at least one
conception of analytic truths: that according to which they are true
by virtue of meaning alone. The two different sets of objections can
be paired off with two different accounts of analyticity. If you
follow Frege and define analytic truths as reducible to logical
truths by substitution of synonyms for synonyms, you may be
attacked by arguments against the objectivity of synonymy. If on
the other hand you favour the conception of analytic truths as true
by virtue of meaning, you may be attacked by arguments which
support a holistic view of language and meaning, and tend to
exclude the possibility that any sentence is true purely by virtue
of meaning. In the next two sections I shall discuss how the failure

---

[1] Hylton (1982) argues that rejection of the ASD need not involve acceptance of the
indeterminacy thesis. In the following sections I argue differently for an equivalent conclusion: rejection of the indeterminacy thesis need not involve acceptance of the ASD.

[2] But see sections 12.6–12.8.

of the indeterminacy thesis affects each of these approaches to analyticity.

12.3 Synonymy and the Fregean definition of analyticity

Suppose the synonymy of whole sentences and of sentence parts were admitted to be matters of fact. And suppose we then defined as analytic those truths that were reducible to logical truths by substitution of synonymys for synonyms. Even so, Quineans would not be forced to concede that we had managed to define a determinate class of sentences. For, as Quine has often insisted, there seems to be no uniquely correct way to define the set of logical truths.

Of course he is willing to admit that the notion of logical truth can be made clear enough for practical purposes. In most contexts where this notion is to be used there is likely to be agreement on which expressions can be counted as logical (e.g., 'not', 'and', 'all'). Agreement on a 'regimented' language is one way of doing this. And given that agreement, logical truth can be defined clearly enough, for example, as a truth which involves only logical expressions essentially, or perhaps as a sentence from which we get only truths when we substitute sentences for its simple sentences ('Truth by Convention', 1936, pp. 73 f., 1960, p. 103, 1970a, chapters 4, 7, 1979a, pp. 132 ff.). However, this is not to say the notion of logical truth is fully determinate; and in fact Quine has consistently urged that it is not. (Cf. 1936, especially secs. vii, ix; 1970a, p. 59: 'Our proposed abstract notion of logical truth depends not only on language but on how we grammaticize it'.) So Quineans who reject the indeterminacy of translation and go on to accept the determinacy of synonymy for both whole sentences and sentence parts are not thereby bound to accept that there is a determinate class of analytic truths.

There is a different but equally well paved route to the same conclusion. Quineans who still accept the radical contention of 'Two Dogmas' that logical laws are subject to revision will see no reason to think that even agreement over logical expressions or linguistic structure would commit them to the existence of a determinate class of logical truths. For they will not concede that such agreement entails agreement over logical principles. To be sure, this contention is at odds with some of Quine's own claims in *Philosophy of Logic* and certain earlier writings, claims which have prompted the charge of backsliding. But *pace* the Quine of chapter 6 of *Philosophy of Logic*, it still seems possible for Quineans to argue for deviant logics; and to the extent that they can do so, the main point of this section is reinforced: acceptance of the determinacy of synonymy need not commit Quineans to acceptance of a determinate analytic–synthetic distinction. (See section 12.5.)

12.4 *Synonymy, inextricability, and truth by meaning*

In chapter 4 I argued that there is no inconsistency in maintaining both that there are objective synonymy relations, and that there are no pure semantic facts. You can insist that synonymy relations hold in virtue of the ways expressions are used, and that the contributions which convention and factual knowledge make to the use of expressions cannot be disentangled. This will make it easier to see how Quineans who accept the determinacy of translation, and with it the possibility in principle of objective synonymy relations, can still reject the idea that any sentences are true by meaning alone—even if we ignore what was said in the last section.

To start with, let us consider the case of logical truths narrowly so called. It is often thought that there is some tension between Quine's readiness to accept that logical truth can be defined acceptably (e.g. in terms of 'structure') and his rejection of the idea of truth by meaning. For if logically true sentences can be *known* purely by knowing their structure, how can it be denied that they are *true* purely in virtue of their structure? Quine faces this challenge in chapter 7 of *Philosophy of Logic*. In that compendious chapter he urges that although knowing a language involves knowing the grammar, and although the logical truths are tied to the grammar and likely to be agreed on by all who know the language, it does not follow that 'it is language that makes logical truths true'. 'Perhaps the logical truths owe their truth to certain traits of reality which are reflected in one way by the grammar of our language, in another way by the grammar of another language, and in a third way by the combined grammar and lexicon of a third language' (op. cit., p. 95).[3] Moreover, he asserts, there does not seem to be any clear way of explaining 'true by virtue of' so that logical truths would come out as true purely by virtue of language, rather than by virtue of 'anything and everything'. There is no

---

[3] This seems to imply, interestingly, that there is a way in which an acceptable grammar of a language could be 'false'.

justification for the view that because logic and mathematics are impartially relevant to all sciences, all the evidence of the senses should be credited to the other sciences, while logic and mathematics are regarded as immune to revision. Rather, these sciences should be regarded as akin to 'the most general and systematic aspects of natural science, farthest from observation' (p. 100).

Now let us ignore what was said in the last section, and suppose the Fregean definition of 'analytic' to have been vindicated (still assuming determinacy of translation). Evidently a Quinean who accepted that definition of 'analytic' would still not be forced to accept that sentences that were analytic in that sense were also analytic in the sense of 'true by language alone'. If the logical truths themselves are not true by language alone, *a fortiori* the same goes for sentences reducible to logical truths by substitution of synonyms for synonyms. It seems that even an acceptable Fregean definition of analytic truth need not cause a Quinean much concern—though of course it would destroy some of the claims in 'Two Dogmas'. Still, I see no reason why Quineans should ignore the points made in the last section, and therefore no reason why even those of them who accept the determinacy of synonymy should feel compelled to accept the determinacy of the class of logical truths. The indeterminacy thesis is not really central to Quineanism: of far greater significance is the inextricability thesis. And I do not claim to have refuted that.

12.5 Translating logic

If there is no indeterminacy of translation at all, there is none in the translation of logic. So if Gavagese and English are inter-translatable, Gavagese classical logicians will be distinguishable from Gavagese intuitionists and other deviants. We shall generally be able to tell which is which by getting them to say which inferences they regard as valid, and why (but see below). In view of the conclusion of chapter 10—that general indeterminacy entails domestic indeterminacy—this outcome should be no more surprising than that English speaking classical logicians can be distinguished from English speaking intuitionists, quantum logicians, and others. However, some comments on this point are called for in view of Quine's occasional support for the idea that translators are bound to impose their own logic on those they are translating: 'fair translation preserves logical laws' (*WO*, p. 59).

First, and most obviously, the fact that some sorts of divergence over logical principles are amenable to determinate translation does not imply that for any sentence X that we understand in a certain way, we could make sense of someone's deliberately denying X understood in that way. I think I know why intuitionists reject the validity of the laws of excluded middle and double negation; and I have some idea of why quantum logicians propose to deny the validity of the distributive laws. So I see no problems over translating people whose logic deviates from our own in those ways. However, I have no conception at all of what someone might mean by denying the law of non-contradiction, and I am not at all clear how anyone could intelligibly be translated as doing so. So it does seem reasonable to assume that if the foreigners' language works atall, they will not be able to operate with logical laws which, if taken seriously, would undermine the whole function of words like 'not', 'and', 'or'. This leads us on to the next comment.

It is one thing to abandon the use of certain classically valid inferences; something else to introduce, as new rules of inference, ones which are actually invalid by classical standards. The former seems to raise no serious difficulties for translation; the latter may well do so. Quine's strictures look most plausible in connection with the latter. However, there is a further distinction to notice.

You might have a translation manual which represented certain foreign *theorists* as proposing what struck you as bizarre logical principles; but it does not follow that your manual must represent the entire foreign population as actually *operating* with such principles in their everyday use of the language. The former need not be problematic: those particular foreigners might be crazy or stupid. The latter is certainly problematic. However, can we really rule out such a possibility a priori? Recalling a distinction noticed earlier (3.5), we might find that in one sort of case the dispositions of the population that interested us permitted us to devise an alternative translation manual which did not ascribe bizarre logic to them. Given translation is determinate, I take it that no such manual could fit the facts better than the first. So we are left with the other sort of case: we cannot translate the foreigners *at all* unless we ascribe a bizarre logic to them. In such a case Quine's maxim that good translation preserves logical laws simply could not be applied except at the cost of saying that *no* manual could accurately render the foreigners' sentences into English. True, that might be the correct way to handle translation between that language *and English*. However, if such a language is a real possibility (a question I need not pursue) then so are a pair of such languages. Given such a pair, exact translation between them, especially if they are as close as Japanese and Korean are said to be, may be possible. Such translation could still 'preserve logical laws' in a sense. But the 'laws' thereby preserved would be unintelligible to us.

These remarks show, I think, that if fair translation must preserve logical laws, it must do so only to the extent to which the utility of linguistic expressions *depends* on their being used in accordance with those particular laws. How far that principle takes us in any particular case depends on the details of that case, and your verdict will depend on your general position. But at any rate we have seen no reason to follow those of Quine's successive treatments of these issues which favour the conservative approach of always trying to render the foreigner as subscribing to classical logic, or even as subscribing to the translators' own logic, whatever that may be. Quineans who accept determinacy of translation can happily follow the radical Quine of 'Two Dogmas' and *The Roots of Reference*, who allows even logical laws to be subject in principle to revision.[4]

12.6 Synonymy

In some of the above discussions it has been useful to assume that determinacy of translation renders synonymy unproblematic. But that was just a temporary expedient: there is much to be said against the assumption. Certainly determinacy of translation would eliminate some Quinean qualms about synonymy, but it leaves others unassuaged. In this section and the next two I shall try to see what the true position is.

Quine has attacked the notion of synonymy on three main counts. First, synonymy cannot be *defined* both clearly and without recourse to that tight circle of related notions which includes analyticity, necessity, and proposition (TDE, *WO*). Second, synonymy is not an objective matter of *fact*: the question whether two expressions mean the same has in general no determinate answer except relative to some agreed scheme of translation (*WO*, OR,

---

[4] For discussion of Quine's oscillations see Susan Haack, 1977.

FM). Third, the appeal to synonymy, or at any rate the appeal to meanings, has slight, if any, *explanatory* value (*WO*, MVD).

The second of these lines of attack does appear to be undermined by the conclusion that translation is not subject to Quinean indeterminacy. If translation is determinate in the relevant sense, then it is after all a question of fact whether two sentences mean (exactly) the same. However, it is important not to overestimate the implications of this conclusion. Bear in mind that chapters 10 and 11 imply only that exact translation is determinate. How much exact translation is possible remains moot. *Homophonic* translation is certainly exact, and so is translation between any pair of languages as closely alike as English and the Martian of chapter 11, such as, no doubt, Japanese and Korean, Mandarin and Cantonese. But that conclusion by itself does nothing to help us decide how far exact translation between different languages is possible; and Quineans who accept that translation is determinate in the relevant sense may well argue that very little is possible. To concede that there is no Quinean indeterminacy of translation is not to concede that there are many cases of exact interlinguistic synonymy.

Given that synonymy of whole sentences is determinate as far as it exists, we might define synonymy of sentence-parts as follows: an expression is synonymous to another expression if the substitution of the one for the other in a sentence always yields a synonymous sentence. (Cf. TDE, pp. 37 f., 1978, p. 2, 1979a, pp. 133, 138.) So if there are objectively synonymous sentences, there seems to be no theoretical difficulty over the objective synonymy of sentence-parts. But that blocks only one of the three prongs of Quine's attack on synonymy. Let us next look at the difficulties over the definition of synonymy of whole sentences.

12.7 Can synonymy be defined?

The determinacy of translation does nothing to help us devise a *definition* of synonymy that would be acceptable to Quine. 'I ask no more, after all, than a rough characterization in terms of dispositions to verbal behaviour', he has said (*WO*, p. 207). But the restriction to behavioural terms seems just as crippling for the case of synonymy as it is now generally agreed to be for the case of propositional attitudes. The sort of behaviour that a given person is disposed to produce in relation to a given sentence at a given time will generally depend on their total mental state at that time, so that no specifiable sorts of behaviour will necessarily be linked with a given belief, desire, etc. Since Quine is surely right to link meaningfulness with utility in communication, which in turn is explicable in terms of propositional attitudes, the project of defining synonymy in purely behavioural terms seems doomed.

It seems clear that there is no conflict between Quine's objections to defining synonymy and acceptance of determinacy of translation. If you accept the latter you must certainly accept that each expression (type) is objectively an exact translation of, and so means the same as, *itself*. (For the discussion throughout is about translation manuals for given languages, so that the fact that on occasions we have to translate individual utterances non-homophonically does not generate exceptions to the last remark.) So you must concede that type-identity of expressions is a *sufficient* condition for their synonymy. But unless you are also prepared to settle for a thoroughly eccentric explication of synonymy, you will not concede that type-identity is also necessary for synonymy. It seems you are free to insist with Quine that there is no criterion— necessary and sufficient condition, in his usage—for the cut-off point where the degree of affinity between a pair of *non*-identical terms is sufficient to allow them to be interchanged *salvo sensu* (cf. 1979a, p. 138).

I conclude that Quineans who accept the determinacy of translation can happily continue to endorse the claim that synonymy cannot be satisfactorily defined (that is, they can accept thesis VI in my list).

It is perhaps worth adding explicitly that this means that Quineans who accept determinacy of translation are not thereby bound to accept that the notion of propositions (or 'intensions' generally) as non-linguistic entities is adequately clear. Even without the indeterminacy there are sufficient Quinean difficulties over the notion.

12.8 Synonymy and explanation

To reject the indeterminacy thesis is to accept that sameness of sentence meaning is sometimes a matter of fact (cf. section 12.6). It is to reject one of Quine's three main complaints against the notion of meaning. However, we have seen that rejecting the indeterminacy thesis is quite compatible with endorsing another of his complaints: that meaning could not be defined or analysed in acceptable terms. It remains to be seen whether rejecting the indeterminacy thesis is also compatible with endorsing the third complaint: that the notion of meaning lacks explanatory power.

Consider the following exchange:

Q. Why does knowing French help us to get on with French speakers?

A. Because knowing French involves knowing the meanings of their utterances, and so helps us to tell what they believe, desire, intend, etc., which in turn helps us to understand and predict their actions and co-ordinate our behaviour with theirs.

Certainly A _seems_ to be explanatory. But in fact it is just the sort of thing that Quine calls 'spurious explanation, mentalistic explanation at its worst' (MVD, p. 87). He picks out three levels of explanation of verbal and other behaviour: the mental, the behavioural, and the physiological. The mental is 'the most superficial', 'scarcely deserving the name of explanation'; the physiological is 'deepest and most ambitious, and it is the place for causal explanations'. Unfortunately intelligent discourse is so varied and so complicated that we tend to despair of adhering to the standards of natural science in coping with it, and resort to mentalistic semantics. But we must resist this temptation: we must not just 'surface listlessly in the Sargasso Sea of mentalism'. Instead we must strive to base our attempts to understand language on behavioural dispositions, which are, after all, realized (my word) in physiological states yet unknown. So the second, behavioural dispositional, level of explanation is 'what we must settle for in our descriptions of language, in our formulations of language rules, and in our explications of semantical terms' (MVD, p. 88).

At first sight you might think that if the indeterminacy thesis is false, Quine's strictures against the explanatory power of the notions of meaning and intentional explanations generally must be mistaken. If translation is determinate, then permissible statements of sameness of sentence meaning convey matters of fact. And surely one cannot rule out a priori that any matters of fact could in principle be used in explanations. Moreover, as we have seen, to reject the indeterminacy thesis is to be committed to holding that permissible statements of sentence synonymy are strictly implied by the totality of truths statable in terms of physics. (I am pretending that the fact-stating truths are all underlain by those statable in terms of physics.) It follows that there is a sense in which permissible statements of sentence synonymy are ways of stating certain *physical* facts—physical facts which cannot, however, be adequately paraphrased in purely physical terms, nor even in purely physiological terms. If these statements do state physical facts, and if they cannot be satisfactorily replaced by statements at the physical or physiological levels, then surely they must be conceded to have considerably greater explanatory power than Quine admits.

However, his disparagement of mentalistic idioms in general and mentalistic semantics in particular does not depend wholly on the indeterminacy thesis. Admittedly Quineans who reject the indeterminacy thesis cannot regard the notions of meaning, synonymy, etc., with the extreme contempt evinced by Quine himself in 'Mind and Verbal Dispositions'. The indeterminacy thesis would have vindicated that contempt in a very satisfying way: by entailing that what had been assumed to be explanatory facts were not matters of fact at all.[5] But those who reject it can find other reasons for refusing to concede much explanatory power to the idioms in question.

One familiar worry is that it is obscure how much latitude can be allowed in the translation or paraphrase of statements ascribing propositional attitudes, when the ascription contains words not in the person's own vocabulary. Another concerns the difficulties over referential opacity—difficulties over the substitutivity of identity and quantifying into opaque contexts. These difficulties lead him to conclude: 'All in all, the propositional attitudes are in a bad way. These are the idioms most stubbornly at variance with scientific patterns' (MVD, p. 92). These difficulties illustrate his dominant thought: mentalistic idioms, if they are explanatory at all, are so only in a superficial way, being too loosely and obscurely connected with underlying physiological realities to be capable of supplying scientifically adequate explanations. (He could have increased his doubts, perhaps, by endorsing the view that these explanations are just *redescriptions* of the behaviour they are supposed to explain.) The practical utility of these idioms is not in dispute. The point is that we employ them impressionistically, so to speak, in ignorance of the underlying realities. Again the

---

[5] Quine puts considerable weight on the indeterminacy thesis in MVD. See pp. 90 f.

comparison with colour concepts is helpful. The colour concepts are useful in everyday life, but most of us employ them in great ignorance of the complicated underlying physical and physiological realities; and they hardly figure at all in natural science (NNK, p. 70)

To say that is not, of course, to endorse these Quinean misgivings. But perhaps it is enough to show that Quineans who reject the indeterminacy thesis are not thereby bound to accept that mentalistic idioms have much explanatory power. There is no Quinean indeterminacy over the colour concepts either, but it does not follow that colours (rather than the underlying physical and physiological mechanisms) have much explanatory power.

12.9 Conclusion

I have been arguing that the failure of the indeterminacy doctrine leaves most of Quine's other views undisturbed. Those positions which seemed to support it actually do nothing of the sort (chapters 2, 4-6, and 7). Nor is it the only support for some of his most important claims. Even his objections to the notions of synonymy, analyticity, and the idioms of propositional attitude have emerged largely unscathed. So if you accept the arguments of chapters 10 and 11, Quineanism without the indeterminacy is still Quineanism. Jettisoning that rotten plank from the Neurathian ship is easier than might have been expected.

If the arguments of chapters 10 and 11 are rejected, it is still worth knowing how little support for the indeterminacy doctrine there is in Quine's other doctrines, or indeed anywhere. But even if the arguments of the last two chapters are sound and recognized as such, I should not expect them or any arguments to bring the extinction of the indeterminacy doctrine. Like all sceptical doctrines, it feeds our craving for radically disturbing, mystifying ideas. It takes us to an abyss where we cannot possibly know what others think or feel—and not for the reassuring reason that the contents of everyone's thoughts and feelings are inaccessible to outsiders, but for the utterly disorientating reason that it is never a matter of fact what those contents are. That idea seems likely to haunt philosophy for many more years.

Appendix A

Versions and Perversions of the Indeterminacy Doctrine

This Appendix lists the main variants of the indeterminacy doctrine that are discussed in the text, and some different theses with which it is occasionally confused. The references give some of the places in Quine's works where a particular version appears to be stated, and places where that version is discussed in this book. Let me emphasize once again that I have attacked only I, II, III and IV, which make up the indeterminacy doctrine.

I. Our ordinary notion of sameness of meaning is such that rival teams of linguists, applying this notion to a given pair of languages but deliberately disregarding all constraints of simplicity and practicality, could produce rival manuals of sentence translation which fitted all the physically statable evidence (or facts), yet were mutually incompatible.

(The main indeterminacy thesis. Supposed to hold for exact translation, and even for interpretation within a single language. FM, p. 193, TPT, p. 23, chapters 3, 10, 11.)

Ia. As I, with 'behavioural dispositions' substituted for 'physically statable evidence (or facts)'.

(Weaker than I. OR, p. 29, TPT, p. 23, section 3.1.)

Ib. As I, with 'speech dispositions' substituted for 'physically statable evidence (or facts)'.

(Weaker than Ia. WO chapter 2 passim, section 3.1.)

Ic. As I, with 'dispositions to assent to and dissent from sentences under various kinds of stimulation' substituted for 'physically statable evidence (or facts)'.

(Weakest of all. WO, p. 54, 1968b, p. 313, section 3.1.)

II, IIa, IIb, IIc. As I, Ia, Ib, Ic, with 'schemes of reference' substituted for 'manuals of sentence translation'.

(The inscrutability of reference. Appears to imply I (see section 5.9). WO, pp. 51-7, OR passim, TPT, pp. 16-22, chapter 5.)

III. Relations of sameness of meaning for sentences—even for exact translations—are not generally matters of fact.

The non-factuality thesis. *WO*, p. 73, FM, sections 3.1, 3.10, and 12.6.)

IV. Statements of sentence synonymy make sense only relative to a scheme of translation.

(The relativistic thesis. *WO*, pp. 75, 221, section 3.12.)

V. There is no set of constraints statable in Quine-acceptable terms which, applied to the totality of Quine-acceptable evidence, determines a uniquely correct scheme of sentence translation between a given pair of languages.

(*WO*, chapter 2, section 3.2.)

VI. Sentence synonymy cannot be defined or analysed in Quine-acceptable terms.

(Presumably implied by V. Related to the Brentano–Chisholm thesis. *WO*, p. 221, 1974a, p. 329, section 1.10.)

VII. Different criteria for sameness of meaning can yield conflicting results.

(A truism: sections 1.1(*f*), 3.10, and 7.3.)

VIII. Translation manuals which agree in their assignments of truth values to sentences, even in all possible worlds, can conflict with one another. (Sections 3.8, 3.11, and 5.5–5.7.)

IX. Schemes of reference for a given language which agree in their assignments of truth values to sentences, even in all possible worlds, can conflict with one another.

(Contrast with II. Cf. Putnam 1981, p. 33, sections 5.6–5.8.)

X. In translation between conceptually distant languages there is not generally any fact—as to which of two inequivalent rough versions of a given sentence (or term) is correct—to be right or wrong about.

(Another truism. SO, pp. 5 f., 25, OR, p. 29. See section 1.1(*c*).)

XI. For some pairs of (*a*) sentences ((*b*) terms) offered as translations of one another, the behaviour of speakers of the translated language gives no basis for saying either that the proposed translation is acceptable, or that it is not acceptable.

(Common or garden indeterminacy of (*a*) sense, (*b*) reference. See section 1.1(*d*).)

XII. There can be empirically equivalent but mutually incompatible theories of the world.

(The underdetermination thesis. RIT, NNK, ESW, chapter 6.)

Appendix B

Language and Dispositions

In his discussion of the indeterminacy thesis Quine treats language as 'the complex of present dispositions to verbal behaviour, in which speakers of the same language have perforce come to resemble one another'. 'Reckon a man's current language by his current dispositions to respond verbally to current stimulation' (*WO*, pp. 27-8). I want to comment on this approach, which is open to interpretations that seem to damage his overall position (cf. 9.5 above), and has also seemed objectionable on other grounds. I shall argue that it is acceptable in spite of some difficulties.

First some general points. Although Quine thinks talk of dispositions can be useful he excludes the idiom from an ideal language of science (*RR*, p. 11). Some dispositions, such as solubility in water, are unproblematic because we know the underlying mechanisms: we can explain the dispositions in terms of molecular or other structure. In other cases, such as dispositions to assent to sentences, we posit dispositions because we believe there is some underlying mechanism even though we might never discover what it is. In general we talk in terms of dispositions when we do not know the full explanatory story behind the behaviour in question (*WO*, pp. 222-5, *RR*, pp. 8-15, MVD. See also section 1.7).[1]

In spite of these disarming provisos Quine may still seem vulnerable to a familiar general objection. This is that there is no principled way to avoid the absurdity that each particular bit of behaviour might as well be put down to a disposition to produce just that bit of behaviour in just that situation. But this is not a serious problem: the absurdity is not genuine. After all, he is committed to holding that each bit of behaviour results from the interaction of a complex mechanism (or organism) with the environment. So he must also hold that at any given time that organism's behaviour is a function of its state at that time and whatever impinges on it at that time. Saying it has a 'disposition' to produce just that behaviour in just that situation can therefore be seen as no more than a restatement of that commitment. But note: the commitment does not require Quine to maintain either that the organism must always have possessed that particular disposition, or, connectedly, that an appeal to the disposition would have any explanatory value.

The appeal to such a disposition would have had explanatory value

---

[1] Quine has sometimes stated that the disposition is *identical* with the underlying or other mechanism (e.g. MVD, p. 92). I believe this is an error but will not discuss it because it does not affect my points. (I think we ought to say only that the mechanism constitutes or underlies possession of the disposition.)

only if the disposition had been a (more or less) enduring trait of the organism. An illustration may help. Consider a pocket calculator. It is so constructed that when, for example, the '4' key is pressed, a 4 appears on the display panel. This always happens (except when the display is full). So we can say the device is disposed to show a 4 whenever that key is pressed, and this disposition is an enduring feature. It follows that the appearance of a 4 on the display can on occasions be explained by reference to that disposition. But now suppose I have just keyed in some digits and other symbols, and when I press the 'percent' key (but not the '4' key) a 4 is again displayed. The machine certainly does not have an enduring disposition to show 4 whenever the percent key is pressed. Still, it could be said to have had a disposition to show 4 when the percent key was pressed *in that situation*, simply because its internal workings are such that, once it had been got into that situation as a result of my earlier work on the keyboard, pressing that key was bound to produce a 4. Having that particular disposition was thus only a transitory state of the machine, and for that reason has no explanatory value because reference to it leaves its own existence unexplained. In contrast reference to an enduring disposition—even when there is no explanation of its existence—gives us the satisfaction of knowing that what occurred resulted from some permanent feature of the object in question.

I think these illustrations, and similar ones drawn from full-blown computers, help to validate Quine's (guarded) appeals to dispositions, especially when we bear in mind that in his best statements he makes explicit allowance for what can be called 'higher order' dispositions— dispositions to acquire or lose other dispositions (see below). Consider a computer running a program that is unknown to us, but involves interactions with the user. We want to explain what is going on. Observing its operations we might first conjecture that whenever something of type *F* was put in, the program produced a response of type *G*. Then we might notice exceptions which led us to add 'except when *H* or *J*, when the response is *L* or *M*'; and so on. We could be described as feeling our way towards a characterization of the programmed machine's dispositions—and at the same time as feeling our way towards an outline of the program. Now our rough and ready hypotheses in terms of dispositions can be useful. But in such cases they can also become unmanageably complicated. Nevertheless the existence of the program itself proves that in principle our talk of dispositions could be recast in a completely explicit and thoroughly explanatory form.[2] When such ex-

---

[2] The existence of the program also shows, incidentally, that there may be more illuminating explanations of behaviour than those in terms of the system's detailed physical structure. As cognitive psychologists optimistically hope, perhaps we do not need to look for actual physiological mechanisms in the human case: perhaps there are higher levels of description analogous to those at which a computer's program can be used to describe and

amples are kept in mind it is hard to see how there could be any serious general objections to Quine's talk of dispositions.

However, there are one or two more particular difficulties. One is this. Our current dispositions to respond to current stimulation will reflect only part of our knowledge of our language because they will fail to do justice to, among other things, our ability to revise our opinions, hence our dispositions, as a result of reflection. Consider two contrasting sorts of interrogation. One is exemplified by tests of factual knowledge, for example, zoological knowledge, with questions like 'What is the animal in the photograph?' This sort of interrogation might reasonably be expected to discover some of a person's current dispositions to respond verbally to current stimulation. The other sort of interrogation is exemplified by a leisurely interview in which people are invited to offer their thoughts at length, with due time for reflection, and questions like 'How would you tackle inflation?'. To the extent that this second type of questioning succeeds in inducing people to reflect, to revise their views, and indeed to arrive at new conclusions, it can hardly be regarded as eliciting only their 'dispositions to respond verbally to current stimulation'. For the ability to revise one's first-order dispositions to respond cannot itself be represented by a first-order disposition to respond. Clearly it brings people's knowledge of their language into play in ways the first kind of questioning generally does not.

Of course Quine is aware of this difficulty. In chapter 1 of *Word and Object* he discusses ways in which sentences stand in complex relations of interconnection with other sentences, as well as with non-verbal stimulations. Dispositions to assent to or dissent from some sentences will be conditional on dispositions relating to others (see especially *WO*, pp. 11–17, 56 f.). And in 'Methodological Reflections on Current Linguistic Theory', where he takes issue with Chomsky, he mentions 'dispositions to make or accept certain transformations and not others; or certain inferences and not others'; and also counts, among 'acceptably clear dispositions', dispositions on the part of English speakers to conform to 'any and all of the extensionally equivalent systems of grammar that demarcate the right totality of well-formed English sentences' (MR, p. 444). Thus whatever we take Quine to mean by his phrase 'dispositions to respond verbally to current stimulation', we cannot reasonably assume the dispositions are only first-order dispositions. They must be taken to include dispositions to acquire and lose other dispositions.

The point that the dispositions cannot be just first-order dispositions to assent to or dissent from sentences is less obvious than it would otherwise have been because of Quine's use of the word 'assent'. We

explain its behaviour. Contrary to what Quine has suggested dispositions need not be a 'physiological hypothesis' (*RR*, p. 13).

tend to assume that having a disposition to assent to a sentence X must be tantamount to holding X true, and that this in turn must be tantamount to having the (or a) belief expressed by X. Having made those two assumptions it is natural to assume further that assent to, say, a stimulus analytic sentence necessarily involves a grasp of its implications, hence a tendency to revise one's belief in the light of experience. But such assumptions are quite unwarranted if we take seriously the project of explaining possession of a language in terms of possessing a complex of dispositions. Quine's talk of dispositions to assent to and dissent from sentences is not a way of smuggling back intentional idioms. He cannot properly require— nor does he—that giving 'assent' consists of anything over and above uttering a token of (what we classify as) a standard sign of assent, such as 'Yes' or a nod. (He spells this out in MVD, p. 91, where he calls such utterances 'surface assent'.)

The conception of possession of a language as a complex of dispositions to verbal behaviour has been fiercely attacked by Chomsky as 'either empty or wrong'.[3] I do not find Chomsky convincing, partly because he ignores Quine's readiness to include higher-order dispositions.[4] But he does show that Quine's conception will bear elucidation; and he usefully focuses attention on Quine's failure to explain just how the total dispositional system is supposed to be related to the much narrower set of dispositions to assent to or dissent from queried sentences under various stimulations.

Quine certainly treats the first-order dispositions to assent to or dissent from queried sentences under various patterns of stimulation as specially important. Does he think they are important because they somehow represent the rest of the totality? That is what he seems to imply in some passages (e.g. WO, p. 28, 1968b, RR). Or is his view—and this is inconsistent with the first—rather that the importance of the first-order query-and-assent dispositions consists simply in the fact that it is only by discovering what they are that we can hope to discover the rest of the totality? Other passages seem to imply this (e.g. WO, p. 47, MVD, p. 88). We have already seen that the first view is mistaken. It does not follow that the second is correct, still less that Quine holds it. But the procedure of query and assent is at any rate plausibly described as what primarily enables us to 'tap the reservoirs of verbal disposition' (MVD, p. 88).

Chomsky's attack on the idea of possession of a language as a complex

---

[3] Chomsky, 1975, p. 198. Cf. p. 194, and 1969, p. 57. For Quine's contributions to this debate later than 1968b, see MR, especially pp. 444 f., and RR, especially p. 15.

[4] He ignores this in his *Reflections on Language*, for example, pp. 191 ff. Consequently nothing he says comes near to showing that, as he claims, a person's possession or incorporation of a generative grammar cannot be described as a complex of dispositions. See also section 7.2.

of verbal dispositions fails: he has not shown that it is 'empty or wrong'. But that does not entail it is not empty or wrong. And there is another set of considerations which may well seem to prove it so: considerations of the sort widely held to have exploded the project of translating talk of propositional attitudes in terms of dispositions.

In general a person's dispositions to behave cannot be regarded as the product of some limited department of their mental life, but must be seen as resulting from the combined workings of the totality. So, in particular, there can be no reason to assume that any two people who speak the same language will have exactly the same verbal dispositions. What they will say, or assent to, or dissent from, in any given situation, will depend not just on their knowledge of the language but on their current beliefs, desires, moods, etc.—and these might well result in some of them even refusing to assent to the observation sentence 'Red' when queried in the presence of something red. Now for the reasons given earlier I discount Quine's occasional tendency to write as if dispositions to assent to and dissent from sentences exhausted all verbal dispositions worth bothering about. Further, in view of his qualms about all talk of dispositions that is not firmly anchored in established physical fact (as is talk of sugar's solubility in water), I see no point in ascribing to him the view that *every* English speaker would at *any* time assent, for example, to 'Rabbit?' whenever a rabbit was in full view, regardless of the speaker's total mental state. It is enough for his purposes that most English speakers in ordinary circumstances would do so. So his use of the notion of first-order verbal dispositions to respond to queried sentences under stimulation is not undermined by the general anti-behaviourist considerations mentioned. As to the higher-order dispositions, it is clear enough that the ways they manifest themselves may vary from person to person, depending on other internal factors. So I see no reason why Quine should be worried by the objection.

One last difficulty. Quine's complex of speech dispositions is one 'in which speakers of the same language have perforce come to resemble one another' (*WO*, p. 27; cf. p. 45). That there is some such resemblance is trivially true; but what does it amount to? One natural interpretation of his words would be as follows:

(1) For any given language L, there is a complex of dispositions to verbal behaviour C_1, such that having C_1 is necessary and sufficient for knowing L.[5]

But this will not do. For one thing, if any substantial quantity of higher-order dispositions, including dispositions to make inferences, were to be included, that would imply that differences of 'factual' beliefs were incompatible with identity of language. For my higher-order dispositions

[5] Dummett assumes this interpretation (1974a, pp. 360 ff.).

will depend on the 'factual' beliefs I happen to have, and if they differ from yours, then on this account we shall not count as speaking the same language. But if the higher-order dispositions were not included, justice would not be done to our knowledge of language, for the reasons noticed earlier in this Appendix. The attempt to draw a sharp boundary round these dispositions would seem to prevent, say, genuine intellectual rebels from being counted as speakers of the same language as those they were rebelling against. And there is another weighty consideration. The inextricability thesis is incompatible with the attempt to specify a set of dispositions both necessary and sufficient for a person to know the language. Possession of such a set of dispositions would constitute precisely that distinct linguistic knowledge which the inextricability thesis rules out. We therefore cannot assume that Quine is committed to (1). Instead we can perhaps take him to be committed to something weaker, for example:

(2) For any given language L, each speaker S^i of L has a complex of dispositions to verbal behaviour D^{li}, such that (*i*) having D^{li} is sufficient for speaking L, and (*ii*) for each pair of speakers of L, S^j and S^k, their respective complexes of dispositions to verbal behaviour D^{lj} and D^{lk} resemble one another.

How do their respective complexes of dispositions to verbal behaviour resemble one another? Mere resemblance in first-order dispositions would not be enough for the reasons noticed earlier. But actually to specify the sorts of resemblance that are relevant would demand a much more detailed working out of the sorts of higher-order dispositions involved than Quine or anyone else has offered. *Faute de mieux*, then, he would perhaps be willing to allow the question of what degrees and kinds of resemblance are required in particular cases to be decided by our linguistic litmus paper: competent linguists.

Bibliography

Bach, Emmon, 1974, *Syntactic Theory*, New York: Holt, Rinehart and Winston.

Baker, G. P. and Hacker, P. M. S., 1983, *Wittgenstein: Meaning and Understanding*, Oxford: Blackwell.

Bechtel, P. William, 1980, 'Indeterminacy and Underdetermination: Are Quine's Two Theses Consistent?' *Philosophical Studies* 38, 309-20.

Bennett, Jonathan, 1976, *Linguistic Behaviour*, Cambridge: Cambridge Univ. Press.

Blackburn, Simon, 1976, Critical study of Guttenplan, 1975, in *Philosophical Quarterly* 26, 354-62.

—— 1984a, *Spreading the Word: Groundings in the Philosophy of Language*, Oxford: Clarendon Press.

—— 1984b, 'The Individual Strikes Back', *Synthese* 58, 281-301.

Boorse, Christopher, 1975, 'The Origins of the Indeterminacy Thesis', *Journal of Philosophy* 72, 369-87.

Bradley, M. C., 1969, 'How Never to Know What you Mean', *Journal of Philosophy* 66, 119-24.

—— 1976, 'Quine's Arguments for the Indeterminacy Thesis', *Australasian Journal of Philosophy* 54, 24-49.

Chomsky, Noam, 1957, *Syntactic Structures*, The Hague and Paris: Mouton.

—— 1965, *Aspects of the Theory of Syntax*, Cambridge, Mass: MIT

—— 1969, 'Quine's Empirical Assumptions', in Davidson and Hintikka, 1969, 53-68.

—— 1975, *Reflections on Language*, London: Fontana/Collins

—— 1980, *Rules and Representations*, Oxford: Blackwell

Churchland, Paul M., 1979, *Scientific Realism and the Plasticity of Mind*, Cambridge: Cambridge Univ. Press.

Cohen, L. Jonathan, 1962, *The Diversity of Meaning*, London: Methuen.

Cooper, David E., 1975, *Knowledge of Language*, London: Prism Press; New York: Humanities.

Davidson, Donald, 1967, 'Truth and Meaning', *Synthese* 17, 304-23.

—— 1974, 'On the Very Idea of a Conceptual Scheme', *Proceedings of the American Philosophical Association* 47, 5-20. Reprinted 1984 (to which page references apply).

—— 1974a, 'Belief and the Basis of Meaning', *Synthese* 27, 309-23.

—— 1974b, 'Radical Interpretation', *Dialectica* 27, 314-28.

—— 1974c. 'Replies to David Lewis and W. V. Quine', *Synthese* 27, 345-9.

—— 1975, 'Thought and Talk', in Guttenplan, 1975, 7-23.

—— 1977, 'Reality without Reference', *Dialectica* 31, 247-58. Reprinted in Platts, 1980 (to which page references apply).

—— 1979, 'The Inscrutability of Reference', *Southwestern Journal of Philosophy* 10, 7-19.

—— 1984, *Inquiries into Truth and Interpretation*, Oxford: Clarendon.

—— , and Hintikka, Jaakko (eds.), 1969, *Words and Objections*, Dordrecht: D. Reidel.

—— , and Harman, Gilbert (eds.), 1972, *Semantics of Natural Language*, Dordrecht: Reidel.

Dennett, Daniel C., 1978, *Brainstorms*, Hassocks, Sussex: Harvester.

Duhem, Pierre M. M., 1914/1954, *The Aim and Structure of Physical Theory*, translated by P. P. Wiener from the second edition of *La Théorie Physique*, Paris, 1914, (First edition 1904.)

Dummett, Michael A. E., 1973, *Frege: Philosophy of Language*, London: Duckworth.

—— 1974a, 'The Significance of Quine's Indeterminacy Thesis', *Synthese* 27, 351-97.

—— 1974b, 'Reply to W. V. Quine', *Synthese* 27, 413-16.

—— 1976, 'What is a Theory of Meaning? (II)', in Evans and McDowell, 1976.

—— 1978, *Truth and Other Enigmas*, London: Duckworth.

Evans, Gareth 1975, 'Identity and Predication', *Journal of Philosophy* 72, 343-63.

—— 1982, *The Varieties of Reference*, Oxford: Clarendon Press.

—— , and McDowell, John (eds.), 1976, *Truth and Meaning*, Oxford: Clarendon Press.

Field, Hartry, 1973, 'Theory Change and the Indeterminacy of Reference', *Journal of Philosophy* 70, 462-81.

—— 1974, 'Quine and the Correspondence Theory', *Philosophical Review* 83, 200-28.

—— 1975, 'Conventionalism and Instrumentalism in Semantics', *Nous* 9, 375-405.

Frege, Gottlob, 1884/1959, *The Foundations of Arithmetic*, tr. J. L. Austin, Oxford: Blackwell.

Friedman, Michael, 1975, 'Physicalism and the Indeterminacy of Translation', *Nous* 9, 353-74.

Furley, D. J., 1958, 'Translation from Greek Philosophy', in *Aspects of Translation*, The Communication Research Centre, University College London, London: Secker and Warburg, 52-64.

Gardner, Michael R., 1973, 'Apparent Conflicts between Quine's Indeterminacy Thesis and his Philosophy of Science', *British Journal for the Philosophy of Science* 24, 381-93.

Goodman, Nelson, 1965, *Fact, Fiction and Forecast*, second edition, Indianapolis: Bobbs-Merrill. (First published 1955.)

Grayling, A. C., 1982, *An Introduction to Philosophical Logic*, Brighton: Harvester.

Gross, Maurice, 1972, *Mathematical Models in Linguistics*, Englewood Cliffs, NJ: Prentice-Hall.

Guttenplan, Samuel (ed.), 1975, *Mind and Language*, Oxford: Clarendon Press.

Haack, Susan, 1977, 'Analyticity and Logical Truth in *The Roots of Reference*', *Theoria* 2, 129-43.

Harman, Gilbert, 1969, 'An Introduction to "Translation and Meaning", Chapter Two of *Word and Object*', in Davidson and Hintikka, 1969, 14-26.

Hellman, Geoffrey, 1974, 'The New Riddle of Radical Translation', *Philosophy of Science* 41(1974), 227-46.

Hodges, H. A., 1952, *The Philosophy of Wilhelm Dilthey*, London: Routledge and Kegan Paul.

Hook, Sidney (ed.),1969, *Language and Philosophy: a Symposium*, New York and London: New York Univ. Press, Univ. of London Press.

Hookway, Christopher, 1978, 'Indeterminacy and Interpretation', in C. Hookway and Phillip Pettit (eds.), *Action and Interpretation*, Cambridge: Cambridge Univ. Press.

Hylton, Peter, 1982, 'Analyticity and the Indeterminacy of Translation', *Synthese* 52, 167-84.

Katz, Jerrold J., 1972, *Semantic Theory*, New York: Harper and Row.

—— 1979, 'Semantic and Conceptual Change', *Philosophical Review* 88, 327-65.

Kelly, L. G. (ed.), 1969, *Description and Measurement of Bilingualism*, Toronto: Univ. of Toronto Press.

Kirk, Robert, 1973, 'Underdetermination of Theory and Indeterminacy of Translation', *Analysis* 33, 195-202.

—— 1977a, 'More on Quine's Reasons for Indeterminacy of Translation', *Analysis* 37, 136-41.

—— 1977b, Review of Guttenplan, 1975 in *Mind* 86, 609-11.

—— 1979, 'From Physical Explicability to Full-Blooded Materialism', *Philosophical Quarterly* xx, 229-37.

—— 1982a, 'On Three Alleged Rivals to Homophonic Translation', *Philosophical Studies* 42, 409-18.

—— 1982b, 'Physicalism, Identity and Strict Implication', *Ratio* 24, 131-41.

—— 1983, 'Quinean Indeterminacy and Forcing', *Erkenntnis* 20, 213-18.

—— 1985, 'Davidson and Indeterminacy of Translation', *Analysis* 45, 20-4.

Kripke, Saul A., 1982, *Wittgenstein on Rules and Private Language*, Oxford: Blackwell.

Lenneberg, E. H., 1953, 'Cognition and Ethnolinguistics', *Language* 29, 463-71.

Levin, Michael, 1979, 'Forcing and the Indeterminacy of Translation', *Erkenntnis* 14, 25-31.

Lewis, David K., 1970, 'General Semantics', *Synthese* 22, 18-67. Reprinted in Davidson and Harman, 1972.

—— 1974, 'Radical Interpretation', *Synthese* 27, 331-44.

Lyons, John, 1968, *Introduction to Theoretical Linguistics*, Cambridge: Cambridge Univ. Press.

—— 1977, *Semantics*, vols. 1 and 2, Cambridge: Cambridge Univ. Press.

Massey, Gerald J., 1978, 'Indeterminacy, Inscrutability, and Ontological Relativity', in *Studies in Ontology, American Philosophical Quarterly Monograph Series No. 12*, 43-55.

Matthews, Robert J., 1979, 'Are the Grammatical Sentences of a Language a Recursive Set?', *Synthese* 40, 209-24.

McDowell, John, and Evans, Gareth, (eds.), 1976, *Truth and Meaning*, Oxford: Clarendon.

McGinn, Colin, 1977, 'Charity, Interpretation and Belief', *Journal of Philosophy* 74, 521-35.

—— 1981, 'The Mechanism of Reference', *Synthese* 49, 157-86.

Montague, Richard, 1974, *Formal Philosophy*, New Haven and London: Yale Univ. Press.

Nida, Eugene A., 1964, *Toward a Science of Translating*, Leiden: E.J.Brill.

Papineau, David, 1979, *Theory and Meaning*, Oxford: Clarendon.

Peck, Arthur L., 1953, *Aristotle: Generation of Animals* (translation etc.), London: Heinemann, and Cambridge, Mass: Harvard Univ. Press.

Platts, Mark (ed.), 1980, *Reference, Truth and Reality*, London: Routledge and Kegan Paul.

Putnam, Hilary, 1961, 'Some Issues in the Theory of Grammar', *Proceedings of Symposia in Applied Mathematics* 12. Reprinted 1975b (to which page references apply).

—— 1962, 'The Analytic and the Synthetic', in Herbert Feigl and Grover Maxwell (eds.), *Minnesota Studies in the Philosophy of Science*, vol. III, Minneapolis: Univ. of Minnesota Press. Reprinted 1975b, 33-69 (to which page references apply).

—— 1975a. 'The Refutation of Conventionalism', in M. Munitz (ed.), *Language and Meaning*, New York: New York Univ. Press. Reprinted 1975b, 153-91 (to which page references apply).

—— 1975b. *Mind, Language and Reality: Philosophical Papers, Vol.2*, Cambridge: Cambridge Univ. Press.

—— 1980, 'Models and Reality', *Journal of Symbolic Logic* 45, 464-482. Reprinted 1983 (to which page references apply).

—— 1981, *Reason, Truth and History*, Cambridge: Cambridge Univ. Press.

—— 1983, *Realism and Reason*, Cambridge: Cambridge Univ. Press.

Quine, Willard van Orman, 1936, 'Truth by Convention', in O. H. Lee (ed.), *Philosophical Essays for A.N. Whitehead*, New York and London: Longmans, 90-124. Reprinted 1966, 70-99 (to which page references apply).

—— 1951, 'On Carnap's Views on Ontology', *Philosophical Studies* 2, 65-72. Reprinted 1966, 126-34 (to which page references apply).

—— (1951), 'Two Dogmas of Empiricism', (TDE), *Philosophical Review* 60(1951), 20-43. Reprinted 1953, 20-46 (to which page references apply).

—— 1953, *From a Logical Point of View*, Cambridge, Mass: Harvard Univ. Press.

—— (1958), 'Speaking of Objects', (SO), *Proceedings and Addresses of the American Philosophical Association* 31, 5-22. Reprinted 1969c, 1-25 (to which page references apply).

—— 1959, 'Meaning and Translation', in R.A. Brower (ed.), *On Translation*, Cambridge, Mass: Harvard, 148-72.

—— 1960, 'Carnap and Logical Truth', *Synthese* 12, 350-74. Reprinted 1966, 100-25 (to which page references apply).

—— (1960), *Word and Object*, (*WO*), Cambridge, Mass. New York and London: MIT and Wiley.

—— 1964, 'Ontological Reduction and the World of Numbers', *Journal of Philosophy* 61, 209-16. Reprinted 1966, 199-207 (to which page references apply).

—— 1966, *The Ways of Paradox and Other Essays*, New York: Random House.

—— (1968), 'Ontological Relativity', (OR), *Journal of Philosophy* 65(1968), 185-212. Reprinted 1969c, 26-68 (to which page references apply).

—— 1968a, 'Propositional Objects', *Critica* 2, 3-22. Reprinted 1969, 139-60 (to which page references apply).

—— 1968b, 'Replies', *Synthese*, 264-321. Reprinted in D. Davidson and J. Hintikka (eds.), 1969, *Words and Objections*,Dordrecht: Reidel 1969 (to which page references apply).

—— 1969a, 'Existence and Quantification', see 1969c, 91-113.

—— 1969b, 'Linguistics and Philosophy', in S. Hook (ed.), *Language and Philosophy*, New York and London: New York Univ. Press and Univ. of London Press, 95-8.

—— 1969c, *Ontological Relativity and Other Essays*, New York and London: Columbia Univ. Press.

—— (1969), 'Epistemology Naturalized', (EN), see 1969c, 69-90 (to which page references apply).

—— 1970a, *Philosophy of Logic*, Englewood Cliffs: Prentice-Hall.

—— 1970b, 'Grades of Theoreticity', in L. Foster and J. W. Swanson (eds.), *Experience and Theory*, London: Duckworth, 1-17.

—— (1970), 'Methodological Reflections on Current Linguistic Theory', (MR), *Synthese* 21, 386-98. Reprinted in D. Davidson and G. Harman (eds.), *Semantics of Natural Language*, Dordrecht: Reidel, 442-54 (to which page references apply).

—— (1970), 'On the Reasons for Indeterminacy of Translation', (RIT), *Journal of Philosophy* 67, 178-83.

—— 1974a, 'Comment on Donald Davidson', *Synthese* 27, 325-9.

—— 1974b, 'Comment on Michael Dummett', *Synthese* 27, 399.

—— (1974), *The Roots of Reference*, (RR), La Salle: Open Court.

—— (1975), 'Mind and Verbal Dispositions', (MVD), in Guttenplan, 83-95.

—— (1975), 'The Nature of Natural Knowledge', (NNK), in Guttenplan, 67-81.

—— (1975)'On Empirically Equivalent Systems of the World', (ESW), *Erkenntnis* 9, 313-28.

—— (1977), 'Facts of the Matter', (FM), in R. W. Shahan and K. R. Merrill (eds.), *American Philosophy from Edwards to Quine*, Norman: Univ. of Oklahoma Press, 176-96.

—— 1978, 'Use and its Place in Meaning', *Erkenntnis* 13, 1-8.

—— 1979a, 'Cognitive Meaning', *The Monist* 62, 129-42.

—— 1979b, 'Comments on Newton-Smith', *Analysis* 39, 66-7.

—— 1981a, *Theories and Things*, Cambridge, Mass. and London: Harvard Univ. Press.

—— (1981) 'Things and their Place in Theories', (TPT), in 1981a, 1-23.

—— 1981b, 'Empirical Content', in 1981a, 24-30.

Romanos, George D., 1983, *Quine and Analytic Philosophy*, Cambridge Mass. and London: MIT

Rorty, Richard, 1972, 'Indeterminacy of Translation and of Truth', *Synthese* 23, 443-62.

—— 1980, *Philosophy and the Mirror of Nature*, Princeton, NJ: Princeton Univ. Press.

Rosenberg, Jay F., 1974, *Linguistic Representation*, Dordrecht: Reidel.

Stich, Stephen P., 1972, 'Grammar, Psychology, and Indeterminacy', *Journal of Philosophy* 69, 799-818.

Stockwell, Robert P., 1977, *Foundations of Syntactic Theory*, Englewood Cliffs, NJ: Prentice-Hall.

Strawson, Peter F., 1959, *Individuals*, London: Methuen.

Tuana, Nancy, 1981, 'Taking the Indeterminacy of Translation One Step Further', *Philosophical Studies* 40, 283-91.

Wallace, John, 1979, 'Only in the Context of a Sentence do Words have any Meaning', in Peter A. French, T. E. Uehling, H. K. Wettstein (eds.), *Contemporary Perspectives in the Philosophy of Language*, Minneapolis: Univ. of Minnesota Press, 305-25.

Wittgenstein, Ludwig, 1953, *Philosophical Investigations*, translated by G. E. M. Anscombe, Oxford: Blackwell.

Wright, Crispin, 1980, *Wittgenstein on the Foundations of Mathematics*, London: Duckworth.

Index

Index

Index

objective and subjective, 20-2
objectivity in semantics, 17
observation sentences:
  defined, 38-9
  as not determinately translatable except
    in special cases, if Quine is right, 43
    n. 7
  translation of, 70-3
  as 'stopping points', 95
  and underdetermination of theory, 145-6
observationality, 38-9, 72
occasion sentences, 38, 42
ontological relativity, 127-30
  does not support inscrutability or in-
    determinacy, 128-30
optimism about semantics, argument from,
  201-2
ordinary notions of meaning, translation,
    etc. are intimately enmeshed with other
    intentional notions, 54, 72
  lack objectivity according to Quine, 63,
    77
  see also non-factuality thesis

Papineau, D., 189 n., 203 n.
Peck, A., 5 n. 3
pegged observation sentences (variety of
    standing sentences), 52 n. 4, 133
Peirce, C. S., 82, 83, 84
'perfect actor' objection to behaviourism,
  10-11
permissibility (of translation manuals), see
    fitting the evidence
permutation theorem, 116-17
  Putnam and, 117
  supports neither indeterminacy nor in-
    scrutability thesis, 118-27
philosophy, as part of the scientific enter-
    prise according to Quine, 15
phonetic and phonological analysis, 42, 154
physicalism, 19, 21, 45
  assumed by Quine, 51
  undisturbed by collapse of the in-
    determinacy thesis, 239
physics:
  assumed to be extensional, 21
  realism about, and indeterminacy thesis,
    28, 49-50, 135-9

does not impose any particular scheme of
    semantic concepts, 46
posits, 28, 89
possible worlds semantics, 31
predicate letters, 180-1
'pressing from above', 133-52 passim
  non-sequitur in argument in 'On the
    Reasons', 144-6
  seems to be a failure, 152
'pressing from below', 106-32 passim
  based on unsound arguments, 111-16,
    118-27, 131
  see also inscrutability thesis
pronunciation, 154
proof theory, 112-13
propositional attitudes:
  as not generally matters of fact according
    to Quine, 9-11, 15
  and psychological reality, 12-13, 156-8
  and systems of dispositions, 232
propositions not automatically legitimated
    by determinacy of translation, 246; see
    also museum myth
proxy functions, 113-14
psychological reality, 156-8, 194-5
psychology and linguistics, 137
pure semantic knowledge:
  ruled out by inextricability thesis, 85
  unnecessary on holistic view, 87
  ruled out on Quine's reductionist as-
    sumption, 88
  possible on revised version of in-
    extricability thesis, 99-100
  contrasted with pure knowledge of syn-
    onymy, 101
  as not required for translation of theoret-
    ical expressions, 104-5
  and synonymy, 242
pure translation, 34, 35, 76
Putnam, H.:
  and metaphysical realism, 28 n. 11, 29,
    124
  and natural kind words, 93-4
  and permutation theorem, 117, 118, 123-
    4, 125-7
  on grammar, 160
  on internalism and reference, 232-4

Index

Index

translation (*cont.*)
of observation sentences, 39, 70-3, 145-6
of terms, 41
aims of, 52-4, 73-4
as right or wrong about what?, 103
of theories, 104-5
shown to be determinate between initial segments of English and Martian, 220-4
shown to be determinate between extensions of determinately translatable languages, 224-8
and preservation of logical laws, 243-5
of deviant logics, 243-5
see also exact translation, translation manuals
translation manuals, 32-6
do not necessarily involve a theory of meaning, 32-3
are concerned with pure translation, 34
help speakers of one language to get on with those of another, 54
help with explanation of behaviour, 54, 63
face the evidence as a whole, 67
and agreement over truth values, 67-8
incompatibility (rivalry) between, 68-9, 74-5
as verbal items, 124
triangle argument, 187-8
truth-functional connectives, 40
truth conditions, argument from, 188
truth values:
agreement over, as not enough for empirical adequacy of translation manuals, 67-8
contradictory assignments of, as not required for indeterminacy thesis, 69
Tuana, N., 33 n., 40 n.

underdetermination thesis (thesis XII), 44, 50, 252

an undeniable version, 133
a revised version, 133
as 'real ground' of indeterminacy doctrine, 133, 140-1
and identity of theories, 150-1
undisturbed by collapse of indeterminacy thesis, 239
untranslatable sentences, 209-10, 229-30
untutored notions of reference and synonymy, 118
use of language, 8-9
utility in communication:
contrasting bases for, 90
and Dummett's objections to inextricability thesis, 95-8
and the middle way, 96-8
as a matter of degree, 96
and logical laws, 244-5

Wallace, J., 117 n., 118 n.
weak inscrutability:
illustrated by Japanese example, 107-11
irrelevant to Quinean indeterminacy, 109
consistent with museum myth, 110 n.
does not support (strong) inscrutability thesis 110-11
Wittgenstein, L.:
and Quine, 22-8
as not seeming to think translation is indeterminate, 23, 27
and justification of claims about meaning, 26-7
as seeming to think that form of life etc. determine meaning and translation, 28
on rule-following and form of life, 213-14
Wright, C., 28 n. 10

Zermelo, E., 114, 115

276